NORTH CAROLINA IN THE ANXIOUS AGE

NORTH CAROLINA IN THE ANXIOUS AGE

People, Places, and Policies That Will Shape the North Carolina Economy through the Turbulent Twenty-First Century

Michael L. Walden

The University of North Carolina Press
Chapel Hill

This book was published with the assistance of the Luther H. Hodges Jr. and Luther H. Hodges Sr. Fund of the University of North Carolina Press.

Designed by April Leidig
Set in Warnock by Copperline Book Services

Cover art: Fishing pier in Frisco, NC. © Adobe Stock / JoeStock

Library of Congress Cataloging-in-Publication Data
Names: Walden, Michael L. (Michael Leonard), 1951– author
Title: North Carolina in the anxious age : people, places, and policies that will shape the North Carolina economy through the turbulent twenty-first century / Michael L. Walden.
Description: Chapel Hill : The University of North Carolina Press, [2026] | Includes bibliographical references and index.
Identifiers: LCCN 2026028182 | ISBN 9781469697918 cloth | ISBN 9781469697925 paperback | ISBN 9781469684796 epub | ISBN 9781469697932 pdf
Subjects: LCSH: North Carolina—Economic conditions—21st century | BISAC: BUSINESS & ECONOMICS / Development / Economic Development | BUSINESS & ECONOMICS / Economic History
Classification: LCC HC107.N8 W348 2026
LC record available at https://lccn.loc.gov/2026028182

Again, to Mary,
for her support, guidance, wisdom,
and being a loving partner

CONTENTS

ix List of Illustrations

xiii Preface

1 CHAPTER 1
The New Demography

13 CHAPTER 2
The New Economic Geography

25 CHAPTER 3
The New Workforce

43 CHAPTER 4
The World with AI

55 CHAPTER 5
Education and the Evolution of Tasks

67 CHAPTER 6
Restructuring Education in the Anxious Age

77 CHAPTER 7
Another New North Carolina in the Anxious Age?

103 CHAPTER 8
Managing Energy Use and the Climate in the Anxious Age

121 CHAPTER 9
North Carolina's Position in the Nation and World During the Anxious Age

133 CHAPTER 10
North Carolina in 2050

145 CHAPTER 11
An Agenda for the Anxious Age

147 Acknowledgments

149 Notes

177 Index

ILLUSTRATIONS

GRAPHS

xxii Graph 1.1. Difference between North Carolina and US population growth rate by year, 2015–2024

xxii Graph 1.2. Contribution of net births (births minus deaths) to North Carolina population growth, 2015–2024

2 Graph 1.3. Contribution of net in-migration to North Carolina population growth, 2015–2024

3 Graph 1.4. Contribution of foreign immigration to North Carolina population growth, 2015–2024

6 Graph 1.5. Change in populations of demographic cohorts, 2015–2023

7 Graph 1.6. Change in populations of ethnic and racial cohorts, 2015–2023

28 Graph 3.1. JOLTS data for North Carolina and the United States, 2021–2025

28 Graph 3.2. Labor force participation rate in North Carolina, 2015–2025

30 Graph 3.3. Projected growth rates in age groups in North Carolina, 2021–2050

105 Graph 8.1. Trends in North Carolina annual total energy usage and per capita energy usage, 2015–2023

106 Graph 8.2. Trends in North Carolina annual total CO_2 emissions and emissions per 100,000 population, 2000–2023

113 Graph 8.3. Life-cycle carbon footprint of alternative primary fuel sources for electricity generation

114 Graph 8.4. Duke Energy's forecasted primary energy mix for achieving net-zero CO_2 emissions in North Carolina in 2050

123 Graph 9.1. Relative cost of living in the US, North Carolina, and selected states, 2008–2022

125 Graph 9.2. Average hourly wage rate in the US and North Carolina after adjusting for cost-of-living differences, 2008–2022

135 Graph 10.1. Past and projected alternative trends of prosperity in North Carolina as measured by real gross domestic product

137 Graph 10.2. Medium and low earnings as a percentage of high earnings in North Carolina

137 Graph 10.3. Percentages of high-, medium-, and low-earnings employment of total employment in North Carolina

MAPS

6 Map 1.1. North Carolina counties with the youngest population and counties with the oldest population, 2023

8 Map 1.2. Black percentage of total county population, 2018

8 Map 1.3. Hispanic population of total county population, 2020

9 Map 1.4. Asian population in North Carolina counties, by size, 2018

18 Map 2.1. North Carolina counties with the lowest broadband access, under 75 percent of household access in 2021

20 Map 2.2. Difference between net in-migration in 2018–2019 and in-migration in 2022–2023 in North Carolina counties

21 Map 2.3. Potential remote commuting zones around North Carolina's major metropolitan regions based on a forty-five-minute one-way commute

88 Map 7.1. Locations of major economic announcements in technology, 2021–2024

90 Map 7.2. Locations of major economic announcements in pharmaceuticals, 2021–2024

93 Map 7.3. Locations of major economic announcements in warehousing, 2021–2024

94 Map 7.4. Locations of major economic announcements in manufacturing, 2021–2024

TABLES

31 Table 3.1. Change in inflation-adjusted hourly wage rates for economic sectors in North Carolina in years before, during, and after the pandemic

46 Table 4.1. Employment change in major economic sectors in North Carolina, 2012–2024
51 Table 4.2. Expected job changes from AI in North Carolina occupations, based on 2023 job totals
61 Table 5.1. Top twenty and bottom twenty occupations adversely impacted by AI
62 Table 5.2. Top twenty and bottom twenty industries adversely impacted by AI
81 Table 7.1. Relative size of basic North Carolina industries, 2005, 2019, and 2023
83 Table 7.2. Forecasted changes in the relative importance of industries to North Carolina during the Anxious Age
89 Table 7.3. Major economic announcements in North Carolina, 2021–2024: Technology
91 Table 7.4. Major economic announcements in North Carolina, 2021–2024: Pharmaceuticals
93 Table 7.5. Major economic announcements in North Carolina, 2021–2024: Warehousing
94 Table 7.6. Major economic announcements in North Carolina, 2021–2024: Manufacturing
107 Table 8.1. Distribution of primary energy sources in North Carolina
108 Table 8.2. Predicted North Carolina total energy usage in 2030 and 2050 under different assumptions of future energy efficiency
108 Table 8.3. Predicted North Carolina total energy usage in 2030 and 2050 under different assumptions of future energy efficiency and AI impacts
124 Table 9.1. Cost-of-living differences between the nation and designated North Carolina metropolitan areas in 2008 and 2022
129 Table 9.2. Cost increases in North Carolina and the US for factors impacted by growth

PREFACE

I have written two books about the North Carolina economy, both published by the University of North Carolina Press. The first, *North Carolina in the Connected Age*, published in 2008, focused on the remarkable transformation of the state economy in the late twentieth and early twenty-first centuries. North Carolina's economy moved from one dominated by the "Big Three"—tobacco, textiles, and furniture—to an economy with new leaders such as technology, pharmaceuticals, finance, food processing, and transportation parts manufacturing, all components of the new "Big Five." In particular, the expansion of the relatively new industries of technology and pharmaceuticals during this time period indicated that North Carolina was now in the vanguard of economic change in the country.

The industry shifts in the state economy during what I dubbed the "Connected Age"—my term for the digital age—had numerous ramifications, particularly for the state's population, workforce, and relative prosperities of urban and rural regions. North Carolina moved from trailing the nation in population growth prior to the Connected Age to exceeding the country in population growth during the Connected Age.[1] People moved to North Carolina because of job opportunities in new industries, a lower cost of living, and the spread of air conditioning to deal with the state's hot and humid summers.

The Connected Age required new workforce training for the skills necessary for emerging industries like technology, pharmaceuticals, and finance. As a result, there was a surge in post–high school training in the state, including four-year universities and two-year community colleges. The percentage of the workforce with more than a high school degree jumped from 8.5 percent in 1970 to 46 percent in 2020, a faster gain than in the nation.[2]

The growth in new businesses, population, and prosperity was centered in the state's metropolitan areas, while at the same time many rural areas were losing population due to the shrinkage of the "Big Three" sectors, which were centered in rural areas. From 1970 to 2020, when the state's population increased by over 100 percent, populations of sixteen of the state's one hundred counties increased by less than 20 percent; ten of these counties actually lost population. By contrast, the population of Wake County (home of Raleigh) jumped 393 percent, that of Mecklenburg County (the location of Charlotte) surged 215 percent, and that of Durham County rose 145 percent. Rapidly urbanizing counties around the core metro counties also experienced triple-digit population growth. As a result, the state's urban/rural divide widened from a crack to a cavern.[3]

In my second book about North Carolina, *North Carolina Beyond the Connected Age*, published in 2017, I shifted to the future for the state economy, with my focus set on 2050. The decline in the birth rate had already begun, but I expected North Carolina's population would continue to grow as a result of in-migration of individuals from other states. Still, as in most other states, the relative size of the state's elderly population would increase, due both to the natural aging of residents and the continuing influx of retirees from other states choosing North Carolina as their retirement home. North Carolina's popularity as a retirement destination would particularly create more growth in coastal counties.

I also saw urbanization expanding as metropolitan regions attracted even more residents and geographically grew outward to incorporate previously rural counties. As a result, I predicted that the urban/rural divide would become even larger.

Like most futurists at the time, I forecasted that technology would continue to disrupt the labor market. Led by the enhanced capabilities of computer technology, more physically oriented and routine-oriented occupations would become at risk as their tasks could increasingly be performed by machines, while problem-solving jobs would not be impacted and would continue to increase. I advocated for the need of education—particularly higher education—to implement more efficient methods of training and to be ready for rapid changes in their curricula as the tasks performed by workers changed.

As North Carolina moved through the decades to the mid-twenty-first century, I expected the economy to be increasingly dominated by services, and even more so by higher-value-added services such as the professions, finance, and the application of technology. Since the locations both of firms in these fields and of education and training for the firms' occupations were in metropolitan areas, I expected that this trend would add to the dominance of metro regions in the state economy. I expected the Triangle (Raleigh-Durham–Chapel Hill) and the Triad (Greensboro–Winston-Salem–High Point) regions to expand toward each other and incorporate the rural counties along US Route 64.

I foresaw North Carolina devoting more attention to climate change as the twenty-first century progressed. The state would move away from fossil fuels toward renewables; ultimately, natural gas would be the remaining fossil fuel supplying a significant degree of energy.

But the accuracy of any forecast is hampered by one unassailable fact—the occurrence of unexpected events. And beginning in 2020, North Carolina, the country, and indeed the world experienced perhaps the greatest modern time unexpected event—the COVID pandemic.

Apart from its role as a major medical event, COVID unleashed several reactions that have caused numerous forecasts to be reevaluated. Among those at the top of the list is remote work. Prior to the pandemic, only 8 percent of the workforce was engaged in either part-time or full-time remote work. During the pandemic this rate jumped to 60 percent. While the remote working rate in early 2025 is near 30 percent—based on the percentage of total hours worked remotely—several experts expect it will remain in this range.[4] One study ranked North Carolina as the tenth-best state for remote work, and another analysis ranked the Triangle region of the state as second in the nation for remote work, behind only Boulder, Colorado.[5]

The pandemic increased concerns about high-density living, where infectious diseases can spread more rapidly. As a reaction to this concern, together with the experience working remotely during the pandemic, remote work likely will be maintained at a significantly higher level than prior to COVID. If so, remote work could be a game changer for the future state economy. For example, remote work would allow workers to live in rural regions, where housing costs are much lower than in cities. Remote work would reduce commuting, thereby helping the environment, and hence decrease the need for new transportation projects, particularly roads. With their increased presence at home, working parents could devote more time to child-rearing. Consequently, remote work may be part of the answer to housing affordability, the urban/rural divide, transportation congestion, pollution, and possibly student achievement.

A corollary to the growth of remote work has been the expansion of home delivery for a variety of consumer products during the COVID crisis. The likely future development of drone delivery of packages will make home delivery even more prevalent. Like remote work, home delivery could further decrease the need for geographic proximity of households to large cities with numerous retailers. Combined, remote work and home delivery have the ability to significantly reduce the significance and importance of large cities and metropolitan regions.

The cracks in metropolitan dominance may already be appearing. In the state's two largest cities, Charlotte and Raleigh, office vacancy rates doubled from prior to the pandemic in 2019 to after the pandemic in 2023, and remained higher than prepandemic levels at over 24 percent near the end of 2024 and projected through 2025.[6] Those leading cities have also been threatened by a noticeable exodus of existing businesses, likely prompted by the decline in foot traffic in their downtowns.[7] Between 2019 and 2023, the number of people visiting downtown Raleigh dropped by 35 percent, and Charlotte's downtown foot traffic was down 25 percent. Although there were improvements in foot traffic in 2024, businesses are still seeing inconsistent activity compared to prepandemic years, especially in the downtown core.[8] Hence, given the combination of remote work, home delivery, and a reevaluation of urban work and living, there is need for a reassessment of how the geographic growth of North Carolina will evolve in the post-COVID period.

The relative power of players in the labor market was also impacted by COVID. After the economy reopened, labor shortages occurred for a variety of reasons, and these shortages resulted in a shift of power from employers to employees. Wages rose substantially, especially in labor-intensive sectors. A question is whether this power shift will continue in the decades after COVID, and what changes and challenges in the labor market in North Carolina will be long-lasting.

One of the most impactful innovations in the future labor market will be artificial intelligence (AI). AI is the application of enhanced machine learning based on the ability of today's technology to conduct rapid analysis of large quantities of data to reach conclusions and recommendations for a wide variety of questions and issues. Some have designated AI the beginning of the world's fourth industrial revolution.[9] Although AI's development began prior to COVID, issues arising during the pandemic related to areas such as the labor market, healthcare, and education prompted an acceleration in efforts to extend and apply AI. It has been estimated that 41 percent of companies increased their development and application of AI during the pandemic.[10] This means AI will likely be applied faster and have a broader range of effects than people thought prior to COVID.

Although our economy has been through previous applications of technology that impacted society—such as the mechanization of agriculture and the application of the assembly line in factories—AI is fundamentally different and will therefore have new impacts. Previous technological applications mainly replaced the physical component of labor. For example, farmers driving a tractor to plow a field were much more efficient than farmers guiding a mule or horse to plow a field. Hence, fewer farmers were needed for plowing. Similarly, using assembly lines to manufacture a product, such as a vehicle, also increased worker efficiency and reduced the number of workers required for a given output level.

AI is different because it replaces the cognitive component of labor. Therefore, AI's impact will apply to service jobs, office jobs, and even numerous highly skilled occupations, including teachers, researchers, accountants, and financial analysts. The implications for North Carolina's labor, training, and educational markets and institutions could be massive.

While my 2017 book discussed climate change and its implications for energy in North Carolina, the focus was on energy usage by consumers and businesses. There was no anticipation that North Carolina would be a major national participant in developing the products and components in the energy transition. However, in recent years the state has created what some call an "energy production corridor" in a mainly rural region between the Triangle and Triad along US Route 64. A multibillion-dollar investment creating thousands of jobs is occurring at the electric vehicle (EV) manufacturer VinFast, the computer chip maker Wolfspeed, and Toyota's largest battery factory. It is expected that scores of supporting companies could also locate in the corridor.

Unfortunately, the development of the energy corridor has hit snags. Financial issues have delayed VinFast's initial production by several years. Similarly, financial issues leading to a bankruptcy and sale to a new investor, as well as questions about federal funding, have raised questions about Wolfspeed's production schedule.

Of course, there have been other non-COVID impacts since the appearance of *North Carolina Beyond the Connected Age* in 2017. An important one is immigration. Although immigration regulation is a national policy, the impacts are seen in almost all states, including North Carolina. Since 2017 we have witnessed three distinct changes in national immigration policy: The first severely restricted immigration, the second implemented regulations and policies resulting in an immigration surge, and the third created strong restrictions and deportations. Predicting which policy will dominate in the future is difficult, but clearly the social and economic implications for North Carolina are important, so a detailed look at alternative immigration futures is recommended.

The world, and especially the economic world, has changed since COVID. Long-run predictions made prior to COVID are no longer valid. Equally important is the realization that we don't know exactly how the post-COVID economic world will be different. But today's outlook goes beyond uncertainty about how events will unfold. There is also a noticeable unease about what the future holds, suggested by the rise in the use of mental health care.[11] This unease is likely a holdover from the COVID period but has also been reinforced by sharp differences over public policy and worry about what AI will do to the job market. Hence, I call the time period we have entered "the Anxious Age."

North Carolina in the Anxious Age will provide two important extensions to *North Carolina Beyond the Connected Age*. First, it will use updated data from a variety of sources for the key demographic, economic, education, labor, and climate indicators, as well as many other metrics that will place North Carolina in the post-COVID period. Comparing these data to pre-COVID data will permit a comprehensive analysis of how the state has changed since the pandemic.

Second, the updated data will provide a base for forecasting changes through future decades considering the key macro changes discussed above following the outbreak of the pandemic. As a result, *North Carolina in the Anxious Age* will give a fresh perspective on how North Carolina's economy has recently performed, as well as informed forecasts about how the state's economy will perform to the mid-twenty-first century.

The discussion and forecasts included in *North Carolina in the Anxious Age* are presented in eleven chapters.

Chapter 1, "The New Demography," documents new demographic trends in North Carolina, especially since COVID, and the likely paths of those trends through midcentury. Lower birthrates, greater household diversity, a faster-aging population, and more reliance on both in-migration and immigration for population growth are some of the important topics discussed. The impacts of these factors will be used to foresee future population trends in the state.

Chapter 2 is titled "The New Economic Geography." North Carolina's economic geography could be profoundly impacted in the Anxious Age, raising numerous questions. How will remote work, faster home delivery, and the rising costs of living in metropolitan areas alter household choices of where to reside? Will there be a revival of lower-density rural counties and a stagnation—or even contraction—of big cities? What would such a shift do to the financing of public services when workers live and work in different counties, or perhaps even in different states? Will businesses follow workers who choose rural residences? What characteristics of rural regions will be prominent in attracting remote workers? What will North Carolina's urban/rural divide look like in 2050?

Chapter 3, "The New Workforce," looks at possible changes in employment. With the pandemic shifting more power to workers, how will the balance of power between employers and employees evolve in the Anxious Age? Could the ongoing development of labor-saving workplace technology reduce workers' bargaining power, or will a slower-growing—or even a falling—workforce keep employers in stiff competition for employees? Trends and implications for freelance ("gig") workers and a possible thirty-two-hour workweek will also be explored. Do organized labor unions have a future in North Carolina that will shift the balance of power in the labor market?

Perhaps the most important question to be addressed during the Anxious Age will be worker skills. In Chapter 4, "The World with AI," the focus is on how the dominant technology innovation of the Anxious Age, artificial intelligence, will change the skill needs in the economy and disrupt occupations and careers. How the skills needed in the economy will change is examined. Estimates are provided for the impacts of AI on specific occupations in North Carolina.

The conclusions from chapter 4 directly lead to the topic of chapter 5, titled "Education and the Evolution of Tasks." As the nature of work tasks and skill requirements are altered, education and training programs in North Carolina will have to adapt in several ways. The content of education and training will need to follow the growth in some skills and the decline in others. It will also be important that curricula changes follow at the same pace as skill changes in the marketplace. This will require rapid resource reallocations made by education providers.

A complementary issue is how the model for delivering education and training might change during the Anxious Age. This question is the focus of chapter 6, "Restructuring Education in the Anxious Age." Specifically, what changes might AI create in how education is delivered? Also, will there be changing roles for public, private, and employer-based providers of education and training?

Chapter 7, "Another New North Carolina in the Anxious Age?," examines how the structure of North Carolina's economy will likely change in future decades. The dual forces of remote work and AI could create a new economic transformation in North Carolina, similar to the shifts from farming to manufacturing and manufacturing to technology in earlier periods. As with the previous re-creations of the state economy, another transformation will result in new economic sectors and alterations in existing economic sectors; some will grow, others will contract. What will be the dominant economic sectors in North Carolina in 2050? The chapter will outline possible future pathways for the economy's sectors.

Chapter 8, titled "Managing Energy Use and the Climate in the Anxious Age," addresses questions of energy consumption in a changing world. Like all states, North Carolina will continue to be a consumer of the new energy technologies being developed and implemented to address climate change. A key question discussed in the chapter is the speed at which the state can make the energy transition, given the challenges of the state's growing power usage resulting from rising population, the new demands for power from AI, and shifting energy policies from the federal government. Also, could the state's new role as a producer of clean energy inputs and products assist with and speed the energy transition in North Carolina?

Could this new role create new industries and jobs—particularly in rural areas—during the Anxious Age? But will North Carolina's production of clean energy components in the Anxious Age continue to be dependent on federal funding? These and related issues will be addressed in the chapter.

North Carolina's position in the nation and the world is addressed in chapter 9. As North Carolina's population and economy expand, the state's relative position in the nation and world will become more prominent. North Carolina will be a bigger player on the national and world stages. But while growth brings benefits, it also brings costs. The chapter examines these trade-offs and asks if there are ways to enjoy both the benefits of growth while limiting the consequent disadvantages. What new kinds of policies will need to be implemented to achieve this dual outcome?

Chapter 10, "North Carolina in 2050," collects the conclusions of the previous chapters to present a picture of North Carolina at the maturation of the Anxious Age in 2050. What will the picture of the state look like? Has prosperity spread, both individually and geographically? Have workers successfully transitioned to the AI-dominated economy? Has housing affordability improved, heath care become more affordable, income inequality narrowed, and the environment become cleaner, while at the same time providing the energy needed by a growing state? What will be the most important policies necessary to achieve these goals? In summary, where will North Carolina be at the culmination of the Anxious Age?

The final chapter, "An Agenda for the Anxious Age," gives a concise summary of the proposals for action presented in the book to address the numerous issues and challenges North Carolina is facing during the Anxious Age. While the chapter will be most useful for public and private leaders and groups in the state, all North Carolina residents who are interested in the state's future, and particularly in the state's future opportunities and challenges, should find its proposals useful for discussion, debate, and perhaps implementation.

It is my hope that *North Carolina in the Anxious Age* will provide valuable and useful insights into the past, current, and especially future North Carolina economy, hopefully insights that will make us less anxious and more excited and optimistic about the future.

One technical note is in order. The latest data available while the book was written during 2024 and 2025 are used. Often the latest data availability varies for different measures.

NORTH CAROLINA IN THE ANXIOUS AGE

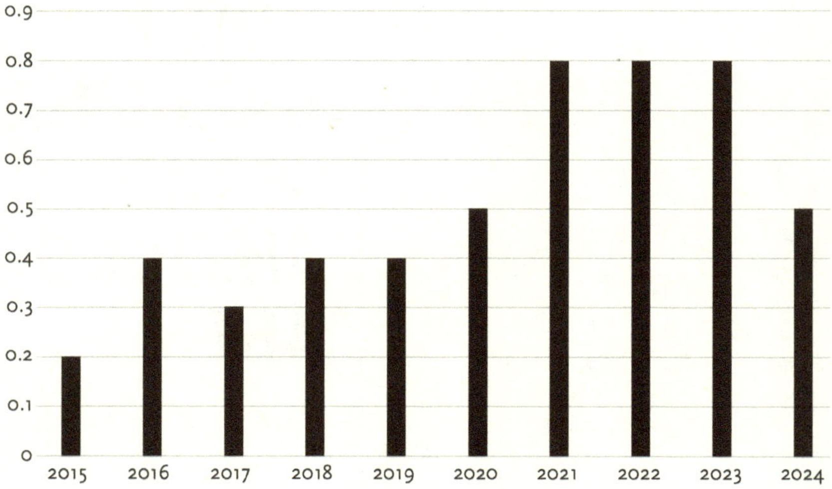

GRAPH 1.1. Difference between North Carolina and US population growth rate by year, 2015–2024 (in percentage points). Source: US Census Bureau.

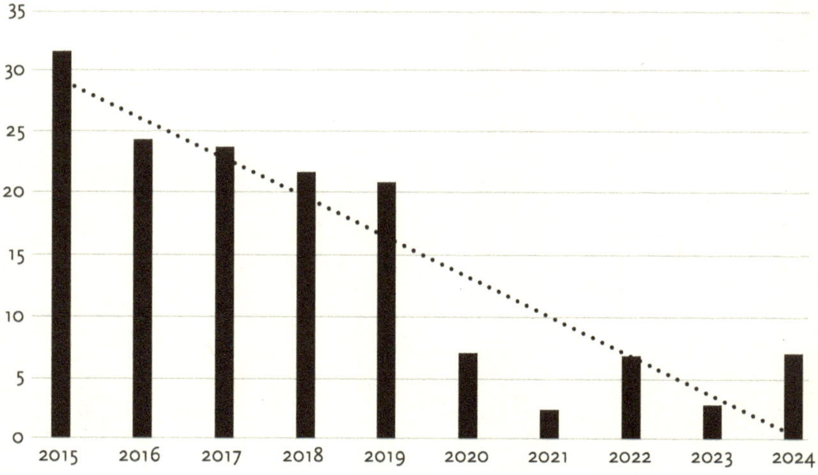

GRAPH 1.2. Contribution of net births (births minus deaths) to North Carolina population growth, 2015–2024 (in percentage points), with trend line. Source: US Census Bureau.

1

THE NEW DEMOGRAPHY

COVID Turning Point?

For years, North Carolina has been one of the fastest-growing states in population in the country. Consistently since the 1970s, the state's annual population growth rate has exceeded the nation's rate.[1] Between 1970 and 2020, only eight states had faster population growth rates than North Carolina, and since the pandemic (2020–23) just seven states have beat North Carolina in population growth rate. In 2024 North Carolina ranked as the ninth-most-populous state. Among surrounding states, only Georgia had a higher ranking, at number 8.[2]

Graph 1.1 shows recent annual differences in population growth rates between North Carolina and the nation. Interestingly, during the pandemic year of 2020 and the recovery years of 2021, 2022, and 2023, North Carolina's growth rate edge over the nation increased, effectively doubling from the prepandemic years. In 2024 North Carolina's growth rate margin moderated.

To illustrate why North Carolina's population growth rate increased after 2020 when COVID emerged, graphs 1.2, 1.3, and 1.4 show the three contributors to North Carolina's population growth in recent years: net births (births minus deaths), net in-migration from other states, and foreign immigration. The contributors are shown as a percentage of the annual total population change. Dotted lines on the graphs indicate trends in the measurement over the time period.

There are several key takeaways. Graph 1.2 clearly shows a significant declining trend in the contribution of net births that began the pandemic but accelerated afterward. The contrast is extraordinary. In 2015 net births contributed almost 32 percent to the state's total population growth, while in 2024 the contribution was just over 7 percent. There was a rebound in 2024, perhaps due to a recovery in births after the pandemic in the immediate post-COVID years.

Interestingly, the reason for the decline in net births has not been a decline in the number of births. Recent annual births in North Carolina during the period 2015 to 2024 have ranged between 117,000 and 122,000, with no discernible trend. Although North Carolina's birth rate (live births per 1,000 people) has declined, particularly among the Black population, as in the rest of the nation, the continuing increase in the state's population of child-bearing women has offset that decline.[3] Rather, the drop in the contribution of net births to population growth is a result of rising annual deaths in North Carolina, reflecting the state's growing elderly population. Annual deaths rose 22 percent from 2015 to 2024.[4]

Graph 1.3 shows the rising trend of the contribution of net in-migration to the state's population growth over the entire period. Indeed, in every year since 2015 net in-migration has accounted for 50 percent or more of North Carolina's population growth. In 2021 the contribution was an astonishing percentage. In 2022 the contribution was over 60 percent, in 2023 it was 70 percent, and in 2024 the contribution moderated to 50 percent.

Foreign immigration has also become more important to North Carolina's population growth. Graph 1.4 shows annual contribution rates between 25 percent and 30 percent in both 2022 and 2023, significantly higher than during the pre-COVID period. The modest 10 percent contribution rate in 2021 likely reflects the impact of mobility restrictions during that

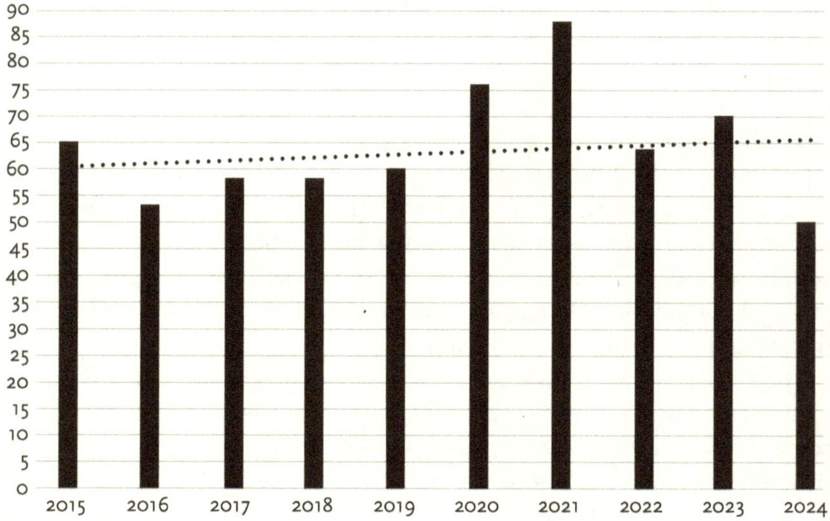

GRAPH 1.3. Contribution of net in-migration to North Carolina population growth, 2015–2024 (in percentage points), with trend line. Source: US Census Bureau.

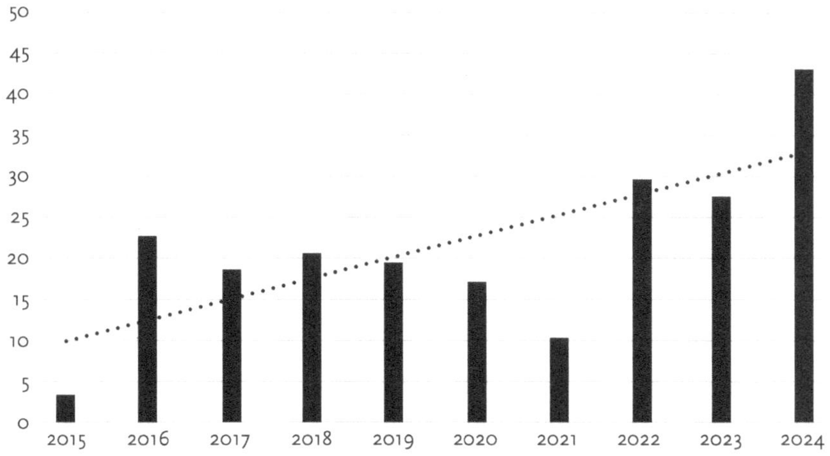

GRAPH 1.4. Contribution of foreign immigration to North Carolina population growth, 2015–2024 (in percentage points). Source: US Census Bureau.

year. But in 2024 the contribution of foreign immigration hit a modern high of 43 percent. With the border restrictions applied by the Trump administration beginning in 2025, it is likely the immigrant contribution to population growth in North Carolina will decrease.

A Real Bounce or a Burst Bubble?

The analysis above suggests that there has been a post-COVID bounce to North Carolina's relative population growth compared to the nation, and that this bounce is likely related to the state's enhanced attractiveness to "outsiders," both domestic and foreign. Why has the state's attractiveness increased, and is the bounce real or will it end as a temporary bubble?

The first stop in answering these questions is to look at the details of who has been moving to North Carolina, and where they have been moving to. Fortunately, a recent detailed analysis is available from the state demographer using annual data for the period 2011 to 2021.[5] Younger people under age thirty-four now lead among individuals moving to North Carolina. And not only are they the leading group, but their propensity to move to North Carolina rose the most over the time period. This is a major shift from earlier decades, when it was older individuals who led the migration to North Carolina.

In terms of income, the analysis found that the likelihood to move to North Carolina is highest among households earning higher incomes. Also, while the propensity to move to North Carolina increased for all income groups over the 2011–21 time period, the propensity rose the greatest for households earning $200,000 or more. A decade earlier, it was also higher-income individuals who outnumbered other groups moving to North Carolina.[6]

What states are in-migrants coming from, and where do they locate in North Carolina? During the 2011–21 period, two states dominated as the source of in-migrants to North Carolina—California and New York—followed by South Carolina, Florida, and Texas.[7] An analysis based on 2022–23 data shows the top destinations for in-migrants to the state were the metropolitan areas of the Triangle (Raleigh, Durham, and Chapel Hill), Charlotte, and the Triad. The relatively smaller regions of Asheville, Wilmington, and New Bern have also been popular destinations.[8] These destination locations suggest a combination of in-migrants moving to North Carolina for work in the large metropolitan areas, and others likely moving for retirement in the mountain (Asheville) and coastal (Wilmington, New Bern) regions. However, some retired in-migrants could also be locating in the large metropolitan areas in order to be close to their working children.[9]

North Carolina may have experienced a recent bounce to its net in-migration due to several studies rating the state relatively high on its performance during the pandemic. For example, an analysis of health, economic, and education factors from two studies, one by the Council on Foreign Relations and the other by the National Bureau of Economic Research, ranked North Carolina in the top third—seventeenth and thirteenth, respectively—on performance during the pandemic period among the fifty states and DC.[10]

While the heightened attraction of North Carolina during and after COVID could be interpreted as a bubble that may burst, other information suggests that the state's attractiveness to newcomers will be ongoing, although with some moderation compared to the COVID period, as indicated by the lower net in-migration rate in 2024. One reason is that North Carolina's high ranking on net in-migration has been occurring for several years.[11] The second is that analysis of factors related to high net in-migration rates among states reveals that North Carolina has many of these factors, including a lower jobless rate than the nation, a modest personal income tax, a cost of living lower than the national average, significant fiscal surpluses in the state budget, and relatively warm winters.[12]

Finally, it is important to note that in-migration to North Carolina is also driven by national factors impacting the number of households who potentially could move to the state. Recently these national forces have been trending in the direction of less household migration. Specifically, older households move less frequently—a relevant fact because the nation's population is aging. Also, reduced housing availability, and data suggesting that today's workers are changing jobs less frequently, could reduce in-migration rates for all states, including North Carolina.[13]

Hence, questions about the trend of household in-migration to North Carolina, combined with unknowns about future birth rates and foreign immigration levels to the state, add to the uncertainty of the Anxious Age.

Age and Diversity

Graph 1.5 shows the path of four age groups from 2015 to 2019 to 2023. The numbers measure the proportion of the category's population in the designated year relative to the category's population in 2015. For example, the value of 1.23 for the population sixty-five and over in 2023 means the population of that age group in 2023 was 23 percent greater than in 2015. All values in 2015 are set at 1.

Graph 1.5 clearly shows that the strongest population growth is in the age group 65 years old and over, with a gain of 23 percent over the time period. By contrast, the population of the 19-and-under age group was almost unchanged between 2015 and 2023, and this group's population actually fell slightly between 2019 and 2023. The 20–24-year-old age group had a 5 percent growth rate between 2015 and 2023, and all the gain happened from 2019 to 2023 after a decline from 2015 to 2019. The gain from 2019 to 2023 was likely due to the aging of the 0–19 cohort into the older 20–24-year-old group. The 25–44-year-old age group had a modest 7 percent increase over the 2015–23 period. Since the 2020 census, North Carolina's median age is estimated to have increased almost one-half year by 2024.[14]

Of course, the median age is not consistent across North Carolina. Map 1.1 shows counties with the youngest median age and those with the oldest median age. Young counties are defined as those with a median age of thirty-seven or lower, and the oldest counties are defined having a median age of fifty or above. The young counties are in fast-growing metropolitan areas with universities, including Mecklenburg (University of North Carolina at Charlotte), Onslow (University of North Carolina at Wilmington), Pitt (East Carolina University), and Watauga (Appalachian State University), and in counties with access to military bases such as Ft. Bragg (Cumberland, Hoke, and Harnett). Older counties are in traditional low-density rural areas in the western mountain and foothills regions (Macon, Cherokee, Clay, Transylvania, Polk, and Alleghany) the northern

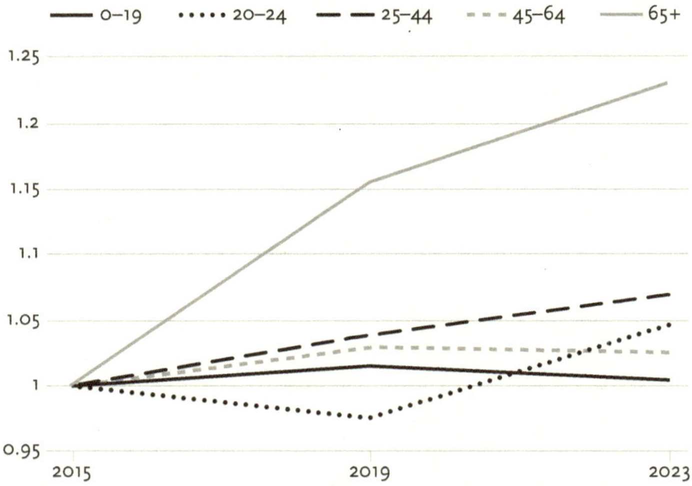

GRAPH 1.5. Change in populations of demographic cohorts, 2015–2023 (values proportional to 2015 value). Source: US Census Bureau, *American Community Survey*.

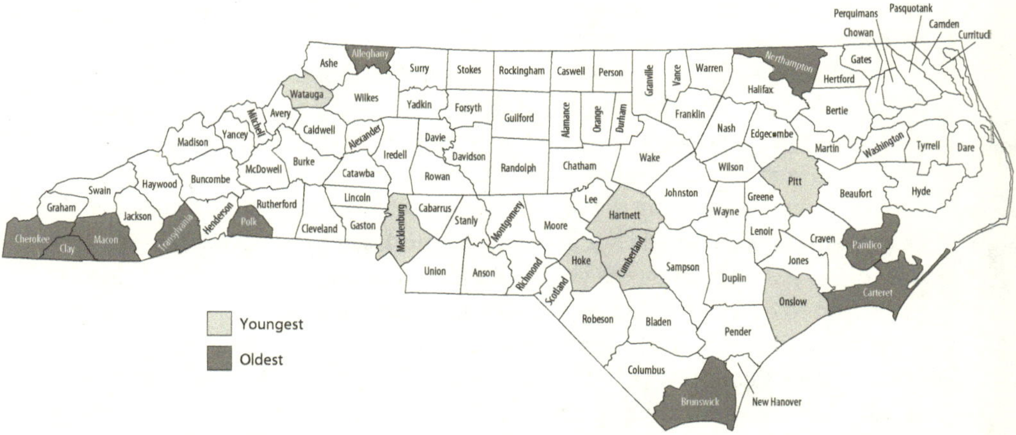

MAP 1.1. North Carolina counties with the youngest population and counties with the oldest population, 2023.

Piedmont (Northampton), and in fast-growing retirement counties on the coast (Brunswick, Carteret, and Pamlico).

Out of the one hundred counties in the state, only five experienced a reduction in median age during the 2015–23 time period. However, if the time period is split between the pre-COVID time period of 2015–19 and the post-COVID period of 2019–23, the contrast is stark. During 2015–19, only

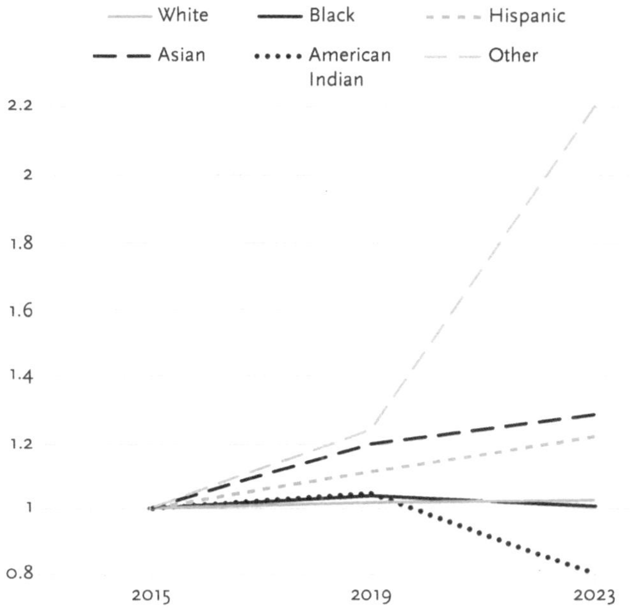

GRAPH 1.6. Change in populations of ethnic and racial cohorts, 2015–2023 (values proportional to 2015 value). Source: US Census Bureau, *American Community Survey.*

three counties became younger. But from 2019 to 2023, one-third of North Carolina became younger, likely a result of deaths from COVID.[15]

Graph 1.6 provides population information for the same years as in graph 1.5, but for ethnic and racial cohorts. The "Other" category includes smaller groups, such as Pacific Islanders, but is dominated by individuals who identify as having mixed races. Indeed, there has been a surge in mixed-race individuals in recent years, so the "Other" category increased over 120 percent between 2015 and 2023.

Among the categories, the Black and white populations were relatively stable over the time period, but with both experiencing a slight decline between 2019 and 2023. The American Indian population dropped significantly—by 16 percent—between 2015 and 2023, but all the loss came after 2019. The Asian and Hispanic populations each recorded consistent gains from 2015 to 2023, with very little difference in the pace of increases for 2015 to 2019 compared to 2019 to 2023.

As with age, there are distinct geographic differences for racial and ethnic components of the North Carolina population. Map 1.2 shows that the Black population has its highest concentration in Eastern North Carolina. Map 1.3

indicates that the Hispanic population has its largest relative share in the "Downeast" counties, where agriculture is dominant. By contrast, the Asian population (map 1.4) is most dominant in the state's largest metropolitan regions: the Triangle, the Triad, and Charlotte.

The major conclusion from examining age and racial/ethnic trends in the years immediately prior to and immediately after the pandemic is that long-run population changes observed over the past several decades in North Carolina appear to be continuing. The state is aging, and the dominance of the white and Black populations continues to narrow. Yet these conclusions still leave important questions unanswered. Will these trends

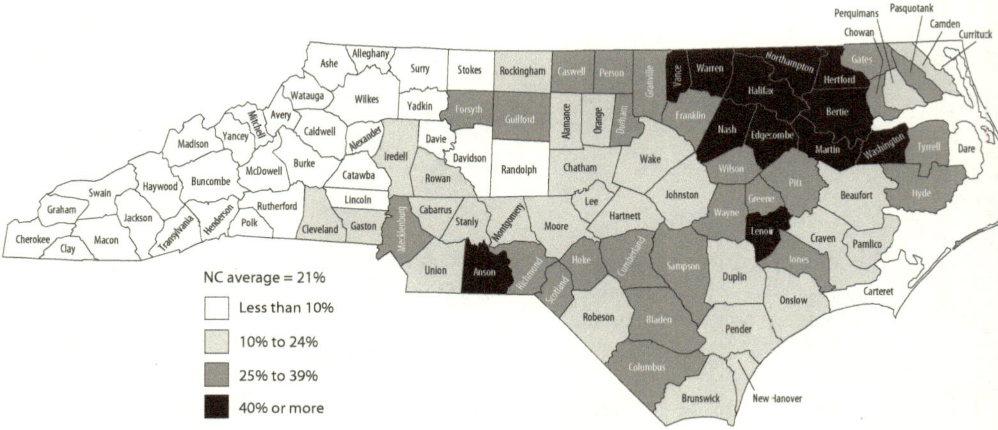

MAP 1.2. Black percentage of total county population, 2018. Source: Carolina Demography.

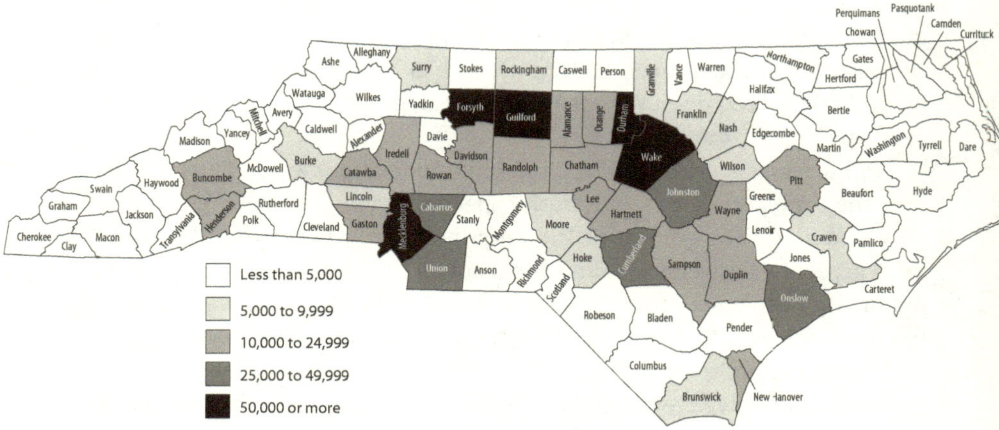

MAP 1.3. Hispanic population of total county population, 2020. Source: Carolina Demography.

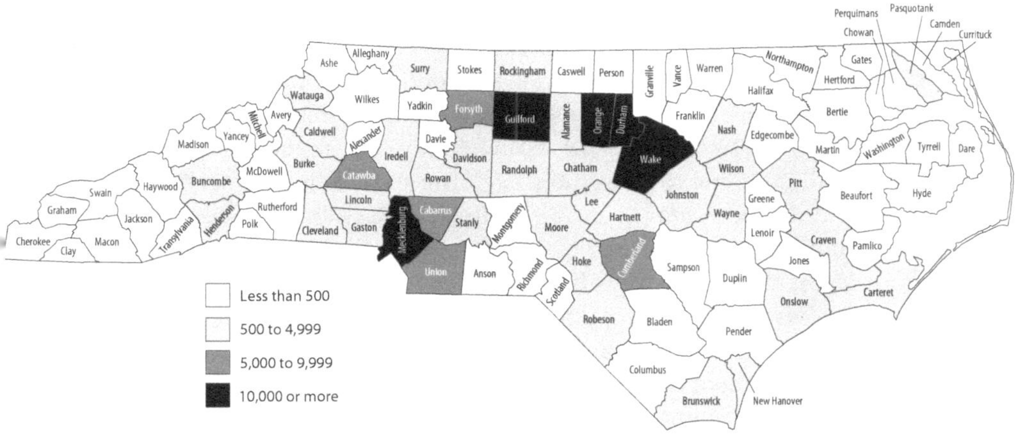

MAP 1.4. Asian population in North Carolina counties, by size, 2018. Source: Carolina Demography.

still persist in North Carolina through midcentury? How could major changes in the three components of state population growth—net internal growth (births minus deaths), net in-migration, and immigration—impact the path of North Carolina's future population? These questions are confronted in the next section.

Alternative Futures of North Carolina's Population

The most recent forecasts from the state demographer of North Carolina indicate that the state's population will continue to increase. Indeed, the growth forecasts have become stronger. In 2015, the official forecasts of the state demographer showed North Carolina's 2030 population at 11.6 million, and the 2050 population was predicted to be 13.4 million. The forecasts developed in 2024 indicate a 2030 population of 13 million and a 2050 population of 14.2 million.[16]

The latest forecasts are also consistent with previous predictions for the state population to continue aging. The 2020 to 2050 growth rate in the population of those aged sixty-five and over is predicted to be twice the increase for the total population and more than 2.5 times the increase for that of those aged zero to seventeen. Trends in the racial and ethnic populations are also expected to persist. For example, the Hispanic population is forecasted to increase its share of the total state population from 11 percent in 2020 to 14 percent in 2050.[17]

But there could be a major point crossed in the 2040s that will bring a new and important element to North Carolina's population future. Graph 1.2 showed a clear downward trend in the contribution of net births (births minus deaths) to population growth. National forecasters predict in the decades ahead the birth rate will remain below replacement levels, meaning deaths will continue to exceed births.[18] The state demographer forecasts that beginning in the 2040s, net births in North Carolina will be a negative contributor to population growth. In other words, in the 2040s there will be more deaths than births. Specifically, it is expected that deaths will exceed births by over 250,000 during the 2040s decade, and by almost 350,000 in the 2050s decade.[19] This means population growth in North Carolina will be totally dependent on migration, both from other states (in-migration) and from foreign countries (immigration). In fact, the same situation will exist for the nation.[20] Still, demography experts forecast the national population to continue increasing at least until 2080, and the same is expected for North Carolina.[21] However, some experts argue that COVID may have had a permanent impact on reducing the birth rate. If accurate, this could be one of the pandemic's most important lasting effects on North Carolina's demography.[22] Indeed, the latest national forecasts indicate the domestic birth rate will continue to fall, decreasing another 4 percent between 2025 and 2035.[23]

Yet with North Carolina's population growth expected to become more tied to both domestic and foreign households moving to the state, it is now more important to consider factors impacting these movements. The nonpartisan Congressional Budget Office (CBO) estimates that annual foreign immigration doubled during the years 2021–24 compared to the decade prior to 2021. But CBO forecasts that the annual number has declined beginning in 2025 and will average 1.1 million for the period 2027–55, one-third of the estimated 3.3 million in 2023 and far lower than the 2.7 million in 2024.[24] Of course, these numbers are speculative because they depend on potential future legislation and enforcement mandates. But if close to accurate, the forecasts imply a significant reduction in the foreign immigration numbers North Carolina has experienced in recent years, dropping from approximately 76,000 annually to 25,000 annually.[25]

While domestic household migration to North Carolina has had a modest upward trend in recent years (graph 1.3), interstate migration of households has been declining nationally for several years.[26] Over time, states losing population can alter policies to slow the losses. At the same time, states such as North Carolina that have attracted population can suffer "growing pains" from fast growth, such as higher housing prices, more traffic congestion, and less open space, changes that could reduce the attractiveness of North Carolina to residents of other states. Therefore, there is the possibility, perhaps even the likelihood, of slower future migration from both domestic and foreign households to North Carolina. This change would moderate North Carolina's future population growth and make the current forecasts too high. The implication is not that North Carolina will depopulate. Instead, the conclusion is North Carolina may not reach the expected 14.2 million population level in 2050. If these forecasts are accurate, North Carolina will still be older and more diverse, but not as populous as once expected.

Population growth importantly depends on motivation: motivation for families to have children, and motivation for households from other states and countries to move to North Carolina. But what is behind these motivations? A major determinant is the economy of the state, and whether the economy incentivizes households to move to North Carolina and grow their family. How will the state be viewed as a place to live, work, and prosper in upcoming decades? Specifically, in the post-COVID world of potential new ways of working and living, will North Carolina's reputation as a place to live and work improve or decline? These and similar questions will be addressed in upcoming chapters.

Summing Up

In the post-COVID decades, North Carolina's population is expected to continue growing, expanding from 10.6 million in 2020, to 11.7 million in 2030, and rising to 14.2 million in 2050. However, with an expectation of ongoing low birth rates and rising deaths from an aging population, population growth will become increasingly dependent on people moving to North Carolina from other states and from foreign countries. In fact, beginning in the 2040s, the annual difference between births and deaths in the state is expected to become negative.

There are legitimate questions as to whether both domestic in-migration and foreign immigration will remain at levels experienced in the first two decades of the twenty-first century. North Carolina may have experienced a temporary bump in domestic in-migration as a result of its relatively better performance during COVID compared to most other states. Also, states losing population to other states could be expected to take policy actions at some point to reduce incentives for residents to leave. Finally, future foreign immigration is expected to decline significantly in upcoming years from its high levels in the early 2020s. These uncertainties create questions about future forecasts of North Carolina's population. While the state will likely have more residents in 2050 than today, the gain could easily be significantly less than official projections show.

However, North Carolina's demographic future is not totally beyond its control. Economic and residential options are key drivers for attracting households to a state, and state policies have some impact on these factors. Chapter 2 looks at how the combination of occupational and residential options—termed "economic geography"—might be altered in North Carolina during the Anxious Age to make the state more attractive and prosperous, as well as less costly for households, particularly those with children. As with numerous outcomes from the pandemic, the potential benefits from the remaking of North Carolina's economic geography will have its origins traced to the COVID years.

2

THE NEW ECONOMIC GEOGRAPHY

Have Urban Areas Reached Their Peak?

COVID has had numerous impacts on our lives, but a strong argument can be made that among the greatest impacts may be those that affect how we work and where we live. If these impacts achieve their full potential during the Anxious Age, they could reverse an important national and state trend that has been ongoing for over a century.

Rural regions were dominant in the early years of the country, including in North Carolina. This is because agriculture was the main industry, and agriculture was—and still is—predominantly a rural industry. But the Industrial Revolution brought the labor-saving tractor to farms and created factories in cities, and these changes shifted the economic geography. Factories needed workers, and now with the oversupply of farmers from the increasingly machine-intensive farm, a massive population movement from rural to urban living was generated. In 1920 the United States first became a majority-urban country.[1] Due to its relatively larger rural population and slower pace in changing to the new manufacturing sector, the conversion to urban dominance in North Carolina did not occur until seven decades later, during the 1990s.[2]

Ever since this rural-to-urban transformation occurred, urban areas have expanded and widened the gap with lagging rural regions. By 2020, two-thirds of the state's population lived in areas classified as urban.[3] Also in 2020, urban areas of North Carolina accounted for an astonishing 88 percent of the state's aggregate economic production (also known as "gross domestic product").[4] These data demonstrate the economic dominance of urban regions in North Carolina, a phenomenon shared with most states.[5]

With the expanding tech sector, the growing importance of colleges and universities, and increased interest by households for access to restaurants and entertainment—all of which are extensively located in cities and metropolitan areas—the common forecast has been that urban areas will continue to outpace rural areas in growth and prominence well into the twenty-first century.[6] Indeed, preferences for urban living, particularly in large cities, appears to appeal to the trend-setting Generation Z.[7]

Then came the COVID pandemic and the reactions it created. Humans have a history of adapting, a trait likely responsible for why humans have survived for millions of years. COVID presented a major new challenge, and we responded by adapting. Several of these adaptations could have profound implications for the geographic urban/rural divide in the Anxious Age.

Geographic Game Changer No. 1: WFH

One of the major reactions to COVID was the work-from-home (WFH) alternative. With lockdowns and stay-at-home orders instituted in most states in early 2020, both employers and employees looked for ways to continue working while still abiding by the mandates. For some—but certainly not all—jobs, a remedy was for individuals to remain at home but connect to their work virtually. This was not a new work method. Before the pandemic an estimated 5 percent of the workforce used WFH, at least partially.[8] But during the pandemic the rate exploded to 61 percent.[9] Office workers and teachers were two of the top professions utilizing WFH. As the pandemic subsided, the WFH rate dropped. But the latest information for 2025 shows that the proportion of weekly WFH hours is still between 25 percent and 30 percent, and experts think the rate will stay in that range.[10] The percentage includes those working at home full-time as well as those working some days at home and some at the worksite, called "hybrid working." Importantly, North Carolina has participated in WFH. In 2023, one study ranked the Raleigh-Cary metro second to Austin in the WFH rate and ranked Charlotte fourth among metropolitan regions.[11]

There has been a vigorous debate about WFH. From an environmental perspective, WFH eliminates commutes to work, thereby helping the climate. One analysis suggests that CO_2 emissions could be reduced by 10 percent if one-third of households worked remotely.[12] With the current average round-trip commute of one hour daily, WFH employees save both time and money, allowing those resources to be devoted to other activities, including sleep![13] The WFH employee also has more opportunity to interact with a spouse, partner, and children. Mothers, who often are the primary care provider for children, may find that WFH helps them keep a job. Even if the WFH is part-time, such as working at home three days and at the employer's location two days, these benefits will occur, though to a lesser degree.

A potentially large benefit from WFH can result from the typical household's largest expense—housing. With the WFH employee likely at home for a significant part of the workweek, many will expand their geographic search for housing to include locations much farther from the employer's location. Typically, this means the employee can take advantage of the "iron law of real estate." The "iron law" simply says the price per square foot of housing will decline as the unit's location moves farther away from significant centers of economic activity, like central cities. The "iron law" occurs because most households prefer to be closer to jobs, schools, medical care, and shopping and eating venues offered by cities. But the savings from a household living in a more remote location can be significant: Research shows that costs for the same-sized house are 45 percent lower in rural areas than in urban areas, and 15 percent less in suburban locations than in cities.[14]

Of course, there are potential and important disadvantages with WFH. In many occupations, frequent collaboration with colleagues is valued for generating ideas and solving problems. While such interaction can still be maintained with WFH through digital contacts, this technique may be an imperfect substitute. Management control and guidance of employees is also less viable with WFH than if both management and employees work at the same site. Also, on a broader scale, some worry about the replacement of in-person contact with humans by digital contact. The concern is about the creation of an "artificial world" and the discarding of the "real world," and what this means for the human experience of interactions with others.[15]

Indeed, one of the original founders of modern economics, Alfred Marshall, emphasized the benefits of what he termed the "gregarious" nature of economic activity. He argued that individuals working together in the same space leads to coordination, specialization, and sharing of knowledge and expertise. These benefits result in greater productivity and financial returns for employers. But beyond these economic benefits, Marshall emphasized additional social benefits through the development of workers' characters, especially regarding relationships between individuals.[16]

Marshall's insights have sparked an analysis of the impact of WFH on worker productivity. The issue has not been settled, as competing studies have found both higher productivity and lower productivity with WFH, leaving the question unsettled.[17] However, two conclusions appear to have been reached. One is that hybrid WFH is better than full-time WFH for maintaining or improving productivity. Another is that hybrid WFH has a significant positive impact on worker retention, perhaps raising the retention rate by as much as 33 percent.[18] To date, no conclusions have emerged regarding the effect of WFH on the character of workers, as noted by Marshall.

Despite continuing debate about WFH, WFH appears to now be a permanent option for many employees. Some futurists see WFH even expanding from mainly office occupations to a variety of occupations with the increased use of artificial intelligence (AI) and the possibility of remotely operated machines.[19] Another point to consider regarding AI—which will be discussed in more depth in later chapters—the debate about whether AI will help or harm remote work. AI could harm remote workers if the technology results in labor downsizing: Remote workers may suffer from the "out of sight, out of mind" effect and become more susceptible to being cut. Conversely, AI workers could benefit if AI creates more tasks that can be performed remotely.[20]

The main conclusion is that WFH has the potential to reduce the advantage of urban regions in household locational decisions, thereby elevating the attractiveness of rural counties and moderating the urban/rural divide during the Anxious Age. The remote jobs, many of which pay well, would generate new spending in outlying areas. The new spending would create more local jobs, a big plus for addressing the high unemployment in rural locations. Many unemployed residents in rural regions could then stay in their locality rather than moving or commuting to find work.

Geographic Game Changer No. 2: New Shopping and Delivery Techniques

Given that households were motivated by the pandemic to reduce personal interactions, and that a number of retail venues have not recovered to prepandemic levels, ways of providing products and services to customers have expanded during the pandemic period.[21] Cyberbuying and home delivery both surged. In 2015, e-commerce accounted for only 7 percent of retail sales. In the year prior to the pandemic (2019), e-commerce had grown to account for 10 percent of retail sales. The rate jumped to 17 percent at the height of the pandemic in 2020, but then eased to 14 percent in 2022 as households became more comfortable with public shopping. However, in recent years cyberbuying has resumed its upward climb, with the data for 2024 showing a 16 percent share of total retail spending and a 21 percent share expected for 2025.[22] There are forecasts that cyber-generated retail sales will exceed one-third of all retail sales by 2027.[23]

Part of the reason for the optimism about e-commerce is its potential interaction with other technology. Currently, cyberbuying has clear disadvantages for purchasing some types of products. Clothing is a good example. While buyers using cyberbuying can guess about needed sizes, mistakes involve time and effort in returning items, even if returns are free.

However, already technology has been developed to create a cyber version of a buyer's body, thereby allowing "cyberfitting" to take place before purchases are made. As advances in AI enhance such cyber "body doubles," cyberbuying will likely be improved and perfected. The idea could be extended to other applications, including creation of cyber "home doubles" for furniture and appliance shopping.[24]

A form of cybershopping for groceries already exists: A household sends a list of needed items to a supermarket, supermarket employees gather the items, and the buyer then picks them at the store or has them delivered. But in a few decades, this process may seem obsolete. In the near future, appliances like refrigerators as well as kitchen cabinets and pantries will be able to monitor the rate of usage of food items and automatically reorder items as needed. Robot home-helpers may even unpack and store the items after they are delivered.[25]

As noted, delivery is often a part of cyberbuying. Unfortunately, delivery can be one of the most expensive parts of the process. The so-called last mile of delivery, dominated by vehicles, can account for almost half of the total delivery cost, as it often involves moving through crowded streets and residential developments.[26]

Once again, the future may have an answer in the form of delivery drones. Drones can avoid crowded streets, can travel faster than vehicles, and are a cheaper method of delivery because they are more energy efficient than vehicles. Drones can also serve remote and rural areas that are currently underserved by vehicle delivery.

But currently drones deliver only 4 percent of annual commercial packages sent in the United States, a result of numerous challenges the technology must overcome.[27] Package load is limited, so larger and stronger drones need to be developed. Regulations need to be established for both drone flights and their landings and takeoffs. Methods must be established to ensure safety and guard against theft.[28] Experts forecast that if these issues can be overcome, drone delivery will substantially increase and possibly become the common method households use to receive packages, especially in rural areas.[29]

Geographic Game Changer No. 3: High-Speed Internet Everywhere

An obvious requirement for remote work is household access to reliable high-speed internet, also termed broadband. Until recently, a clear benefit of living in metropolitan areas has been the greater access to broadband compared to rural areas. However, like many states, North Carolina has improved broadband access through public funding. North Carolina's program is called GREAT, or Growing Rural Economies with Access to Technology. The program provides subsidies to private companies to extend broadband access to underserved—mainly rural—areas.[30] While the GREAT program is certainly positive, map 2.1 shows that approximately one-third of North Carolina's one hundred counties still have broadband access for fewer than 75 percent of their households.[31] Most of these counties are clustered in the mountains, northeast, and southeast, areas where the economies are dominated by agriculture and forestry and where access can be challenging.

Currently, much of the broadband expansion is using the traditional technique of reaching customers by running lines on telephone poles or burying the cable lines. Yet there is an alternative way to provide internet access that avoids ground lines and difficulties related to geographic access. The Starlink company and similar firms have had success in providing broadband using access to satellite connections. Indeed, North Carolina and FEMA have used Starlink to help restore internet service to Western North Carolina after devastation from Hurricane Helene.[32] Satellite internet subscriptions have been increasing, and it is estimated that there are now almost 9 million subscribers to satellite broadband providers in the United States, many of whom are rural.[33] Although this is a fraction of the estimated 115 million total broadband subscribers in the country, the alternative of providing broadband access through a satellite connection is a promising option for the Anxious Age.[34]

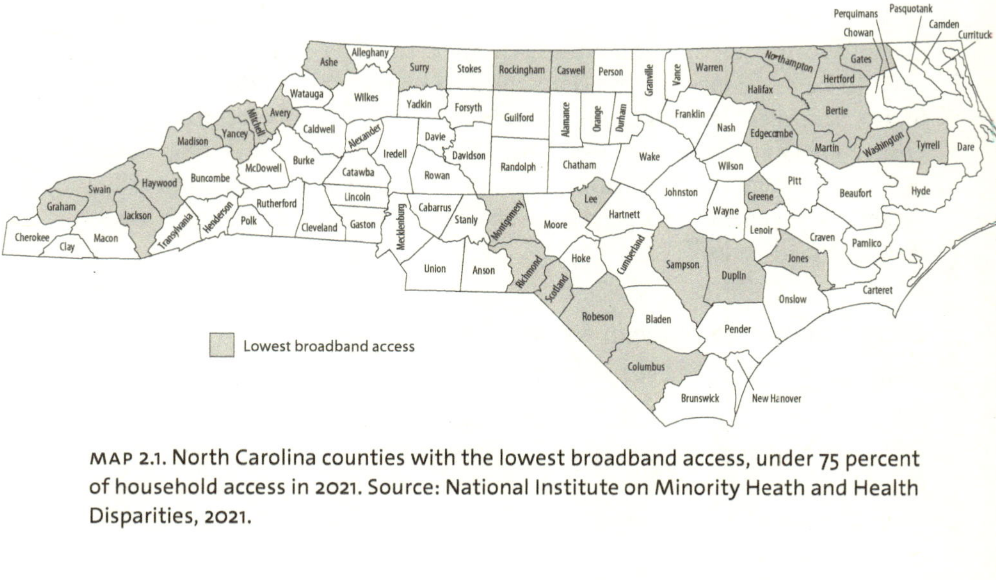

MAP 2.1. North Carolina counties with the lowest broadband access, under 75 percent of household access in 2021. Source: National Institute on Minority Heath and Health Disparities, 2021.

Is There Evidence of Households on the Move in North Carolina?

While there is evidence that remote work has maintained a higher level than it did prior to COVID, there are two follow-up questions. First, have remote workers moved, and second, if they have moved, where have they moved to? More specifically, is there any evidence that remote workers have moved out of large metropolitan areas to lower-density small towns and rural regions? And if the answer is affirmative, has North Carolina participated in the shift?

There is some tentative, but incomplete, evidence that remote workers may have moved, and the evidence in North Carolina is consistent with the national results. At the national level, University of Virginia demographer Professor Hamilton Lombard has tracked domestic migration over the past decade.[35] Domestic net migration captures the movement of households within the country and does not include foreign immigration. Domestic net migration is positive if more people move into the area—like a county—than move out, and negative if more people move out of the area than move in.

Lombard has estimated the domestic movements for areas of different population levels. For the more highly populated regions, Lombard discovered that net in-migration in the most recent years has turned negative: In other words, more people have moved out of the largest populated regions than have moved in. For the regions with lower populations, Lombard found the reverse—more people moving in than moving out. Although Lombard is not able to link these findings to remote work, logic does imply there could be an association.

Using the census data compiled by Lombard that applies to North Carolina, map 2.2 compares changes in net in-migration in North Carolina counties for the prepandemic period of 2018–19 and the same changes in the postpandemic period of 2022–23. Darker-shaded areas on the map are associated with an increase in net in-migration between 2018–19 and 2022–23, and lighter-shaded areas connote a decline in net in-migration between the two time periods.

The figure reveals an interesting pattern for North Carolina. Net in-migration declined between 2018–19 and 2022–23 in the counties that include the cities of the state's top three metropolitan areas: Charlotte, Raleigh, and Greensboro.[36] Also included is Moore County, a major retirement area and home to Pinehurst and national golf tournaments. Furthermore, in the same four counties in 2022–23, net in-migration was actually negative, meaning more people moved out of the counties than moved in. By contrast, several counties near major cities, such as Onslow (close to

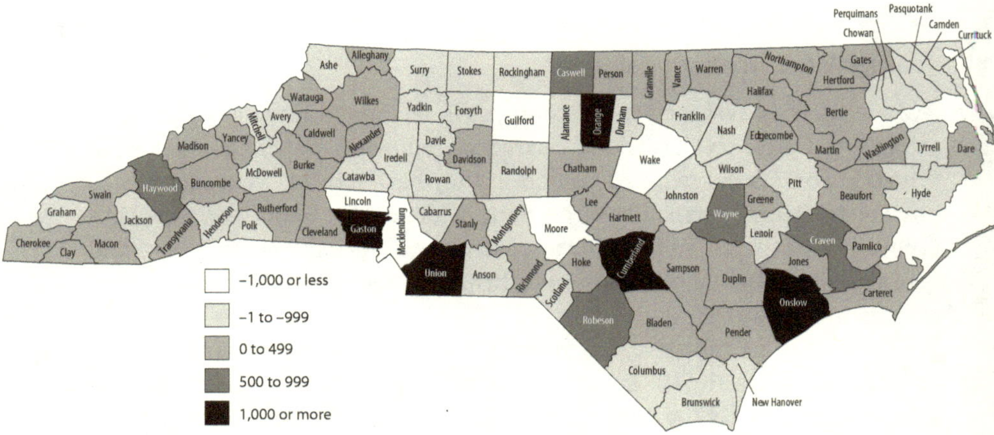

MAP 2.2. Difference between net in-migration in 2018–2019 and in-migration in 2022–2023 in North Carolina counties. Source: US Census Bureau data compiled by Dr. Hamilton Lombard, University of Virginia. Calculations by the author.

Wilmington), Union and Gaston (adjacent to Charlotte), Orange (to the west of Raleigh), and rural counties in the Western NC mountains, had gains for net in-migration. Cumberland County also had an increase in net in-migration, but the county is a special case, as the US military dominates the local economy.

The conclusion is that movers in North Carolina found large cities less attractive and less-populated areas more attractive after the pandemic. But what's the reason? Since age-adjusted deaths from COVID were lower in less-dense areas than in high-density regions, households could have decided that less-dense areas would be safer than more-dense areas in the event of another highly contagious virus.[37] Or it could be that households moved to take advantage of the benefits of living and working remotely, such as lower housing costs, lower transportation costs, and improved time allocation. While the answer is unknown, the implications will likely become clearer during the Anxious Age.

Will the Geographic Game Changers Reshape North Carolina?

The three geographic game changers of remote work, new shopping and delivery techniques, and expanding broadband access together have the potential to reduce the geographic influence and attraction of large cities and metropolitan areas, while increasing the influence and benefits of smaller

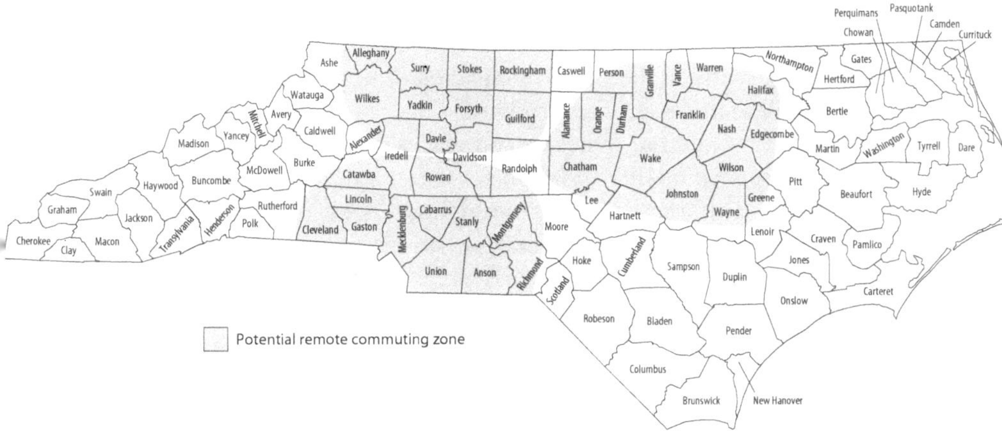

MAP 2.3. Potential remote commuting zones around North Carolina's major metropolitan regions based on a forty-five-minute one-way commute. Source: MapQuest.

cities and rural regions that can offer lower housing prices and open space. As shown, the tracking of household movements after COVID suggests that such a geographic alignment may have begun in North Carolina. If accurate, where might the realignment take place in North Carolina, how would the affected counties be impacted, and what would be the public policy implications?

In addressing the question of which counties in North Carolina might become homes to remote workers, commuting time is of key importance. While all remote workers, by definition, will not commute every day, a hybrid schedule of three working days at home and two days commuting to the worksite is not uncommon.

Surveys show that workers consider a one-way commute of over an hour excessive.[38] Map 2.3 illustrates the one-hour commuting area around the top three metropolitan regions in the state based on Charlotte, Raleigh, and Winston-Salem as the central cities (only the part of each region that lies within North Carolina is shown). The reach not only includes the existing outer ring of the metro areas but also, importantly, includes towns outside the metros, such as Rocky Mount, Wilson, and Goldsboro for Raleigh; Shelby, Rockingham, and Newton for Charlotte; and Wilkesboro, Dobson, and Yadkinville for Winston-Salem. For those who work remotely every workday, the geographic possibilities for where to live are extensive.

While workers moving to these more remote areas benefit from significantly lower home and rent prices, less traffic congestion, more open space, and—in some cases—greater natural amenities, they also, as I already emphasized, give up proximity to more extensive shopping options, colleges and universities, and higher-level medical care, as well as access to transportation such as international airports.[39]

This creates a potential "chicken and egg" situation. Localities that already have upgraded quality-of-life factors are more likely to attract WFH households. Yet at the same time, as more households show interest in the WFH lifestyle, there will be additional incentives for both private and public decision-makers in other localities to increase quality-of-life factors such as retailers, medical care facilities, entertainment venues, expanded higher education facilities, and greater supply of housing to reduce shelter prices. Indeed, several smaller cities surrounding Raleigh, like Cary, Apex, and Holly Springs, and surrounding Charlotte, including Huntersville, Cornelius, and Mooresville, have attracted enough businesses and amenities to be self-sustaining. Many residents of those smaller cities are able to avoid long commutes for work, shopping, and medical care.

Yet if the forces behind remote work continue, one possible outcome is the development of new types of communities in small town and rural areas to attract remote workers. Remote-working developments would focus on attracting remote workers by making reliable high-speed internet available, and the developments would include modest medical clinics and small retailers. The developments could also be constructed so as to facilitate drone delivery for households wanting to use the service. The developments would be privately financed, but with the assistance of local public authorities for sites and necessary zoning changes to allow for amenities such as drone landings. Remote-working households would still benefit from significantly lower housing prices compared to urban locations, less traffic congestion, less commuting, and more open spaces.

It is important to recognize that there would likely be a public finance impact of a major shift to remote work and remote living, especially if the shift results in households leaving metro areas for rural and small-town areas. Certainly, fewer households in urban areas would mean lower total local tax revenues from reduced local property developments and local sales taxes. The reverse would happen in the rural and small-town regions that gained households. Of course, with fewer households in urban areas and more households in rural areas, there would be a reduction in needed urban public service spending and an increase in needed rural/small-town public service spending. But because many public functions incur large "fixed costs"—costs that don't vary with the number of users, like buses on a specified route—there could be a challenging adjustment period. As a result, major publicly supported projects in large urban areas, including arenas, convention centers, public transportation, and school buildings, which were financed with an expectation of a larger population, may be put in jeopardy.

But there could be some countervailing economic benefits to large cities and metro areas resulting from the flight of remote workers. With fewer households living in the city, there could be enough of a drop in housing demand to reduce housing prices in metro regions. Yet such a price decline, although good for buyers, could be a financial disadvantage for owners planning to sell. The declines would also reduce local property tax revenues. Over time, however, with lower real estate prices, less traffic congestion, and reduced pollution, the image of large cities and metropolitan areas as attractive locations to live could be renewed.

Hence, the three geographic game changers could reshape North Carolina's economic geography by spreading the wealth and the population more evenly between urban and rural regions. Such a change could narrow—perhaps even close—the urban/rural divide during the Anxious Age. Yet this major shift would generate large adjustments, including some negative effects for the losing urban areas, as well as new challenges—including many positive changes—for winning rural regions.

Summing Up

There's a saying that the three most important factors for a real estate buyer to consider are location, location, and location. Access to jobs, shopping, medical care, entertainment, and educational institutions is important for households. In the twentieth and early twenty-first centuries this access was largely found in urban areas—the key reason that regions like the Triangle, Triad, and Charlotte have expanded so rapidly in North Carolina. However, combined with the demise of many of the industries that traditionally supported rural North Carolina, the growing dominance of urban North Carolina is a key reason for the large urban/rural divide that has existed in the state.

However, there may emerge a new economic geography in the Anxious Age that ultimately shrinks the urban/rural divide. With the technological changes experienced in work, shopping, and delivery, and with broader internet access during the COVID period and continuing in the post-COVID period, the advantages held by urban regions may be slipping. Remote work continues for a significant percentage of workers, internet access has spread, cybershopping is growing, and drone delivery is on the verge of taking off. If the application of these factors continues—and certainly if it increases—the hold of urban regions on the economy may be broken as households seek new locations providing what they want but at a much lower cost.[40] The benefits of remote living would be especially significant for households with children.

In fact, the latest census data already show that households have been leaving the largest metropolitan areas in North Carolina, while at the same time many rural areas have gained relocating households. If these trends continue, there is potential for numerous North Carolina counties composed of rural and small-town areas to attract remote workers and their families, especially those counties located under an hour of driving time to the center of a metropolitan area. Hence, in future decades we may observe a new type of development spreading across the state—remote-working developments. These developments would be specifically designed and equipped for the remote worker and household.

Yet there is an emerging technology that may possibly work against remote-working developments: driverless vehicles. Driverless vehicles would allow traveling workers to use their commute time in productive ways, including working and even sleeping. This capture of commuting time for other uses would offset some, but not all, of the downsides of travel to work.

Yet even with driverless vehicles, there could still be a significantly altered economic geography during the Anxious Age that would benefit rural and small-town areas at the expense of urban areas. The dominance of the big city may pass as work and life become separated from geography. However, this remaking of where people live, work, and shop will bring a mix of positive and negative outcomes, especially focused on both private and public finances, as a new economic geography is formed during the Anxious Age. But if recognized early enough, the challenges can be managed.

3

THE NEW WORKFORCE

COVID Intervenes in the Labor Force

In the modern capitalist economy of the last five hundred years there has been a continuous competition for power between employers and employees. This competition is over factors such as hours of work, working conditions, vacation time, benefits, and, of course, compensation. The competition exists not only between employer and employees but also between different employers who are hiring employees with the same skill sets. In the twentieth century another set of players entered this competition. Governments—federal, state, and local—have frequently intervened by setting standards related to compensation, working hours, and working conditions.

Just as it did for so many other aspects of our lives, COVID impacted the labor market. Mandated business shutdowns kept an estimated 22 million workers from their jobs for several months.[1] Federal financial support, in the form of stimulus checks and related assistance, sustained furloughed workers. But then a funny thing happened on the way to the recovery. As mandates were relaxed and businesses were reopened, labor shortages emerged. And although the shortages moderated as the pandemic receded, even four years after COVID first struck the country, abnormal labor shortages were still being reported.[2]

These shortages affected the balance of power between employers and employees. With workers now in demand by more employers, workers had greater ability to bargain for higher compensation as well as for more favorable job conditions. Average worker compensation surged, particularly in labor-intensive sectors. For example, between 2019 and 2021, average hourly wage rates rose in sectors like leisure/hospitality by 3.7 percent. In construction the hourly rate was up 3.6 percent, and in other services the increase was 4.5 percent. It is important to note that these gains are all recorded after removing the impact of inflation, which was also beginning to rise.[3] Average vacation and sick leave also increased, and average weekly work hours decreased.[4] Young workers, in particular, would often tell potential employers they needed "purpose and meaning"—as defined by them—in any job before they would consider it.

The improved bargaining position of employees led, perhaps ironically, to efforts to revive labor unions. Labor unions have been in decline for several decades; membership dropped from 33 percent of the workforce in 1955 to 9.9 percent of the workforce in 2024.[5] But since the pandemic, labor unions have had several wins, including some in the South, where unions have been all but nonexistent.[6] Perhaps workers saw unions as a way to transform their improved individual bargaining position into even greater collective power.

A complementary force at work is the declining birth rate. As I discussed in chapter 1, the birth rate is now at below replacement level in both the nation and North Carolina. At some point, the labor force in North Carolina will increase only if people willingly move to the state, from other states as well as from other countries. However, while such movements are uncertain due to the potential influence from individual states' public policies as well as from national public policy, it is certainly reasonable to consider that the future power of labor relative to employers could increase, perhaps so much that a four-day workweek may emerge.

Yet possibly countering this power shift to labor is the looming expectations of technology, especially AI, on the employer-employee relationship. There appears to be universal agreement that AI will have major impacts on the labor market. But the question is whether those impacts will be a net positive or a net negative for the number of jobs. If AI creates more jobs than it eliminates, it could help increase the strength of labor. But if AI eliminates more jobs than it creates, it could weaken labor bargaining.

The future position of labor will also depend on two other elements. One is the evolution of the so-called gig economy, in which workers use digital technology to freelance their employment, often with no protections or benefits. If the relative position of labor strengthens, will gig workers be absorbed with other workers and receive typical benefits and protections? Or, if new technology actually weakens labor's strength, will more workers become gig workers?

The future of foreign immigration will also be important to the labor market in upcoming decades of the Anxious Age. Straightforward economics suggests that a greater inflow of foreign migrants increases labor supply, reduces labor shortages, and thereby moderates the power of employees in negotiating with employers. Also, with a large share of immigrants taking jobs in lower-paid sectors such as construction, hospitality, and food services, the reduction of labor shortages and the weakening of relative labor power would be greatest for lower-skilled and lower-paid workers.[7] Conversely, if foreign immigration is reduced, and especially if large numbers of existing immigrants are deported, labor shortages could strengthen labor power. Some of the answers to these issues and questions will depend on future skill needs, a topic I address in a separate chapter.

Depending on how these competing forces come together, there could also be a dramatic change in work hours. There have already been discussions about the nation moving to a four-day workweek.[8] Could such a shift come to fruition in the Anxious Age?

This chapter discusses each of these topics, focusing on their relevance and impact on the future labor market. The issues have particular relevance for North Carolina. The state is regarded as one of the least labor-friendly states in the country, as demonstrated by its low unionization rate.[9] How the labor component of the economy evolves after COVID and during the twenty-first century will have a significant impact on the level of household prosperity in the Anxious Age.

How Surprising and Long-Lasting Is the Labor Shortage?

The most common measure of labor shortages is in a monthly survey from the US Bureau of Labor Statistics' Job Openings and Labor Turnover Survey (JOLTS). The survey provides the number of job openings as a percentage of employment, referred to as the JOLTS rate. The survey is released monthly for the nation and for each state. Graph 3.1 shows the JOLTS data beginning in the early stage of the pandemic (November 2021) through November 2024 for North Carolina and for the nation.

The impact of the pandemic is clearly seen. In November 2020 North Carolina's JOLTS rate was 4.7 percent and the nation's JOLTS rate was 4.6 percent. Both JOLTS rates continued to rise through 2021 and early 2022; North Carolina's rate reached a peak of 8.6 percent in February 2022, and the nation's top rate of 7.4 percent also occurred in February 2022. But as the pandemic receded, so did the JOLTS rates. However, at the end of 2024 and into early 2025 there was a modest upward movement in the North Carolina JOLTS rate, with a similar but smaller increase in the national rate.

There is a complementary statistic providing other information about the labor market: the labor force participation rate (LFPR), which measures the percentage of potential workers who either have a job or are looking for a job. The federal government, which calculates the LFPR, defines a potential worker as anyone over age sixteen who is not in the military and who is not institutionalized. Prior to the pandemic, North Carolina's LFPR, shown in

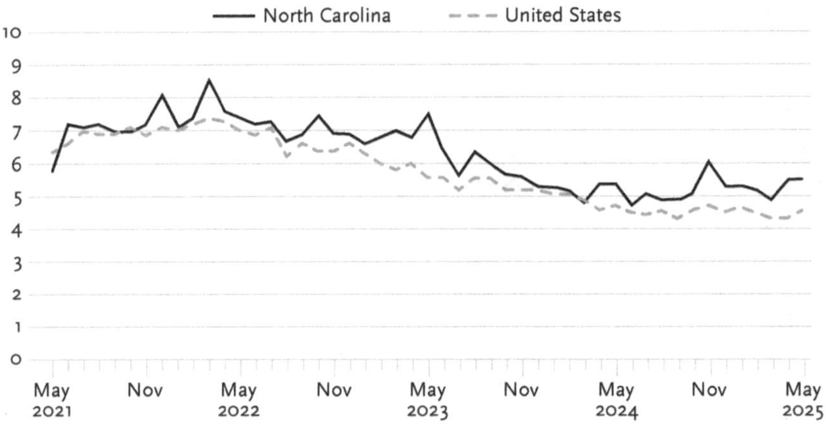

GRAPH 3.1. JOLTS data (job openings rates) for North Carolina and the United States (in percentage points), seasonally adjusted, 2021–2025. Source: US Bureau of Labor Statistics.

graph 3.2, was nearly 61 percent. At the height of the pandemic during the mandated shutdowns, the LFPR plunged to under 57 percent. It recovered to past 61 percent in 2022, but in 2025 the rate had dipped to 59 percent, still higher than during the pandemic but under the prepandemic rate. However, if the state's LFPR in 2025 was at prepandemic levels, over one-fourth of the job vacancies in early 2025 could potentially have been filled.

Hence, the conclusion is that an elevated job shortage has persisted in North Carolina, even several years after the pandemic began. What are the reasons for this job shortage, and what do they imply for the future job market?

The aging population is one major reason. The LFPR has been declining in most states, including North Carolina, since the late 1980s, when the state's LFPR was 69 percent. As North Carolina's population has become older, participation in the state's labor market has been more driven by retirees, because they are counted as in the labor force, meaning they are considered *potential* workers. But if they don't have a job, they are not counted as *participating* in work. Additionally, retirements accelerated during COVID as older individuals worried about the possible impacts of the disease on their health and longevity. Many elderly individuals retired by cashing in on the surge in housing prices following the record low mortgage interest rates that occurred during the pandemic, and selling their homes.[10] In addition, young individuals in their late teens and early to mid-twenties have reduced their participation in paid work, as more are attending college.

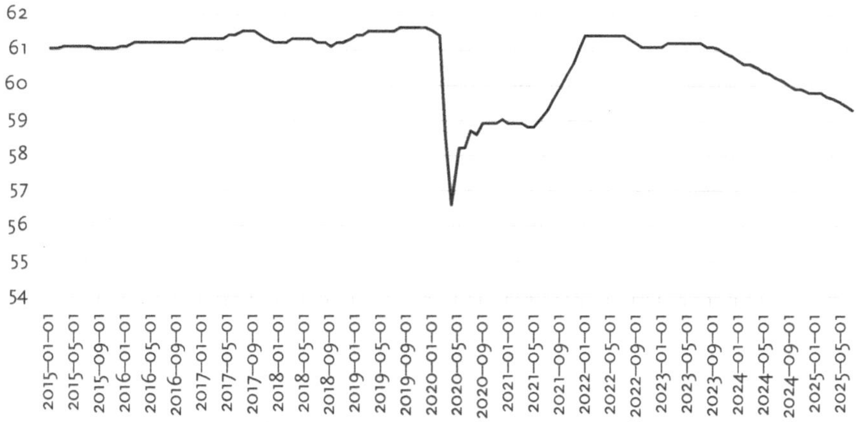

GRAPH 3.2. Labor force participation rate in North Carolina, 2015–2025 (in percentage points). Source: US Bureau of Labor Statistics.

Two other factors are important for explaining the lower LFPR following the pandemic, but they are likely to be temporary. One is the massive financial assistance provided to households during the pandemic and in the immediate recovery from the pandemic. Federal programs supplying stimulus checks and child assistance went to a majority of households. SNAP (Supplemental Nutrition Assistance Program, the successor to food stamps) benefits and health assistance from the Affordable Care Act were also expanded. There were also moratoriums on evictions for households who couldn't pay their rent. Analysts conclude that the size and duration of this financial help may have motivated some households to delay returning to the labor market as the pandemic eased.[11] Federal legislation has already been passed to curtail these COVID-related programs.[12]

A related phenomenon impacting the labor market during COVID was the "Great Resignation," where millions of workers nationally—many of them young—willingly quit their jobs. While these departures certainly may have created worker shortages for individual firms, it is likely that the Great Resignation had very little net impact on the aggregate labor shortage.[13] This is because most of the workers who resigned did so to take an alternative job with better pay and/or better working conditions. The fact that the quit rate was highest in lower-paying economic sectors such as retail, hospitality, healthcare, and government, provides support for the idea that a significant number of workers took advantage of the labor shortages that emerged during COVID to improve their financial position.[14] Indeed, as the pandemic receded, the Great Resignation subsided.[15]

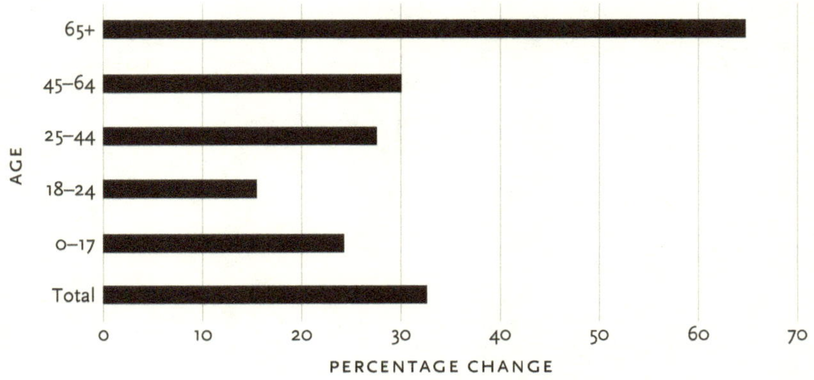

GRAPH 3.3. Projected growth rates in age groups in North Carolina, 2021–2050 (in percentage points). Source: State Demographer of North Carolina.

The major factor determining whether North Carolina will have a labor shortage or labor surplus in the future will be the relative growth of age cohorts. Using the forecasts from the state demographer shown in graph 3.3, it appears there will be a stronger likelihood for a tightening of labor supply than for a loosening of labor supply. Between 2021 and 2050, the state demographer predicts that the oldest cohort (age 65 and over) will increase by 65 percent, twice the rate of the youngest cohort (ages 0 to 17). The three age cohorts of 45–64, 25–44, and 18–24 comprise the major working ages, and each has modest projected growth rates significantly less than for the oldest cohort. The state demographer's forecasts are based on assumptions about migration to the state, both from other states and internationally. As I discussed in chapter 1, an argument can be made that in-migration from both sources could be significantly reduced in the future. Hence, the possibility of future serious labor shortages in North Carolina is real, especially in sectors like construction, agriculture, and hospitality, where labor from foreign immigrants—often undocumented immigrants—is very important.[16] Deportations of existing workers who are undocumented immigrants, which accelerated beginning in 2025, could exacerbate the labor shortages.[17]

Did COVID Create a Shake-Up in Wages?

The labor shortages created by COVID resulted in significant impacts on wage rates. An obvious tactic for businesses experiencing unfilled employment positions is to increase wage rates to make the positions more attractive. This happened as the economy reopened when the pandemic subsided.

TABLE 3.1. Changes in inflation-adjusted hourly wage rates (by percentage) for economic sectors in North Carolina in the years before, during, and after the pandemic.

Sector	2014–19	2019–24	2019–21	2021–23	2023–24
All	9.4	1.3	3.7	−2.3	1.5
Finance	12.3	−0.1	8.4	−17.7	2.3
Information[a]	15.3	8.7	−4.4	3.9	9.5
Professional/business services	7.3	0.3	3.8	−1.7	−1.7
Education/healthcare	4.8	7.7	9.1	−3.3	2.1
Construction	12.6	11.3	3.6	4.1	3.2
Manufacturing	5.7	4.1	0.0	5.7	0.0
Other services	20.3	−0.3	4.5	−7.1	2.6
Transport/trade/utilities	1.5	2.0	1.1	−2.7	3.8
Leisure/hospitality	8.7	11.2	3.7	3.5	3.7

Source: US Bureau of Labor Statistics; calculations of inflation-adjusted hourly wage rates by the author.

[a] The information sector comprises producing, processing, and distributing information, and includes traditional broadcasters as well as web-based information providers. Wage rates for agriculture are not available.

But two questions immediately follow: Where in the economy did the wage rate gains occur? And were the improvements in wage rates temporary, or are they a long-lasting result of COVID?

Table 3.1 shows the changes in the inflation-adjusted hourly wage rates for the major economic sectors in North Carolina during five time spans between 2014 and 2024. It is important to adjust wage rates to account for the impacts of inflation (higher prices) on the purchasing power of workers.

Columns 1 and 2 compare averages of the five wage rate changes for the years prior to the pandemic (2014–19) and the five wage rate changes for the years during and immediately after the pandemic (2019–24). For all sectors combined, as well as for the majority of individual sectors, inflation-adjusted hourly wage gains were lower in the 2019–24 period than in the 2014–19 period, mainly due to the higher inflation rate in the early 2020s. The exceptions were leisure/hospitality, education/healthcare, and transportation/trade/utilities, and the latter sector was dominated by retail trade.

Columns 3, 4, and 5 provide shorter two-year periods for comparison.

With only one exception in the 2019–21 period, gains were made in inflation-adjusted hourly wage rates in the sectors. During the 2021–23 period, however, there was a decline in inflation-adjusted hourly wage rates for all sectors combined as well as for five of the individual nine sectors. The reason is that these years covered the surge in the postpandemic inflation rate. The peak annual rate of 9.1 percent occurred in June 2022. Afterward the inflation rate decelerated, and column 5, covering the 2023–24 period, shows inflation-adjusted wage rate gains for all sectors except professional/business services.

Looking again at column 2 for the pandemic and postpandemic period combined, the top four sectors in inflation-adjusted wage gains were construction, leisure/hospitality, information, and education/healthcare. Examining the job losses during the crucial 2019–21 period when shutdowns were mandated and many workers moved to different occupations as the economy reopened, the stunning 38 percent loss of employees in leisure/hospitality and the significant 8 percent loss in education/healthcare workers were likely factors in driving the above-average wage rate gains in those sectors. Indeed, education/healthcare and leisure/hospitality had the largest boosts in real wage rate gains during the 2019–24 time period compared to 2014–19.[18]

What does this analysis imply? Did the pandemic permanently change the labor force? It is too early to be certain, but there's some indication that it may have helped elevate the wage rates in some low-income sectors. The most prominent example is the leisure/hospitality sector, which traditionally has the lowest hourly wage rate. The average hourly wage rate in this sector increased from being 56 percent of the economy-wide average wage rate in 2019 to standing at 61 percent of the economy-wide average wage rate in 2024. Hourly wages in education/healthcare rose from 98 percent of the overall average wage in 2019 to 103 percent in 2024, and the comparable increase for construction wage rates was from 98 percent to 106 percent of the economy-wide average.[19]

In a market economy where businesses compete for labor, changes in pay rates are ultimately determined by shifts in the need for workers (demand) and the availability of workers (supply). The shutdowns and financial support for households during the pandemic gave lower-wage-earning workers time to evaluate their situation and consider moving to higher-paying jobs. Evidence indicates that many did, in fact, follow this path.[20]

This situation provides an explanation for why North Carolina firms in lower-paying sectors like leisure/hospitality significantly increased their pay rate during the pandemic and postpandemic period. Faced with a reduction in the supply of workers, businesses in the sector needed to increase the financial benefit to employees in order to attract workers. National analysis also supports this conclusion.[21]

But businesses now faced with higher wage costs in the Anxious Age will be motivated to look to technology as at least a partial replacement for labor. There are already examples of this happening, such as the fast-food giant McDonald's experimenting with totally machine-controlled and -operated restaurants.[22] If such efforts are successful, the remaining jobs may be high-paying ones, but the number of total jobs could be dramatically slashed.

Hence, two competing forces will determine wage rates in the future—demographics and technology. Specifically, the trends of an aging workforce and advances in labor-replacing technology will drive wage rates. With a declining birth rate and longer lifespans, our population is becoming older. As we have already seen for North Carolina, the population aged sixty-five and older is forecasted to increase almost three times faster than the population under age seventeen between now and 2050. There's also a big difference forecasted between growth in the sixty-five-and-older population and the prime working-age population between twenty-five and fifty-four.[23] So unless there's a surge in migration to North Carolina from other states or nations, workers will be relatively harder to find in the future. This will motivate businesses to improve wages and working conditions to attract workers, thereby supporting the labor market changes prompted by COVID.

Yet at the same time, businesses facing relatively more expensive labor will be prompted to find ways to reduce their use of labor. The major way to do this is to use more labor-saving technology. Interestingly, we are now on the cusp of new labor-saving methods in the form of AI. It is certainly plausible that AI's success could eventually create labor surpluses, which would lower worker pay and make the impacts from COVID temporary. Think of the future as a race between demographics and technology.

While it may take years to see demographic outcomes and to determine whether machines will replace people in sectors like leisure/hospitality, education/healthcare, and even construction, a long-used method to protect and promote the worker may gain increased popularity and use in North Carolina in the Anxious Age. The method is unions.

Background on Unions

Labor unions are a way for workers to combine their numbers and thereby increase their bargaining power with employers. Members of a labor union operate collectively, rather than individually, when negotiating with an employer. In the absence of a union, an individual worker who doesn't like the wage rate paid by the employer can threaten not to work or even to quit. To the employer, these threats are minor for one person. However, if all workers threaten not to work—that is, threaten to strike—this is a major problem for the employer. Although the employer could dismiss all the workers, it would probably take considerable time and effort to find replacements. In the meantime, work is not done, and the employer likely loses substantial money and customers.

In our country there were labor unions as early as the 1700s, but labor unions began to develop in earnest after the Civil War. Labor unions had setbacks in the 1920s, came back in the 1930s during the Great Depression, again retreated in the 1940s with wartime economic restrictions, and then once again grew after the war. Union membership as a percentage of the total workforce peaked in the 1950s at close to 35 percent.[24]

Several setbacks then began to take a toll on labor unions. Unions had enjoyed success in the growing manufacturing sector as a way to protect workers from being replaced by technology.[25] Then, beginning after World War II, global trade was encouraged as a way to prevent future wars, based on the idea that countries that traded with each other would be less likely to engage in conflict.[26] The North American Free Trade Agreement (NAFTA) between the United States, Canada, and Mexico was passed in 1994, and a comparable worldwide trade agreement, termed the World Trade Organization (WTO), was established in 1995 to further promote trade and worldwide economic growth. Importantly, China joined the WTO in 2001.[27]

Since numerous countries, especially China, have significantly lower labor costs than the United States, a major impact of open international trade has been for many US-based manufacturers to move their production out of the United States, resulting in millions of job losses in the country.[28] In North Carolina, the textile and furniture production industries had been a dominant part of the state economy for decades. Between 1990 and 2024, furniture manufacturing employment dropped by two-thirds, and textile employment plunged an amazing 90 percent.[29]

With the demise of traditional manufacturing in the country in the late twentieth and early twenty-first centuries, union membership collapsed, dropping from its peak of nearly 35 percent in the 1950s to 9.9 percent in 2024.[30] Yet in North Carolina, labor unions have never been strong. Part of the reason was the structure of the Southern economy. Agriculture had long been the dominant industry in the South. Farmers were independent operators who didn't use many hired laborers. Hence, the economic conditions were not attractive for unions to take hold in the South.[31]

After the Civil War, the Southern economy was devastated and people were destitute. The textile industry, mostly located in the New England states, looked to reduce its costs by moving to the South and taking advantage of much lower-cost labor. Anti-labor-union sentiments still persisted, so efforts to unionize workers were unsuccessful. Unfortunately, some of the attempts at unionization led to violence.[32]

In the post–World War II period, numerous states passed legislation to hinder the ability of unions to organize workers, and North Carolina was one of the states. So-called right-to-work laws were passed in twenty-six states, including in North Carolina, in 1947. The major provision of a right-to-work law is that it prohibits all employees from being forced to join a union even if the union was supported by a majority of the workforce. In labor law terms, right-to-work laws prohibit a "closed shop"—a company where becoming a member of a union is a condition of working there.[33]

Impacts of Unions

Researchers have evaluated the economic impact of unions both on union members and on the broader economy of a state, which includes union and nonunion members. These results can be used to inform North Carolina leaders and residents of the potential results of increased unionization in the state.

The most comprehensive recent analysis of the impacts of labor unions is by the Federal Reserve Bank.[34] States that inhibit labor unions, meaning states with right-to-work laws, have lower wage rates and modest reductions in self-reported financial conditions by workers. But countering the decline in union membership and wage levels are increases in job openings and in employment levels.

Yet, interestingly, an MIT study found that right-to-work laws in a state are associated with an improvement in worker satisfaction.[35] There are several potential explanations for this finding. Some workers may place a higher value on individually dealing with employers regarding pay and working conditions, compared to relying on unions to negotiate these relationships. Also, employers could be more motivated to address worker pay and condition disagreements on a personal level, hoping to create the feeling of a partnership with individual workers.[36]

Economic developers in Southern states worry that an increase in union activity and success will eliminate Southern states' current advantage of lower labor costs due to the absence of unions, thereby leading to fewer business starts and slower economic growth in the region.[37] However, there is a counterargument that in the United States, unions have been associated with higher worker productivity.[38]

Will Unions Be Part of North Carolina's Future?

North Carolina has the second-lowest union membership rate in the country: 2.8 percent, two-thirds lower than the national rate and only slightly higher than South Carolina's 1.6 percent rate.[39] So union organizers have a tough road ahead of them in boosting the presence of labor unions in North Carolina.

Yet demographics and politics might be on the side of labor unions. Polls show that younger people are more favorable to labor unions.[40] Even though North Carolina is an aging state, as today's youth move through the aging process and their work career, they may keep their views about unions intact. Additionally, since North Carolina is considered a "purple state" politically, it straddles the Democratic Party / Republican Party split. Because Democrats favor unions at a rate more than two times higher than Republicans do, years in which North Carolina swings Democrat could provide opportunities for boosting unions.[41]

A shift in the state toward being more favorable to labor unions could begin with a repeal of the state's right-to-work law. There is precedent for such an action, as Michigan repealed its right-to-work law in 2023. But even without such a repeal, the recent success of unions in right-to-work states like Tennessee and South Carolina shows that a repeal of the law is not necessary for union success.[42] North Carolina now is home to its first auto manufacturer, VinFast. The United Auto Workers has vowed to unionize every auto manufacturing plant in the country.[43] And with new manufacturing companies like the Wolfspeed chips plant and Toyota's battery facility also locating in North Carolina, there will be more opportunities for unions to organize in the manufacturing sector, where labor unions traditionally have had success.

The challenge for promoting unions in North Carolina will be considerable, as shown by the decisive 75 percent vote by Amazon workers at a warehouse near Raleigh against joining a union in early 2025.[44] In economics there is a long-standing debate between "equity"—meaning improving worker conditions—and "efficiency"—which focuses on maximizing the returns from resources, including labor. Some economists think the two cannot be achieved simultaneously, while others think they can.[45] Labor unions focus on equity, while right-to-work laws promote efficiency. One strategy unions can use is to argue that higher pay and improved working conditions increase worker productivity, as research cited earlier has shown. Depending on the political and economic conditions, debates about unionization in North Carolina are likely in future decades of the Anxious Age.

The Future of Gig Work

The next topic is this chapter is about a labor market method that emerged prior to the pandemic, but about which questions have arisen in the post-pandemic economy. The work method is gig work.

The gig economy began during the recession of 2007–9, sometimes called the Great Recession. During that recession the jobless rate more than doubled, from 4.4 percent to 10 percent, and it didn't return to 4.4 percent until 2017.[46] During that challenging decade, both businesses and workers were motivated to consider innovative methods of hiring. Businesses were looking for hiring methods that would provide them with flexibility and fewer commitments to workers. Workers were just looking for jobs. At the same time, the availability of the recently developed World Wide Web on computers created opportunities for new forms of business interactions.

The gig economy was one of these opportunities. The gig economy is really a freelance economy. Workers engage in short-term, flexible employment opportunities with firms. Common examples are ride-sharing and food delivery drivers, web developers, and graphic designers. But any work task that doesn't require a continuous set schedule, where experience isn't important, and where coordination between multiple workers isn't necessary can be performed by the gig economy.

The major benefit to the worker of the gig economy is flexibility. Workers usually do not have a long-term contract. Workers can often choose when, where, and how much to work. Gig work offers a variety of types of work and skill needs, including foreign opportunities. For workers with family responsibilities, such as care of children or of elderly parents, gig work can be the perfect fit, especially if the work can be done digitally.[47]

But there are major downsides to gig work. One major disadvantage is insecurity: Contracts are often very short term. Benefits like health insurance, retirement packages, and regulations about working conditions are minimal or nonexistent. Also, because gig workers are considered independent contractors, access to unemployment compensation is not available. A 2023 report ranked North Carolina as the forty-fourth-best state for gig work.[48] The index used a combination of working conditions for gig workers, where the state ranked forty-ninth, and gig opportunities and competition, where North Carolina ranked twenty-eighth.

Based on a 2022 survey, there are an estimated 58 million gig workers in the country. Although there is not a separate survey for North Carolina, if the same population proportion applies to the state as in the nation, there are 1.8 million gig workers in North Carolina. The same survey found that immigrants, younger individuals, and lower-income people are more likely to be gig workers. The top reasons for becoming a gig worker are the need for a job, a desire to have a flexible job, the enjoyment of gig work, and the desire to earn money for discretionary spending.[49]

Experts think the gig economy will continue to expand.[50] There is a logical reason for this expectation. The initial start of the gig economy was from technology, based on the ability of the internet to allow remote working as well as mobile working using the internet and cell phones. We are now entering a period where the next technology anchored in artificial intelligence will create both new ways of working and new types of tasks and careers. Each of these results will likely spark further innovations in how employees and employers interact, which is at the core of the gig economy. This topic will be addressed in more depth in chapter 4.

Also, look for increased debates in the upcoming decades about regulations over the gig economy, especially if it grows. This debate will be similar to the one about unions, where the question is equity for workers versus efficiency for employers. And the same question will be important—whether both equity and efficiency can be accomplished simultaneously.

On Deck: Changes in the Standard Workweek?

The common five-day workweek has been around since 1940.[51] That was the year the five-day, eight-hour workweek became standardized by the federal government. The legislation required companies to pay overtime wages for workweeks longer than forty hours. Prior to this, companies were free to set their own workweeks.

The move to a standardized workweek actually got started in 1869, when President Grant guaranteed eight-hour workdays for government employees.[52] Then in the 1920s auto manufacturer Henry Ford brought the five-day, eight-hour daily workweek to his auto factories. Ford reduced workers' hours but maintained their pay, and he concluded that the longer workweeks yielded little benefit to auto production.[53]

We may have entered a new debate about the workweek. US Senator Bernie Sanders has introduced a bill in Congress to reduce the standard workweek from forty hours to thirty-two.[54] The bill would motivate business adoption by requiring time-and-a-half pay for workdays longer than eight hours, and requiring double-time pay for workdays longer than ten hours. The bill would also prevent firms from reducing current hourly pay and benefits with the shorter workweek.

Sanders argues that some European countries—specifically Norway and Denmark—have already adopted workweeks shorter than forty hours. He also points to studies showing that workers are happier and less burned out with the shorter workweek, and that employers are happier too.[55]

Why has this issue popped up? Again, the answer may be COVID. Many workers, especially young workers, are putting more focus on their work-life balance. And although labor shortages have mostly disappeared, shortages could certainly reappear if the labor force continues to grow slowly, as I emphasized earlier in this book. With employers potentially competing for hiring from a smaller pool of people, companies will look for more ways to appeal to existing workers and to motivate people who aren't working to consider a job. Offering a shorter workweek is one way of accomplishing this.

The rise of remote work has also been another factor raising the profile of the workweek. How so? Remote work has allowed workers to spend more time at home, where they can interact with their family, integrate household chores with their work, and enjoy more flexibility to schedule necessities like medical appointments and shopping. Offering a guaranteed shorter workweek, but with the same pay as the longer workweek, is one way of attracting and keeping workers at the office.

So, is a shorter workweek a win-win? Advocates answer yes. Workers will have more time to relax, spend time with their family, handle obligations like doctors' appointments, and simply enjoy a better work-life balance. For two working spouses with children, childcare expenses will be reduced. Also, commutes to work will drop 20 percent, thereby helping reduce traffic congestion and pollution. Some studies also find less stress and better mental health for employees as well as fewer physical issues when working fewer days and hours.[56]

Advocates say businesses will also benefit. Operating a firm four days rather than five days a week will lower costs. Several studies have found that worker productivity increases so much that some businesses will realize increased revenues.[57]

However, not everyone is on board for the shorter week. There are studies reporting that worker stress increases with the shorter workweek as employees try to accomplish in four days what they previously did in five.[58] There's also the possibility that if all firms go to the shorter week, the total amount of business transactions could fall and shrink the economy, as well as create inconveniences for consumers. If all businesses are, for example, closed on Friday, then how does that help families schedule appointments? There's also the same concern as heard for remote work: that the shorter workweek would reduce the time available for worker collaboration, something that is extremely important in many companies.

There are three possibilities about where the workweek debate will go next. One is that legislation such as that proposed by Senator Sanders will ultimately be passed and the four-day, thirty-two-hour workweek will be accepted as the standard in the country, including in North Carolina. Backers say the benefits from the shorter workweek are too great to ignore.

The second possibility is not to reject the shorter workweek but instead to allow individual states or even individual businesses to decide whether to keep the forty-hour week or go to something shorter. That is, if workers and businesses both benefit from the thirty-two-hour, four-day week, then wouldn't we expect them to willingly make the choice of voluntarily instituting the shorter workweek? The third possibility is that the four-day workweek doesn't gain traction and is not implemented.

Expect the workweek debate to heat up in the Anxious Age, both nationally and in North Carolina. One reason is the emergence of artificial intelligence, which has the capacity to take over many worker tasks. In this case, the workweek may shrink simply because there's less work for people to do. This issue will be part of the discussion in chapter 4.

The debate over a shorter workweek may be the most symbolic issue of the Anxious Age. Continuing from COVID, people are still worried about numerous aspects of their lives, and many feel overwhelmed. They don't consider themselves in control of their lives. Having more time to themselves and less time committed to their job is one way of having more control and perhaps feeling less anxious.

Summing Up

The labor market will be one of the most dynamic parts of the national as well as North Carolina economies during the Anxious Age. The pandemic appears to have made permanent changes to the labor market. Labor shortages and mass job resignations motivated many firms to improve working conditions in order to attract employees. Major increases in inflation-adjusted wage rates occurred in lower-paying sectors such as healthcare and hospitality. Whether these wage gains and other employment improvements persist will depend on an ongoing competition between the supply and demand for labor. Like many other states, North Carolina is expected to see modest increases in the working-age population in future decades. Such a trend would be expected to give workers better bargaining power and hence better working conditions and wages. But the likelihood of major technological advances—driven by AI—that could replace labor with machines will reduce the relative need for workers by businesses. Hence, maintaining the pandemic-era gains in inflation-adjusted wage rates for workers will be largely determined by a typical competition between labor supply and labor demand, in this case represented by demographics and technology.

However, a new player in the labor market may emerge in North Carolina during the Anxious Age—labor unions. Legislation such as right-to-work laws, as well as public attitudes, have effectively kept unions from organizing in the state. But recent union gains in neighboring states plus an increased support for unions among younger demographic groups have increased optimism for the future of labor unions in North Carolina. For unions to increase their influence, the long-standing debate between equity and efficiency will need to be confronted. Can unions achieve improved working conditions and compensation for workers, while at the same time increasing worker productivity and not diminishing the attractiveness of North Carolina for business investments? If the answer is yes, then unions could have a positive future in North Carolina's Anxious Age.

The gig or freelance economy, born with the development of the modern tech economy, continues to be popular in North Carolina; it is used by an estimated one-third of the state's workforce. And advances in future technology are expected to increase the use of gig work. Yet gig work, largely unregulated because gig workers are considered independent contractors, has created a debate over equity and efficiency similar to the debate sparked by labor unions. There will likely be moves to require businesses hiring gig workers to provide benefits such as health insurance, access to unemployment compensation, and possibly even retirement plans. There may even be attempts at unionization, as there has been in other states. If such efforts are successful, then the question again becomes how an employer will weigh the benefits of gig work versus the costs.

Finally, look for the question of the standard workweek to emerge as a major issue in the Anxious Age. The debate will be driven both by workers who are increasingly concerned with their work-life balance and by businesses who are looking for ways to attract workers in an increasingly tight labor market. Also, a shorter workweek may be one way to spread a diminished amount of future human work if AI takes over many tasks from humans. A remaining question is whether changes in the standard workweek will be mandated by government, or whether they will be left to individual businesses.

Clearly, our plate will be full of workplace issues and decisions during the Anxious Age. Having a big impact on these issues will be the emergence of a new technology that many think will have game-changing influences on all parts of our lives, including the workplace. That technology is artificial intelligence, or AI.

4

THE WORLD WITH AI

AI Is Different

The next three decades could witness some of the most dramatic and widespread changes to work tasks in our history. AI has the potential to completely rearrange the work performed by humans and the tasks done by machines. This labor market "disruption"—as economists term it—will spare no state, including North Carolina.

There are two major steps in initially preparing for this disruption. The first is an attempt—with an emphasis on "attempt"—to comprehend exactly what AI is and what it will do, particularly to the job market. The second, equally important step is to understand and estimate how AI will impact specific occupations differently, and then to calculate how many jobs may be lost in North Carolina due to AI. This will allow both the state's leaders and residents to prepare for the labor market transformation during the Anxious Age.

Labor market disruption is not new. It has happened often, particularly when major new work technology is introduced. But the newest technology—AI—is different. While we are still learning about its capabilities, many experts say that AI is capable of replacing humans in a wide range of occupations. What makes AI different than the plow, conveyor belt, or even the standard computer is its ability to perform tasks that currently require human cognition, evaluation, and decision-making. This is what makes AI's impact so broad—and also, to many, scary.

The goal of this chapter is to provide some specifics for AI and its impacts, focusing on North Carolina. Quite frankly, many people are confused about AI, hence they fear it. But since AI may be the development that makes the biggest impact on North Carolina during the Anxious Age, it is important that we have as much knowledge about AI as possible. Along the way will be a discussion of the debate over whether AI can dramatically improve our world and standard of living, while also recognizing possible adverse consequences of AI. Also, in light of AI's expected impacts, the chapter addresses the question of whether AI should be regulated. Of course, the focus will be on North Carolina, but most of the conclusions will be applicable to any state or country.

Before beginning these topics, it is helpful to place AI in the context of the technological change that has already occurred in North Carolina's history.

A Brief History of Technological Change in North Carolina

During North Carolina's history, technological developments have had significant impacts on the state's economy. Of course, by the time North Carolina was first settled, food production had already made the important leap from hunting and gathering to crop and livestock farming. But after the Civil War, technology in the form of the water mill played an important role in attracting one of the state's dominant industries of the twentieth century—textiles. Although water mills had been in use for over 1,500 years, North Carolina's numerous rivers where mills could be applied to generate power were a major factor in shifting the textile industry from New England to North Carolina and other Southern states. Later technology like the automated loom further increased the dominance of textiles in the state.[1]

The state's large agricultural industry was revolutionized when the use of man and mule for plowing was replaced by the much more productive and labor-saving tractor. With less labor now needed on the farm, thousands of workers were available for new employment. Fortunately, the displaced workers found jobs in the textile, furniture, and tobacco factories then expanding in the state. Hence, tractor technology changed more than farming in North Carolina.

But with the decline of the textile, furniture, and tobacco industries in the late twentieth century, North Carolina had to remake its economy. Fortunately, the state was able to attract firms in the newest technological field—computers—to such an extent that North Carolina is now a leading tech center, where the term "tech" refers to computer technology and its applications.[2]

Technology also contributed to making one of the state's prominent cities—Charlotte—the second-largest banking hub in the country in the twenty-first century.[3] When in the past states regulated the geographic territory of a bank, most states limited banks to a territory in their immediate vicinity. But both North and South Carolina were different. The two states permitted banks to operate in territory throughout the state. Charlotte, which is on the border of North and South Carolina, attracted banks that served both states. Hence, when the federal government in the late twentieth century permitted banks to have nationwide territories, the Charlotte-based banks used the communication and management technologies they had developed to operate bank branches in large territories to rapidly expand nationwide, and they soon represented the largest concentration of financial activity outside New York City.

One last example of technology's impact on the North Carolina economy is the importance of the state's railroads and ports. Beginning in the 1800s, North Carolina's railroads facilitated the movement of products and people throughout the state and to numerous other states. Railroads also linked with the state's main port of Wilmington to support international trade. Although some of this transportation has been lost to trucking, the current annual economic impact of the state's railroads is still estimated at nearly $20 billion.[4]

The conclusion is that technology has long shaped the North Carolina economy, including the job market. AI will be no different. But before examining both the meaning and impact of AI, it is important to review where the North Carolina labor market stands after the pandemic.

Trends in the Labor Market Before and After the Pandemic

Perhaps the most significant trend in the labor market since World War II has been the shift away from manual and routine occupations to cognitive and analytical occupations. Two reasons have been behind this move. One is continuing development of labor-saving technology in sectors like manufacturing and construction. The second is the expanded use of services, including services such as education, healthcare, and legal assistance, all of which require high-level cognitive decision-making.

When occupations are divided into two categories—cognitive, which require high levels of decision-making, and routine, which require little individual decision-making—the trend toward increased employment in cognitive occupations and decreased employment in routine occupations in North Carolina is evident. As a percentage of total employment, the cognitive occupational share rose from 32 percent in 1980 to 48 percent in 2015 and to 55 percent in 2023. Conversely, the routine occupational share dropped from 68 percent in 1980 to 52 percent in 2015 and to 45 percent in 2023.[5] Complementing the increase in cognitive occupations in North Carolina, occupations that require more formal education, has been the steady increase in adult educational attainment in the state.[6]

Another way of seeing this labor force transformation is to examine

TABLE 4.1. Employment change in major economic sectors in North Carolina, 2012–2024, by percentage.

Sector	2012–16	2016–20	2020–24
Total	9.4	1.4	12.4
Construction	16.7	12.8	18.0
Manufacturing	5.4	−4.0	4.1
Wholesale trade	4.7	0.0	18.3
Retail trade	9.5	−2.4	8.5
Transportation	13.2	21.9	17.4
Information	12.5	1.4	13.7
Finance	11.7	11.7	23.0
Professional and business systems	13.5	0.0	21.5
Education and healthcare	6.4	0.7	17.6
Leisure and hospitality	15.7	−20.0	44.0
Other services	10.3	−1.7	21.3
Government	3.9	−2.0	9.8

Source: US Bureau of Labor Statistics.

employment changes in the major economic sectors in North Carolina. Table 4.1 shows the changes in employment for major economic sectors in the three recent four-year time periods.

Although each sector contains a combination of cognitive tasks and routine tasks, many are dominant in one task type. Manufacturing is a good example, where workers are more likely to engage in routine tasks. In each time period, including the most recent 2020–24 period, manufacturing was among the sectors with the lowest employment gains. By contrast, the information, finance, professional/business systems, and other services sectors were among the sectors with the highest employment gains, especially outside the 2016–20 period, which includes the shutdowns during the COVID pandemic. Generally, tasks in these sectors involve nonroutine activities based on specific situations, therefore requiring unique decision-making. Even a sector like leisure/hospitality, which had large employment gains except for the period including the outbreak of COVID (2016–20), often requires tasks specific to a customer that have not yet been able to be performed by technology.

Yet the changes documented in table 4.1 occurred prior to the widespread implementation of AI. Once the AI technology is broadly applied and used, how will the labor market be affected? Before this question can be answered, the question of exactly what AI is needs to be addressed.

What Is Artificial Intelligence?

The technological development that will most impact the upcoming decades of the Anxious Age is, without a doubt, artificial intelligence, or AI. One-third of businesses have already reported to have begun using AI in their operations, and this usage will likely climb in future years.[7] Even before it has been fully deployed, AI has created different reactions. Some look forward to its availability, and expect it will make life better and easier, even leading to a new renaissance of life. Others have the opposite reaction, worrying AI could lead to a "machine-ruled" world, one where AI has complete control of all facets of our lives.[8]

Yet how should AI be defined? Many people think the concept implies machines that can think and make decisions. It is easy to understand why some come to this conclusion. AI involves three components: significant amounts of data, computer programs to analyze the data and identify patterns and relationships, and conclusions based on the data analysis using the computer programs. This is essentially the process humans use. To solve a problem, we gather information (data), examine the data for information to guide us (analysis of patterns and relationships), and then reach decisions (conclusions).

AI is not a new concept. The term "artificial intelligence" was coined in the 1950s when mathematicians and statisticians began developing the concepts that would allow them to use large amounts of information to develop predictions.[9] For example, if physicians want to use symptoms to predict strokes, they gather information on many individuals—both those who have had strokes and those who have not—and then try to relate their characteristics to the likelihood of having a stroke using simple observation of the data. In the days before the computer, this was extremely time-consuming and painstaking work; I know this from personal experience, since I did similar kinds of analysis in economics before computers became available. Also, because relationships between personal characteristics and stroke probabilities likely change over time, the relationships and predictions could quickly become out of date, which is just a polite way of saying the predictions could become wrong, thereby potentially endangering patients.

This has all changed with today's ability to collect massive amounts of data and perform sophisticated analysis using widely available high-capacity and high-speed digital computers. Continuing with the medical example, large quantities of patient information can be continually collected and analyzed—that is, the results showing relationships between patient characteristics and stroke probabilities are constantly updated. The analysis can also "learn," indicating that the programs run by the computers can keep track of changes in diagnoses as new, better, and more extensive information becomes available.

Hence, the "machine learning" in AI simply mimics human learning. Humans learn by observing, collecting information, looking for relationships, and coming to conclusions. The difference is that machines can do the same much faster, more comprehensively, and more frequently. Therefore, whereas a doctor forty years ago looking for stoke symptoms had to rely on knowledge learned in medical school or from findings in a medical journal that may be years old, today doctors can use the very latest findings about stroke symptoms generated by AI.

Of course, AI will have applications beyond the medical field. In fact, since forecasting the future is necessary in many areas of life, AI will likely be universally applied. For example, manufacturers will use AI to forecast sales, and then use those forecasts to decide on quantities of inputs needed from suppliers. Also, AI will be used by banks to identify fraudulent transactions, thereby protecting honest depositors. The applications of AI are endless.

We hear worries that AI will eventually control humans.[10] Most experts disagree.[11] AI is a tool created by humans. While some interpret the word "artificial" to imply otherworldly or nonhuman, it is important to remember that the computers, computer code, and analytical equations used by AI are all developed by humans. What AI does is controlled by humans. Also, the conclusions and recommendations generated from AI will be evaluated and used by humans. In conclusion, yes, novelists and screenplay authors can create stories of the world being ruled by machines, but we should remember what these artists are doing: They are entertaining audiences.

What Are the Impacts of Artificial Intelligence?

Without downplaying its importance, it is helpful to recognize that AI is just the latest in major technological advances. Electricity, vehicles, air flight, air-conditioning, cell phones, computers, and refrigeration are just a few of the major technological inventions of the twentieth and twenty-first centuries. We now take each of these inventions for granted. But it wasn't long ago that many people didn't have the benefits of these technologies. I can remember my paternal grandmother telling me how thrilled she was when the "lights came on," a result of electricity finally reaching her family farm. The availability of electricity now allowed her to purchase a refrigerator to keep food cold, replacing the "icebox"—literally an insulated box with ice that had to be refreshed regularly. Her home now had illumination with the flick of a switch, and later she was able to purchase an electric-powered washing machine to replace tedious and backbreaking handwashing of clothes.

Technological advances have two major impacts. One is the impact on well-being, also called the standard of living. Usually this is measured by economic productivity, meaning how much output is produced in the economy per unit of input. If an invention increases productivity, then it typically raises the population's average standard of living.

There are three ways inventions like AI can improve productivity.[12] The first is moving a task from being performed by a human to being accomplished by a machine. This is commonly called automation. There are numerous examples of automation in factories, particularly where machines do routine jobs previously done by humans. One AI example is a chatbot used for customer service by many firms. The human customer asks questions of the chatbot and receives AI-generated replies. Automation improves productivity by being able to generate more output than humans in a given period of time.

A second way AI can increase the economy's productivity is not by replacing human workers but by making those workers more productive. Consider again the example of a doctor attempting to diagnose a patient's symptoms. With AI's enhanced ability to successfully relate symptoms to specific illnesses, medical care becomes more productive by increasing the success rate and speed of patient diagnoses.

Third, AI can create entirely new jobs engaged in the objective of making AI itself more productive, consequently making the economy even more productive.

The second major impact of AI is on the labor force. Just as the tractor caused fewer farm jobs but facilitated an increase in factory jobs, major inventions re-sort jobs, causing the loss of some jobs but the creation of others.[13] AI is also expected to do this, but with the question of which side will be larger—job losses or job gains. Three examples of potential new jobs created by AI are AI trainers, who teach companies how to successfully use AI; data detectives who monitor the quality of data used by AI; and cybersecurity analysts who constantly protect the AI machinery and software from online attacks.[14]

Economists agree that the implementation of AI will increase economy-wide productivity, but they disagree on the degree of gain. This should not be surprising, since the widespread implementation of AI is only beginning. Some estimates suggest AI could boost economic output by 7 percent to

16 percent over a decade, while others estimate a much lower gain of under 1 percent.[15] These results compare to estimated decadal gains of 4 percent for cell phones and 25 percent for air-conditioning.[16] Each of these estimates implies additional national economic output of billions of dollars. For North Carolina's economy, the increase would be in the hundreds of millions of dollars.

Perhaps the most important question is the impact of AI on specific jobs, specifically which jobs will multiply and which will suffer losses. Economists are honest in realizing such forecasts are educated guesses, given that a technological change as massive as AI has unpredictable scope.[17] Still, it is helpful to examine estimates to understand the potential range of impacts.

One study separated jobs into the cognitive and routine categories discussed earlier in this chapter.[18] Not surprisingly, routine occupations are expected to significantly decline as a percentage of the workforce. For example, robots directed by AI will replace humans in numerous manufacturing jobs as well as in many tasks performed by humans in warehouses. But the study also predicts a replacement of some human jobs in cognitive occupations. The result, according to the analysis, will be a one-third increase in the unemployment rate. However, one bright spot will be an increase in workers in what the study's authors term creative jobs, including entrepreneurs pursuing new ventures and individuals taking up the fine arts.

The investment firm Goldman Sachs also predicts significant job upheaval from AI's implementation. The company estimates that AI will replace approximately 25 percent of the work tasks in the country, including workers in a wide range of cognitive occupations, including accounting, finance, retailing, research, and analysis, as well as teachers, health professionals, college professors, and writers.[19]

The firm McKinsey Global has released a very detailed analysis of the employment impact of AI.[20] McKinsey predicts that occupations in office support, customer support, and sales, production, and food services will each experience job losses of 10 percent or more due to AI. Table 4.2, which applies to North Carolina these loss rates and loss rates predicted by McKinsey for other sectors, shows the forecasted job declines in North Carolina as a result of AI. The aggregate losses are just shy of half a million, and almost 10 percent of the total state workforce in 2024. However, it is important to remember that if the economy grows faster as a result of AI, new jobs could be created in other sectors for those losing their jobs.

But while faster economic growth resulting from AI could feasibly generate enough new jobs to replace those lost from AI, jobless workers will likely require retraining to be able to perform the new jobs. This means the edu-

TABLE 4.2. Expected job changes from AI in North Carolina occupations, based on 2023 job totals.

Occupational Category	Expected % Change	Number of NC Jobs Lost
Office support	−40	−221,700
Customer service & sales	−23	−112,415
Production work	−12	−39,500
Food services	−10	−42,568
Business & legal professionals	−6	−21,269
Construction	−2	−3,783
Educators	−2	−5,451
Installation & repair	−2	−2,690
Agriculture	−1	−718
Community services	−1	−614
Managers	−1	−29,143
Transportation services	0	0
Creative arts	0	0
STEM professionals	0	0
Property maintenance	0	0
Healthcare professionals	0	0
Total	−10	−479,851

Sources: McKinsey Global Institute; US Bureau of Labor Statistics; author's calculations.

cational and training system in North Carolina will need both the ability and capacity to do this reskilling effort. Will the current educational system need to be restructured to perform this critical task? Or will a significant part of this retraining take place outside the traditional education system?

Also, and just as important, what new skills will be needed in the emerging AI economy? These questions will be addressed in chapter 5.

Do Humans Have Any Advantages over AI?

Even if we accept that AI is not a monster that will take over the world, and that AI will create some jobs to replace those it destroys, there's still the question of whether humans will maintain some advantages AI can't replicate. Fortunately, some thinkers believe that the answer is definitely yes—that humans will maintain some unique advantages.

Ohio State University Professor Angus Fletcher argues that what humans have, and AI doesn't, is "primal knowledge."[21] Primal knowledge was developed during the infancy of humanity, before schools, information, or any type of technology. Humans had to rely on intuition, imagination, emotions, experience, and common sense to solve problems and make decisions. Using these concepts gave humans creativity and flexibility in confronting danger and solving problems. AI is the opposite. AI relies on applying algorithms—a set of rules and computer codes—for analysis and problem solving, leaving virtually no room for flexibility. Each type of analysis and decision-making is important, but only humans can apply both to the same situation. Professor Fletcher calls primal intelligence "natural cleverness that AI can't replicate."[22]

Should AI Be Regulated?

With AI expected to have one of the most impactful influences on people and the economy during the Anxious Age, the question has arisen of whether AI should be regulated. North Carolina is one of the forty-seven states that have proposed or enacted various types of AI regulations.[23]

Most types of AI regulations either proposed or passed fall into one of three categories. The first is regulations to ensure the ethical use of the technology. This primarily means AI should be designed to be transparent and understandable, so that users can understand how the AI results were developed and how the results may be used. The second category is regulations to protect the rights and safety of users. An example is the use of AI to develop "deepfakes," which are digital alterations of user characteristics, including their physical characteristics and physical actions, to create false pictures or videos. The third regulatory category deals with mandating actions to mitigate the negative social and economic impacts of AI. While the first two categories have wide support, there is some AI industry concern that overly strict regulations could impede innovation.[24]

Most existing AI regulations passed or proposed by states, including North Carolina, have been in the first two categories, and this is logical.[25] States want residents' privacy and safety protected in the use of all forms of technology. Forms of AI legislation in North Carolina will likely continue to be offered and debated as AI becomes a larger part of our world in the Anxious Age. What will be more debated is any legislation proposed to address workers losing their jobs due to AI. This issue will be addressed in chapter 5 from the perspective of retraining.

Summing Up

The early period of the Anxious Age has witnessed the continuation of job movements away from routine jobs to jobs requiring cognitive decisions. But a new element will be increasingly introduced into the labor market as the Anxious Age proceeds: artificial intelligence. While not a new concept, AI is now on the verge of becoming a key element in the economy. In short, AI is a process of using large-scale data with high-capacity and rapid computers to process information and develop conclusions with more speed and greater accuracy than humans. AI will increasingly be used to power machines and robots to perform tasks now done by humans. Although AI will certainly be applied to many routine jobs, the big change from the past is that AI will also be used to replace humans in numerous jobs requiring cognitive skills. Hence, AI's impact on the labor market will be much larger than that of many other recent technological innovations.

It is estimated that AI could replace half a million workers in an assortment of occupations in North Carolina, a number equivalent to 10 percent of the state's workforce. Will there be enough new jobs for these people? What skills will be needed for new jobs, if they occur, and how will jobless individuals be retrained for those jobs? Will the structure of education and training need to be reorganized to accommodate these challenges? Will the state and local governments be compelled to provide publicly funded jobs for those not able to be retrained? Or will North Carolina's state and local governments conclude that guaranteed-income programs will be needed to support those displaced by AI, perhaps supported by some type of fee or tax on AI use? The rationale of such a fee or tax would be that the implementation of AI created the chronic unemployment.[26] These are important policy questions related to AI that will dominate many debates during the Anxious Age.

5

EDUCATION AND THE EVOLUTION OF TASKS

COVID and Ongoing Challenges: K–12 Schools

According to the National Assessment of Educational Progress (NAEP) metrics, which many call the gold standard of education assessment, academic performance for North Carolina public school students fell during the pandemic.[1] For example, from 2019 to 2022, fourth-grade reading scores dropped 1.2 percent, fourth-grade math scores fell 2 percent, eighth-grade reading scores dropped by 2.3 percent, and eighth-grade math scores dipped 3.5 percent.[2] This broke a trend of consistent improvement spanning two decades.[3] In three of the four scores, North Carolina's drop was less than the nation's.[4] Educational performance data for 2024 show improvements in North Carolina's scores, but performance has not yet reached prepandemic levels. Again, the state's gains were better than the nation's. Unfortunately, the educational performance gaps between white and Black students and between white and Hispanic students persisted throughout the pandemic as well as in the postpandemic years, in most cases with the gap maintaining or expanding.[5]

Several factors were behind the decline in academic performance, most of which were related to public schools' attempts to substitute digital learning for in-class learning. The factors included shifts in academic schedules as the pandemic progressed, unequal access to technology for students to participate in digital lessons, inconsistent use of digital lessons by students, inadequate preparation and training of both teachers and students for digital learning, and teacher and staff shortages.[6] The learning declines effectively translated into fewer years of time in school for students.[7]

Hopefully the educational recovery from COVID is a short-run problem: The postpandemic evidence does show improvement, though not yet complete recovery.[8] One lingering issue is absenteeism. The absentee rate steadily rose during the COVID years; the rate doubled to a peak of 31 percent in 2022. Since then, the rate has fallen, but in 2024 it was still an unacceptable 25 percent. To compound the concern, the absentee rate is 8 to 10 percentage points higher for Black and Hispanic students than for white students.[9]

The key issue is the longer-run challenge of improving the academic success of all K–12 students. Although there have been clear improvements in the performance of public school students in North Carolina in recent decades, there is still room for improvement. The state ranks near the middle among the states and the District of Columbia in the NAEP scores. In 2024 North Carolina was 34th in fourth-grade reading, 14th in fourth-grade math, 33rd in eighth-grade reading, and 19th in eighth-grade math. Compared to the same measures in 2013, there was a decline in the state's rankings in reading, but an improvement in the state's rankings in math.[10]

North Carolina ranks at the national average for the four-year high school graduation rate, but there are continuing differences in the graduation rate for demographic groups. In 2024 the four-year high school graduation rate was 95 percent for Asian students, 90 percent for white students, 84 percent for Black students, 83 percent for Hispanic students, and 82 percent for economically disadvantaged students.[11]

Although North Carolina has class sizes matching the national average for both elementary and secondary school students, the state lags in resources devoted to public K–12 education.[12] A recent comprehensive study of spending per pupil in all states found that North Carolina ranked forty-eighth among the states and District of Columbia.[13] It is important to note that the calculations were adjusted for differences in the cost of living among the states, which benefits North Carolina, as the state has a lower cost of living than the nation.[14] North Carolina ranked even lower—last—in the percentage of the state economy (GDP) devoted to K–12 spending. But on the positive side, the state ranked nineteenth in targeting state K–12 spending to high-poverty districts.[15]

COVID and Ongoing and New Challenges: Higher Education

Higher education, meaning formal education beyond high school in colleges and universities, has surged in North Carolina. In 2024, 54 percent of adults—people from twenty-five to sixty-four years old—in the state had a higher education degree. This is up from 43 percent in 2017, 38 percent in 2010, and 33 percent in 2000.[16] While part of this increase is a result of workers with a college degree moving to the state during the twenty-first century, the gains are also a response to the dynamics of the state's labor market, particularly the shift from physical skills to cognitive skills in more jobs.[17]

Higher education didn't escape the impacts of COVID. In North Carolina, in-person classes were shifted to remote classes. Fortunately, most UNC System campuses had already established online—also called "distance-learning"—programs. For example, North Carolina State University began its distance-learning program in the 2006–7 academic year, and fifteen years later over 120 academic programs were offered.[18] Hence, unlike K–12 students, many college students and instructors were familiar with online learning when the COVID pandemic occurred. Still, there is evidence of a higher rate of missed assignments by college students during COVID, resulting in a loss of learning.[19] There's also evidence that a concept labeled "pandemic brain" developed among some college students during COVID, where students shifted from deliberative decision-making to impulsive decision-making.[20] Other adverse impacts were found to be distress, depression, and isolation.[21]

While these COVID-related setbacks to college students are expected to be short-lived, there are continuing issues persisting for higher education as well as new issues now emerging.[22] Among the continuing issues are cost, student debt, and the question of how much individuals benefit from a college degree. Relatively new issues are future enrollment levels, increased questioning about the need for a college degree by both potential students and employers of college graduates, and the ability of colleges to shift training to skills needed in the new AI workplace.

Looking first at the continuing issues, North Carolina has a good track record of keeping college student costs under control, especially for public universities. Four-year public university annual tuition and fees rose only 2.5 percent between school years 2018–19 and 2022–23, much lower than the overall rate of inflation. In 2022 North Carolina had the sixth-lowest public university annual tuition and fees. There was a similar pattern for the state's two-year public community colleges. Community college annual tuition and fees rose only 1 percent between school year 2018–19 and school year 2022–23, and North Carolina's tuition and fees in 2022–23 were the third lowest in the country. By contrast, private university annual tuition and fees in North Carolina jumped 18 percent from 2018–19 to 2022–23, almost the same as the overall rate of inflation. In 2022–23, the state's private university annual tuition and fees was the fifteenth most expensive among the states and District of Columbia.[23]

A major reason for North Carolina's success in keeping public four-year and two-year higher education tuitions and fees low is the high percentage of higher education expenses funded by the state. For example, in 2023 the State of North Carolina funded 71 percent of higher education costs, the ninth-highest percentage among the fifty states and the District of Columbia.[24]

College students in North Carolina continue to use debt to finance their education. Total college debt among students in the state has been increasing, reaching $51 billion in 2023. The state's $37,000 average debt per student is very close to the national average.[25]

Recent studies indicate that the financial returns from a college degree continue to be substantial, yet with a downward trend. A large national study based on examining the outcomes of 5.8 million graduates and nongraduates during 2017–20 found that the four-year expenditures for tuition, fees, and books combined with half of graduates' nontuition other expenses yielded a continuing boost in annual salary of 9.5 percent for females and 8.8 percent for males over what they would have earned without the degree.[26] While the annual return is substantial and actually comparable to the long-run average returns from investing in stocks, the same calculations for the earlier 2009–12 cohort yielded higher annual rates of return of 10.1 percent for females and 9.3 percent for males.[27] Also, the study found that the rates of return varied among majors, and engineering and computer science degrees had the highest returns.[28] Similarly, a study of UNC System graduates found significant variation among majors in the monetary benefits from a college degree.[29]

It is important to note that while the average financial rate of return to a college student is positive, there can still be students who financially lose from attending college, meaning their rate of return is negative. One recent study found that 23 percent of students with a bachelor's degree had a negative rate of return, which implies that their degree actually lowered their salary compared to their earnings without the degree. The same study found that 43 percent of master's degree recipients also suffered a negative rate of return from their investment in the degree.[30]

The new issues for higher education may be more daunting than the ongoing issues. Higher education enrollment steadily rose in the six decades following World War II, a result of the country's growing population and affluence, as well as the shift away from physical skills to more jobs requiring cognitive skills. But recently enrollment in public higher education institutions has fallen in the nation. From 2019 to 2024, national enrollment was down almost 10 percent. While the pandemic accounted for a significant portion of the enrollment reduction, the downward trend in higher education enrollment began much earlier than the pandemic.

Enrollment peaked in 2010. Between 2010 and 2019 (the year before the pandemic), national enrollment in higher education fell 6.7 percent.[31] There have been similar trends for enrollments in both public and private higher education institutions.[32]

Although the numbers have been better for North Carolina, the same enrollment trends are evident. Between 2017 and 2022, enrollment in state public higher education institutions rose a mere 0.1 percent. Without the pandemic, enrollment would have continued to climb. But over the long run prior to the pandemic (2012–19), enrollment declined 1 percent.[33] Still, by 2025 enrollment had fully recovered from the pandemic and set a record high.[34]

There are two factors behind these changes, both nationally and in North Carolina. As discussed in the first chapter, one is the decline in the birth rate and the consequent reduction in the growth rate of college-going individuals. After 2025, some experts predict that a persistent decline in higher education enrollment will start.[35] Depending on the levels of in-migration and international immigration to North Carolina, enrollment drops may be prevented or curtailed in the state. However, movements of people to North Carolina from other states and nations remain highly uncertain.

Although demographic trends clearly present challenges for higher education, the second factor affecting enrollment may be more important. This is the apparent drop in the status and perceived importance of a college degree held by both college-age people and businesses. A study of college-age people found a variety of reasons for skipping the pursuit of a college degree, including stress, affordability, a desire to immediately earn money, and alternative ways of learning skills. Noted among the latter are earning a license or certificate, and using media such as YouTube for education.[36] Young men, especially, appear to be questioning the value of a college education.[37] In fact, there's been a broad-based reduction in the attractiveness of a college education. A Gallup poll of US adults in 2024 showed that only 36 percent have a "great deal or quite a lot" of confidence in higher education, although in 2015 the positive rating of college was 57 percent.[38]

There has been a parallel drop in attitudes about the importance of a college degree among businesses. A total of 45 percent of companies in 2024 said they plan to eliminate college degree requirements for certain positions, joining companies who have already done so. The number of jobs requiring a bachelor's degree dropped from 51 percent in 2017 to 44 percent in 2022. Many companies are substituting their own in-house skill training for college training. For example, in 2017 Amazon spent $700 million to retrain one hundred thousand workers, almost a third of their workforce.[39]

The major implication from this shift in attitudes about the value of higher education by both potential students and employers of those students is that higher education needs to alter its structure. Higher education has a reputation for opposing change, but given AI's likely impact on shifting skill needs, higher education may need to change just to survive in the Anxious Age.[40]

AI's Uneven Impact on Occupations, Industries, and Jobs

The first step in reforming both K–12 and higher education is to consider how the skills needed for the Anxious Age will be different from those in the past. While there is no certainty in answering this question because AI is continuing to evolve, there already are some broad conclusions that can be expected.[41]

A study by Edward Felten, Manav Raj, and Robert Seamans meticulously analyzed how individual occupations will be impacted by AI.[42] Table 5.1 shows their findings for the top twenty occupations impacted by AI and the bottom twenty occupations impacted by AI. The researchers made the same classification for industries; the results are shown in table 5.2. Note that their measures do not necessarily suggest job losses. In some cases, AI will substitute for tasks done by workers, while in other cases AI could make workers more productive and hence more valuable.

Examining both table 5.1 for occupations and table 5.2 for industries shows one clear distinction. The top occupations and industries projected to be most impacted by AI are predominantly white-collar occupations and industries, while the top occupations and industries projected to be least impacted by AI are predominantly blue-collar occupations and industries. "White collar" is shorthand for office and desk jobs that mainly require cognitive abilities rather than physical abilities, whereas "blue collar" is shorthand for jobs in outdoor or indoor production facilities that mainly use physical abilities but still require some individual decision-making.

The occupations and industries significantly affected by AI include many financial, mathematical, legal, and educational occupations and industries. The tasks in these jobs tend to be highly structured, with rules and established relationships that can be modeled mathematically and statistically. These are exactly the kinds of tasks that lend themselves to AI. For example, bookkeeping follows well-defined rules. And while investing patterns are much more variable and unpredictable, investment data are perfect for statistical analysis to determine patterns and recommendations.

The occupations and industries expected to be less impacted by AI have two different characteristics. First, several involve tasks using close personal interactions that are valued in the job, like dancing, personal training, and bartending. While it may be technically possible to replace the humans in these occupations with AI-controlled robots, the robots likely

TABLE 5.1. Top twenty and bottom twenty occupations adversely impacted by AI.

Top Twenty	**Bottom Twenty**
Genetic counselors	Dancers
Financial examiners	Fitness trainers & aerobics instructors
Actuaries	Painters, paperhangers, plasterers, stucco masons
Purchasing agents, except retail, wholesale, & farm	Reinforcing iron and rebar workers
Budget analyst	Pressers, textile, garment, and related jobs
Judges	Brick, block, & stone masons, tile & marble setters
Procurement clerks	Dining room & cafeteria attendants, bartenders
Accountants and auditors	Fence erectors
Mathematicians	Roof helpers
Judicial law clerks	Meat processors & packers
Educational administrators, postsecondary	Landscapers & groundskeepers
Clinical, counseling, & job benefit specialists	Athletics & sports competitors
Financial managers	Loggers
Compensation, benefits, & job analyst specialists	Structural iron & steelworkers
Credit authorizers, checkers, & clerks	Cement masons & concrete finishers
History teachers, postsecondary	Terrazzo workers & finishers
Geographers	Rock splitters, quarry
Epidemiologists	Plasterers & stucco masons
Management analysts	Brick & block masons
Arbitrators, mediators, & conciliators	Roofers

Source: Edward Felten, Manav Raj, and Robert Seamans, “Occupational, Industry, and Geographic Exposure to Artificial Intelligence: A Novel Dataset and Its Potential Uses,” *Strategic Management Journal* 42, no. 12 (2021): 2195–2217, https://doi.org/10.1002/smj.3286.

TABLE 5.2. Top twenty and bottom twenty industries adversely impacted by AI.

Top Twenty	Bottom Twenty
Securities and investments	Farming
Accounting, tax preparation, & bookkeeping	Building management
Insurance and employee benefit funds	Foundation and structure contractors
Legal services	Food processing
Agencies, brokerages, & insurance activities	Building finishing
Nondepository credit intermediation	Warehousing & storage
Other investment pools & funds	Textile mills
Insurance carriers	Rail transportation support
Software publishers	Sawmills
Nonfinancial intangible asset leasers	Water transportation
Management of entertainers & athletes	Logging
Credit intermediation	Specialty contracting
Computer system design & related activities	Waste collection
Consulting services	Postal service
Monetary management	Highway & bridge construction
Office administration	Truck transportation
Information services	Apparel mills
Data processing	Seafood processing
Business computer & management training	Local messengers & delivery
Grantmaking & giving services	Utility system construction

Source: Edward Felten, Manav Raj, and Robert Seamans, "Occupational, Industry, and Geographic Exposure to Artificial Intelligence: A Novel Dataset and Its Potential Uses," *Strategic Management Journal* 42, no. 12 (2021): 2195–2217, https://doi.org/10.1002/smj.3286.

can't deliver the same quality of personal interactions; indeed, the robots may deter human interactions. Second, many of the occupations and industries involve construction and outdoor tasks. Again, workers doing these tasks often encounter unique or special circumstances, some of which can be unexpected and therefore aren't easily programmed or solved by AI. The tasks sometimes include the need for careful dexterity beyond the capabilities of machines.

Several other studies have similar findings, including one from the Organisation for Economic Co-operation and Development, and an analysis jointly done by Barclays and IBM.[43] For example, the Barclays-IBM study found that human skills in time management and prioritization would become the most valued capabilities after AI became widespread, and therefore they would be least likely to be replaced by AI. By contrast, STEM-based human skills, which have been highly promoted in occupations during the twenty-first century, would be the most de-emphasized and easily replaced by AI.[44] To add to the distinctions, urban counties are expected to be more adversely impacted by AI than rural counties.[45]

The conclusion is that some occupations and industries using cognitive skills that can be easily replicated by complex computer programs will be prime candidates for being accomplished by AI rather than humans. This certainly doesn't mean all such tasks will be taken over by AI, but likely some percentage will. By contrast, skills involving situations with special and unexpected variations, plus skills requiring emotional interactions, will be less threatened, and possibly even elevated, by AI.

There are other skills and jobs impacts from AI not directly addressed by tables 5.1 and 5.2. One is the impact from data centers that will be built to conduct AI analysis. It is estimated that close to thirty of these multimillion-dollar centers will be constructed across the country, including in North Carolina.[46] However, the centers will likely be highly capital intensive and built around data storage units and large computers. Hence, full-time employees at a data center will likely number under fifty. Still, the centers should generate large state and local tax revenues, which when spent could result in additional jobs.[47]

AI will also produce a second, more indirect job impact. This will be in job substitutions between workers in the same industry, but with different skill levels. Healthcare is a good example. Consider a medical office with doctors and physician assistants. Currently, doctors do the analysis of symptoms to determine the diagnosis and treatment of patient problems. Using AI, physician assistants will be able to derive diagnoses and treatments. This could result in the medical office using fewer higher-paid doctors and additional lower-paid physician assistants. As an added bonus, the cost of medical care could drop.

Could AI Be the Answer to Growing Income Inequality?

Interestingly, the potential for AI to create substitutions between highly skilled workers and less-skilled workers—as in the above example with doctors and physician assistants—has led some economists to think that another result could be a narrowing of income inequality. For most of the past fifty years, income inequality has increased, both nationally and in North Carolina.[48] This means the income gains of higher-paid workers have exceeded the income gains of lower-paid workers.

Could AI reverse this trend during the Anxious Age? One viewpoint says it could.[49] This could happen if AI reduces the value of cognitive jobs while possibly increasing the value of routine jobs. Following the above medical office example, prior to AI only highly trained (and highly paid) doctors could perform symptoms analysis and treatment recommendations. Now, using AI, physician assistants can do both, and possibly do it better than doctors not using AI. In essence, AI has increased the value of physician assistants and decreased the value of doctors. Since in economics, value translates to earnings, the earnings of doctors would therefore be expected to increase more slowly, while the earnings of physician assistants would be expected to increase more rapidly. The result would be a narrowing of the earnings gap between doctors and physician assistants.

In effect, AI is a substitute for human knowledge that can be used by individuals with less knowledge and training. As a result, in many industries AI could be a leveler between workers with different training backgrounds. And if skill differences are narrower, earnings differences will be too.

Summing Up

Education is a prime factor behind a successful society and economy. Yet continuing issues facing education as well as new issues prompted by AI suggest that education at all levels will undergo a shake-up during the Anxious Age.

For numerous reasons, K–12 education experienced major challenges during COVID and the pandemic's aftermath, challenges the sector is still trying to overcome. At the same time, North Carolina continues to face the goal of improving its K–12 educational outcomes relative to other states, plus improving performance for all demographic groups.

Higher education in North Carolina has ongoing issues of costs and student loans, although North Carolina's situation in these issues is much better than in most states. As a result, the new challenges faced by higher education may be more important to North Carolina. Included are the prospects of declining enrollments, concerns over increases in the public's negative views on the relative benefits of a college education, and the increased popularity of alternative ways of educating college-age youths.

Studies show that AI will impact occupations and industries in different ways. Most adversely impacted will be jobs in industries relying on cognitive tasks that AI can perform, often better than workers. Many financial, mathematical, legal, and educational occupations and industries are in this category. While the output of the industries may not contract, jobs could decline.

Least adversely impacted from AI will be jobs and industries involving tasks with special and unexpected variations, especially those performed outside, as well as skills requiring emotional interactions. Indeed, AI's impact in these sectors could even be positive if the personal interactive nature of the tasks makes the industries relatively unique to what is common in the AI-dominated economy.

Perhaps one unexpected and positive impact of AI could be the technology's influence on reducing income inequality. Widening differences between the incomes of higher-paying occupations and lower-paying occupations have been issues in both the nation and North Carolina. Yet as AI potentially reduces the value of higher-paying cognitive tasks and increases the ability of lower-paying occupations with less training to perform those tasks, the pay gaps could shrink.

This analysis suggests one major conclusion. As AI changes tasks, occupations, and industries during the Anxious Age, both the types of education and training needed, as well as how that education and training will be provided, will likely be significantly altered during the decades ahead. But several questions will need to be answered. What will these changes look like, and what will be their effects on what is taught, how teaching occurs, when teaching occurs, and how teaching and training are financed during the Anxious Age? These are the important topics of chapter 6.

6

RESTRUCTURING EDUCATION IN THE ANXIOUS AGE

New Challenges

A key conclusion of the previous chapter was that all education—including K–12 and higher education—will likely need to be restructured to address both ongoing issues and new issues created by AI. The changes may need to be transformative—or "radical," by some interpretations. The purpose of the restructuring is to ensure that both existing workers and new workers have the kind of training now required in the AI-led economy during the Anxious Age.

This chapter also addresses a sobering question. Even after the educational innovations, what if there are still not enough jobs for everyone when AI has entered all segments of the economy? Rather than typical unemployment of 2 percent to 5 percent, what if AI takes over so many jobs that unemployment rises above 20 percent? What will people do, and how will they finance their lives? The chapter concludes with possible answers to this troubling question.

Individualized Learning in K–12

North Carolina's K–12 schooling continues to face the challenges of recovering from COVID learning loss, improving student academic performance, and reducing the ongoing inequality of academic outcomes across many demographic characteristics.[1]

Reducing class sizes, improving teacher pay, and increasing per pupil spending have been the standard recommendations for advancing K–12 education, and numerous studies suggest that these efforts can work.[2] While attention should certainly still be given to these tactics, they may not be good enough for education in the Anxious Age. So, what might be the answer? The answer could be individualized learning facilitated by AI.

It is well known that students learn in different ways. Experts say there are at least eight learning styles. Visual learners like to have information presented visually, such as through graphs, diagrams, and charts. Auditory learners do better hearing information. Kinesthetic learners learn best by doing. Individuals who learn best with the reading and writing style prefer reading the information and then following up by writing the same information. Logical and analytical learners look for connections, patterns, and causes behind them to understand material. Social and linguistic learners perceive concepts best when they socialize in a group and jointly discuss the information. Solitary learners are the opposite: They learn best by themselves. Last are nature learners, who use the calmness of the outdoors to facilitate understanding. To complicate matters even more, individual learning can be a combination of several of the eight styles.[3]

Schools and teachers are aware of these different learning types, and there are often efforts by individual teachers and teaching assistants to address them. But with an average class size of at least fifteen to twenty students, it is effectively impossible for teachers to facilitate individual learning types. But here's where AI comes in. Salman Khan, founder of Khan Academy, a website that develops and provides educational videos, envisions "AI teaching tutors" for each student.[4] The AI tutor will first ascertain the learning category of the student, and then will utilize that style in moving students through the lessons. For students who learn best in a social situation, a student's AI tutor will connect the student to similar students, sometimes from other schools. Similarly, for students who best learn outdoors, the AI tutor can simulate an outdoor setting. As the AI tutor's interaction with the student continues, AI can perceive (some say "learn") more about the student's progress and incorporate that information in the tutoring.[5] An additional advantage of the AI tutor is that student learning can continue at home or at any other location away from school that has internet access. Although preliminary existing studies suggest that AI-assisted learning techniques can benefit students, more analysis needs to be done before AI tutors are recommended universally.[6]

Teachers will still be needed even if AI tutors are adopted. Teachers will introduce topics, summarize the learning objectives, give examples of the usefulness of the information to motivate interest, and monitor students as they advance through the lessons. In fact, AI tutors will allow teachers to devote more time to students, because AI will also do the paperwork, including grading now done by teachers.

Of course, teachers will require training in AI so they understand how learning is facilitated by the technology. Protections will also be required to shield the individual student information held by each AI tutor. Also, computers will be required for each student to access the AI tutor. While many schools already provide computers, including laptops and iPads, not all do. In some schools, new funds will need to be allocated, or existing funds would need to be reallocated, to utilize the AI tutor. However, if the educational benefits are substantial and educational inequality is reduced, the investment would be well worth it.

It should be remembered that the AI tutor will be a tool, not a replacement for the teacher. Teacher-student interactions will still be encouraged and facilitated by AI. Indeed, AI can provide new insights for the teacher about each student.

Higher Education in the Anxious Age: What, How, When?

Higher education everywhere, including in North Carolina, faces three questions during the Anxious Age: what to teach, how to teach, and when to teach.[7] These questions are motivated by numerous issues, including the cost, relevance, and accessibility of higher education. The questions have persisted for decades, but they will be more urgent in the Anxious Age due to AI.

What to Teach

The first consideration is what will be taught in future colleges and universities during the Anxious Age. With AI likely to alter tasks in occupations, higher education institutions—particularly at the four-year university level—will need to rethink the tasks required for a particular major or degree. For example, in STEM fields like computer science and engineering, several of the current tasks involved in the fields will likely be accomplished by AI. This means that what constitutes necessary training for a computer science or engineering degree will need to evolve in the Anxious Age as AI continues to change the nature of work in these fields. An important development will be inclusion of training in how to manage and utilize AI.

In fact, universities may decide to restructure at least some of their curricula away from teaching toward particular occupations to instead teaching skills for particular tasks. Then students can develop their individualized task portfolio and shop the market for jobs matching that portfolio.

Consider, for example, the construction of a hotel. The process now requires three primary occupations—architects, engineers, and a variety of construction trades, such as carpenters, concrete workers, bricklayers, electricians, and plumbers, all of which today are heavily labor intensive. While some of the construction trades will possibly be replaced by technology, such as the robot bricklayers already being used in some countries, humans will continue to do much of the work due to unique features and situations in many building projects that can't be anticipated by technology.[8]

For the other two occupations involved in hotel construction—architecture and civil engineering—there are tasks that are vulnerable to accomplishment by AI. For a hotel project, architects design the building, pick the design elements like materials and finishes, allocate the use of space based on the needs of the client, and develop budgets for each of these components. Engineers then take the architect's plans and implement them, but giving close attention to structural requirements and feasibility. Among these tasks performed by the architect and engineer, the optimal allocation of space in the hotel, the evaluation of structural requirements and feasibility, and keeping all activities within a set budget are tasks that likely will be easily accomplished by AI.

The result is that the major tasks left for architects and engineers in hotel construction will ultimately be creative design and personal interactions with the client. Indeed, it may occur that the architect and civil engineering professions will be combined. Training in the merged "architect–civil engineering" occupation would focus on the design task and on classes assisting with the task of communicating with clients and resolving disputes.

The shift from teaching toward occupations to teaching for tasks will not be easy. The transition will involve a restructuring of departments and colleges, the shrinking of some academic offerings such as STEM, the expansion of others like psychology, and possibly big changes in what professors teach because of the broad impacts AI will have in almost all disciplines. With such fundamental changes potentially being massive and touching the core of academic professions, this restructuring could be contentious, disruptive, and difficult. Some have recommended mandates requiring all college teaching programs to incorporate job-ready skills.[9] This transformation of universities will last for several decades as AI continues to develop and be implemented throughout the Anxious Age.

Two-year postsecondary education programs, such as community colleges in North Carolina, should make the transition to AI much more smoothly, because community college programs have typically been task oriented. Indeed, North Carolina's community colleges often develop specialized programs to teach skills needed by new companies moving to the state.[10]

Will humanities programs, including languages, history, literature, and art, suffer from the influence of AI in the Anxious Age? Actually, some futurists think just the opposite, expecting that such programs might flourish, because the humanities deal with deep, thoughtful questions about life, humanity, and purpose—the opposite of the pragmatic and logical ideas considered with AI. There will still be a need for many firms and occupations to employ workers with training in humanities to provide exactly what AI can't. While AI will excel at production efficiency and pricing to maximize profits, complementary workers with humanities backgrounds can provide subtler information, such as about the psychology of buying and of product enjoyment. The expectation is that many companies will seek a balance between the largely mathematical and logical AI and the subjective and introspective humanities.[11]

How to Teach

Four-year higher education institutions implemented cyberlearning, often called distance learning, prior to the pandemic, and when the pandemic occurred, this learning technique even became popular. The popularity has remained after the pandemic. In 2022, 54 percent of college students took some online courses, and 26 percent were exclusively enrolled in distance learning. Although these rates are lower than during the pandemic, eliminating the pandemic years reveals an upward trend in the use of online learning in colleges during the 2012 to 2022 decade. A big advantage of distance learning is its lower cost. Data from 2022 show online courses are 28 percent less expensive than in-person courses.[12]

The question for four-year institutions during the Anxious Age is whether to keep distance learning as an option but continue to emphasize in-person learning, or to reverse the emphasis, focusing on expanding distance learning and thus relegating in-person learning to a secondary spot.

There are arguments for both approaches. One supporter of giving priority to distance learning is Michael D. Smith, a professor of information technology and marketing at Carnegie Mellon University. In his 2023 book, *The Abundant University*, Smith sees three advantages for digital learning in higher education: expanding the opportunity for college education to more individuals, lowering costs, and enhancing equity due to more individuals having a college degree.[13] Smith argues that universities use limited enrollment to keep prices (tuition) high. Moving to more digital learning would significantly expand enrollment capacity and greatly increase the possibility of a college education to many more individuals, especially those who wouldn't otherwise consider college. Plus, as I have already pointed out, digital learning is less expensive than in-person learning, so average college costs would decline.

Of course, there are rebuttals to arguments promoting online college education. One is that cyberlearning won't work for all students. This is certainly true, which is why both online and in-person classes should be options. There's also the argument that "deep thinking," also called "critical thinking," can only be encouraged in classes with other students and a teacher present. However, some analysis suggests that students rarely learn beyond the material presented in a classroom.[14]

AI may also impact higher education in two possible ways. First, AI will certainly become part of the higher education curriculum. Since AI will impact most occupations and will restructure a wide variety of tasks, it will be necessary for almost every college graduate to understand how to use AI, interpret its output, and remain aware of its limitations.

The second possible use of AI is in the college classroom, both in-person and virtual. Although there may be some colleges that resist, students will likely be permitted to utilize AI as a tool for research papers and similar requirements in higher education.[15] The difficulty of enforcing a ban on AI usage is just too great. Plus, there is the reality that once employed, graduates will use AI for similar tasks.

A major question is whether AI will be used in college classrooms in ways similar to its proposed use in K–12 classrooms to facilitate learning by students with different learning types. Today the answer is likely no. But if in future decades of the Anxious Age AI becomes widely used as a teaching tool in K–12 schools, its application as a tool for learning could also become typical in higher education. There have already been some studies of using an "AI tutor" in college classes, and the results have been positive.[16]

Calls for higher education reform have occurred in the past, but with few results.[17] So what's different today? Why can we now have more confidence that major changes will be made to higher education? There are two factors in the Anxious Age that could drive change in higher education. First is concern over slow growth—possibly even negative growth—in the college-age population of the future. Second is the decline in the rate of return to college students and the consequent drop in college-going intentions. Expanding digital offerings is a way to address both of these issues in higher education.

There's a companion issue to the "how to teach" question for both K–12 and higher education. At the K–12 level, data for the latest year (2023–24) show that three-quarters of students attend public schools, and one-quarter attend privately run schools or home schools. While public schools still dominate, the recent enrollment trends have been falling for public schools and rising for the alternatives. Furthermore, public school enrollment in North Carolina between 2019 and 2026 is predicted to drop 3 percent.[18] There has also been an expansion of the existing voucher programs to include more households, which could further adversely impact public school enrollment.[19]

At the higher education level, there's also been an increase in alternative providers to the traditional public and private universities and colleges, including apprenticeships, certifications, and on-the-job training.[20]

The debate over public schools versus private alternatives at both K–12 and higher education levels and whether public money should help fund the alternatives will likely intensify in the Anxious Age. One possible positive outcome could be that competition between public and private providers spurs innovation in how education is provided. For example, the competition might motivate the use and testing of AI and the technology's ability to improve student achievement at the K–12 level, as well as prompting traditional universities and colleges to reevaluate both their educational program content and delivery methods in the context of changes during the Anxious Age.

When to Teach

Since our modern age, which I will define as starting after World War II, we have followed a standard educational pattern. Starting at age five in kindergarten, or possibly a year earlier in preschool, students move through elementary school and high school and increasingly into a two-year college or four-year university. Indeed, the most recent data indicate that 61 percent of high school graduates enroll in higher education. It has also been typical for graduates of both high school and college to work most of their careers in their chosen field. Further education after graduation has not been typical.[21]

In recent decades, this pattern has been changing. As discussed earlier, more college-age students are forgoing higher education. Also, increasingly college graduates are changing careers during their work life.[22] Both trends suggest a greater need for lifelong education opportunities.

But even without these trends, the need for expanded lifelong education would be driven by another important factor, and once again it is AI. AI will not only change the labor force during the next decades of the Anxious Age; it will also continue to evolve and expand and create ongoing "disruption" to occupations and tasks in later decades. It may not become uncommon for Anxious Age workers to be retrained and retrofitted for new skills and tasks several times before retirement.

In this new educational reality of the "when" of higher education potentially occurring numerous times in a work career, North Carolina should reconsider how it assists higher education. Rather than subsidizing students who attend state institutions, an alternative is to provide all high school graduates with a lifetime educational fund they could use at any educational institution in the state anytime in their lives. Such a funding mechanism would be of enormous help to workers faced with the workplace upheaval expected during the Anxious Age. Public and private educational alternatives, including on-the-job training, will offer added flexibility for workers seeking new skills. Of course, the state would provide some ongoing certification for the approved training options.

In this new system, with the use of public funding of higher education now controlled by the student, the dynamics between students and educational institutions will change. Although the funds are still publicly provided, institutions will look at potential students as controlling the use of those funds. Higher education institutions will therefore be more motivated to convince students they have the educational programs that will successfully train them for a viable career. Also, the institutions will be motivated to deliver on that promise rather than face negative publicity.

What If There Aren't Enough Jobs?

Even with expanded lifetime educational options, some futurists forecast that there may simply not be enough jobs for humans in the Anxious Age.[23] Depending on a person's viewpoint, this dream or curse would fulfill the forecast of the famous and influential economist John Maynard Keynes. In the 1930s Keynes predicted that technology eventually would perform most job tasks, thereby freeing humans for lives of leisure and self-improvement. Ironically, Keynes envisioned his prediction happening in a hundred years, which would put it in the 2030s.[24]

There are two important immediate questions prompted by Keynes's vision. First, with no work, what income source would people use to pay for their everyday needs? Second, what would people do with their time?

There are two possible answers for the first question. People could live off their earnings from investments in companies performing all of society's work. However, this assumes that at some point in their lives, people would have funds to invest, either from past work or from inheritances. Alternatively, government—likely federal and/or state governments—could tax companies and distribute the funds to people for investing. In particular, AI companies, whom some would call "responsible" for the lack of sufficient jobs, could be targeted for taxation. The second answer is again for government to tax revenues from all sources, but this time using the funds for a guaranteed income paid directly to individuals.[25] Such guaranteed incomes are called annuities.

Both of these approaches would need to address questions about what to tax, the level of tax rates, the size of payments to individuals, and how the payment might change with the recipient's age and other characteristics, including health condition.

Regarding the matter of how people would use their time without the need to work, Keynes envisioned people pursuing learning, culture, and the fine arts. To be honest, though, many people—in fact, probably most people—would not follow this direction. Therefore, another, or at least a companion, idea would be for government to create public sector jobs addressing broad issues like preserving and maintaining open spaces and parks, assisting the disabled, and protecting the climate. Higher education institutions, now with lower enrollments, could take on a new role of developing skills and pursuits that allow people to enjoy their lives beyond work.

Summing Up

Education, including K–12 and higher education, could experience tremendous change during the Anxious Age, prompted by lingering issues such as cost and performance, technology reshaping how education can be delivered, the remixing of the labor market putting the emphasis on tasks over occupations, and the need for workers to remake themselves possibly several times over their work careers.

The big questions for education will be what to teach, how to teach, and when to teach. As discussed in the prior chapter, AI will alter many tasks and consequently redefine occupations. Hence, students, particularly in higher education, will master skills used for particular tasks and market themselves with a mixture of skills that can be applied to numerous redefined occupations. Many current occupations as we know them now will be restructured in the Anxious Age.

In terms of the "how" of education, the biggest change will likely occur in K–12. Although young students learn in different ways, in the current system, where one teacher instructs twenty to thirty or more students, it is impossible to modify teaching techniques for different learning modes. AI could be a big game changer for addressing this issue. AI learning assistants, termed "AI tutors," could be established for each student and be programmed to teach in the mode best for the student. Teachers will supervise and augment the learning. AI will also relieve the teacher of grading and other paperwork. Teachers will have more time for student interaction, thereby making their job more rewarding. While more research needs to be done, initial analysis of "AI tutors" is promising.

While the shifts may not be as dramatic as in K–12, teaching methods will also be revamped in higher education. The most significant change will be the expansion of distance learning, for two reasons. Distance learning will make higher education more available to more students. Distance learning will also reduce costs in higher education. Although in-person classes will still be used, they will play a secondary role to distance learning.

Higher education has a reputation for resisting change, but two factors will prompt acceptance of the change needed in the Anxious Age. One is the need to expand the reach of higher education due to the ongoing decrease in the college-age population. Another is to counter the decline in the perceived value of higher education among a rising number of individuals.

The traditional model of formal education ending at college will be discarded in the Anxious Age. Why? Because technology will continually and quickly change what is needed of workers. Workers will likely need to reskill—or at least tweak their skills—several times in their career. This reality will prompt two further changes. Higher education will have an additional role of continuing education for workers. Indeed, reskilling could become the most prominent role of higher education. Second, the state may consider redirecting the funds currently provided to higher education, shifting that money toward individual lifelong education grants for each high school graduate. Workers would be allotted a certain financial amount and would be able to draw on the funds as needed when new training is required.

Every time North Carolina's economy has been remade, education has also had to change. This chapter has outlined the necessary changes in education that will need to be considered as the state navigates the Anxious Age. But specifically, how will North Carolina's economy be reshaped to create another "new North Carolina" during the era? Chapter 7 answers this question.

7

ANOTHER NEW NORTH CAROLINA IN THE ANXIOUS AGE?

North Carolina is embarking on its fourth economic generation. The first generation was based on farming. The second was led by manufacturing. The third, and current, generation has been sparked by the development and evolution of information technology. The fourth generation, which is just beginning and will dominate the Anxious Age, is being shaped by two factors: the emergence of artificial intelligence and its impacts, and the development of a new energy sector. Both factors will have important and lasting effects on North Carolina's structure and on the success of its residents. This chapter focuses on those impacts as well as on the strategies that could spread economic prosperity to more of North Carolina. Two of these strategies are "corridor development" and "remote work hubs."

The Three Acts of North Carolina's Economic Generations

It is always useful to look at the past before examining the future. State economies are driven by industries that sell much of their output to buyers outside the state, including foreign buyers. These industries, called "basic industries," define each economic generation.

ACT 1: THE LAND-BASED ECONOMY

The first economic generation in North Carolina was based on the land; it comprised crop farming, forestry farming, and mineral mining. Farming in North Carolina included many crops, but two dominant cash crops were tobacco and cotton: Both were key exports to other states and to foreign countries.[1] Even after the devastation caused by the Civil War, the state's tobacco and cotton production maintained large national shares of both crops well into the late nineteenth century.[2]

North Carolina's forestry farming was based on its ample supply of pine trees. Pine trees yielded several products, including resin (also called pitch), tar, turpentine, and lumber. Pine lumber was strong and affordable, and pine tar was a popular sealant against damage from moisture and insects. Indeed, the origin of the term "Tar Heel" to describe a North Carolinian was a reference to workers extracting tar from pine trees.[3]

Gold was discovered in Western North Carolina in 1799, which prompted the first gold rush in the young United States.[4] The gold boom persisted for several decades. But by the 1840s, the boom subsided, especially as new gold supplies were discovered in California.

ACT 2: THE BIG THREE ECONOMY

As technology created more efficient methods of building products, North Carolina entered its second economic generation, built around factory manufacturing. The technology allowed the state to take several of its key land-based products, including tobacco, cotton, and forestry, and transform them into the next step of final products. Hence, tobacco products such as cigarettes were made in factories using the state's tobacco crop, a textile and apparel manufacturing industry was developed using locally grown cotton, and furniture and paper manufacturing industries were built from North Carolina's lumber. Beginning in the late nineteenth century and extending well into the twentieth century, the "Big Three"—tobacco, textiles, and furniture/paper/lumber—dominated the state. Indeed, at their peak, the Big Three accounted for almost one-fourth of all jobs and all economic production in the state.[5]

ACT 3: THE BIG FIVE ECONOMY

The late twentieth and early twenty-first centuries brought big changes to North Carolina's economy. Health concerns caused declines in the relative importance of tobacco products. At the same time, increased foreign trade prompted by the North American Free Trade Agreement and the entry of China to the World Trade Organization exposed the state's textile and furniture industries to lower-cost foreign competition. By the end of the first decade of the twenty-first century, employment in the Big Three had fallen an astonishing 75 percent from the early 1990s.[6]

Fortunately, North Carolina's leadership actively worked to remake the state's economy by developing new economic sectors. In agriculture, tobacco was replaced by meat production, specifically hogs and chickens. Replicating what was done with tobacco in marrying leaf production with the manufacturing of final products like cigarettes, a food processing industry was developed, with meat processing as the leader.

A pharmaceutical industry was launched from the state's substantial background in chemical production. The experience Charlotte-based banks had in operating branches in large geographic areas allowed the city's banks to grow when nationwide branch banking was approved in the 1990s, and Charlotte has become the nation's second-largest banking center.[7]

Last, the state's reputation as probusiness and the presence of high-profile community colleges and universities for skill training allowed North Carolina to recruit transportation-related firms in auto parts, aircraft engines, and aircraft assembly, as well as firms in the increasingly dominant industry of technology. In 2023, the new "Big Five"—information technology; chemical-based products, including pharmaceuticals; food processing; transportation; and banking—accounted for over 19 percent of total state economic production (gross domestic product) compared to only 2 percent of total state production from the Big Three.[8]

There are several lessons from this review through the economic generations. One is that change is inevitable. As documented here, in its relatively short lifespan North Carolina's economy has undergone three distinct phases. Each phase has prompted shifts in how and where people work, needed skills and training for workers, and often in how and where people live. The best example of the last impact is the massive shift of population in North Carolina from rural areas to urban ones.

A second lesson is that economic change is prompted by technological change. The steam engine, electricity, gas-powered engines, assembly line, computer, and related digital devices are major examples of technological change prompting the vast economic shifts in North Carolina. We are now on the verge of a new technology—AI—that Microsoft founder Bill Gates has called the most important technological advance in decades.[9] The Anxious Age will be dominated by changes created by AI.

The third lesson is that while moving into the next economic generation will likely be beneficial to the state, just as the past transitions have been, there will certainly be both short-term and long-term losers. Short-term losers will be workers and firms that lose earnings as the new economy develops and modifies the distribution of production, sales, and jobs. Over time, however, workers and firms can adapt through new production methods and new worker training, thereby enabling them to recoup their economic losses. For example, in the late nineteenth century, Pony Express riders could train to become telegraph operators, and stagecoach owners could invest in trains. We will see the same kinds of shifts during the Anxious Age.

Yet, perhaps for the first time, there may be net job losses from the economic transitions in the coming decades. If—as some fear—AI eliminates more jobs than it creates, we may come to live in a Keynesian world of permanent job shortages, where a life of constant leisure is underwhelming for many.

Hints of the Next Transition

Table 7.1 shows three snapshots of the North Carolina economy: in 2005 as the Big Five economy emerged, in 2019 just prior to the COVID pandemic, and in the postpandemic year of 2023, the latest year with available data. The purpose of the table is to determine whether shifts are already occurring that point to act 4 in the state's economy.

There are several key takeaways from the table. The Big Five industries have continued to dominate the state economy both before and after the pandemic. The Big Five increased its spread over the Big Three by 5.5 percentage points between 2005 and 2023. Among the Big Five sectors, food processing's share jumped over 75 percent between 2005 and 2023. Although transportation manufacturing's share held relatively steady, a look behind the numbers shows different trends for its two subsectors. North Carolina's traditional auto parts manufacturing experienced a 50 percent share reduction between 2005 and 2023. By contrast, the new aeronautical sector, comprising parts and engine production and assembly, doubled in relative size between 2005 and 2023. The other components of the Big Five had some fluctuations but changed little between 2005 and 2023.

Conversely, the former Big Three of tobacco, textiles/apparel, and furniture/paper/lumber continued a trend of diminished economic impact on the state economy. Between 2005 and 2023, the collective share of the Big Three plunged almost 75 percent.

There is a third collection of industries in table 7.1 labeled "Other Basic Industries." These are basic industries that have not been recent leaders in North Carolina's economy but have the potential to be leaders in the Anxious Age. Mining is the quarrying and production of mineral-based commodities. Although the state's most famous mined product, gold, long ago faded, the state has other important minerals such as pure quartz, phosphorus, and lithium, each of which plays a major role in the production and use of renewable energy. Hence, their economic impact on the state's economy could become very significant if renewable energy expands in the Anxious Age, a topic I will explore in chapter 8.

With one of the largest military bases in the world—Fort Bragg—located near Fayetteville, and together with several other installations in the state, the military has the potential to be an economic driver. Although table 7.1 shows that the military's relative importance to North Carolina's economy

TABLE 7.1. Relative size of basic North Carolina industries, 2005, 2019, and 2023 (% of GDP).

Industry	2005	2019	2023
Big Five–based industries			
Information technology	1.8	2.0	1.7
Pharmaceuticals and chemical products	4.3	2.8	4.0
Food processing	1.4	2.6	2.5
Transportation manufacturing	1.1	1.5	1.0
Banking	6.8	6.4	6.5
Total	15.4	15.3	15.7
Big Three–based industries			
Tobacco products[a]	3.8	0.7	0.6
Textiles and apparel	1.5	0.5	0.4
Furniture, paper, and lumber	1.9	1.2	1.0
Total	7.2	2.4	2.0
Other basic industries			
Mining and quarrying	0.2	0.1	0.2
Military	2.3	2.0	1.8
Tourism	3.9	4.9	4.5
Farming	1.2	0.6	0.8
Total	7.6	7.6	7.3

Source: US Bureau of Economic Analysis; Travel Industry Association.

[a] Estimates based on cigarettes sold in the US and percentage of US tobacco grown in North Carolina.

since 2005 has fallen, worldwide geopolitical challenges and uncertainties persisting during the Anxious Age will keep military expansion a distinct possibility in coming decades.

Tourists drawn to North Carolina's wonderful beaches, mountains, golf courses, and beautiful rural regions can bring both people and money to propel the local economy. Table 7.1 indicates tourism's economic impacts have been hovering between 4.5 percent and 5 percent in recent years, but up from 2005. In 2023 tourism was more economically important than the Big Three sectors combined, as well as being larger than each of the Big Five sectors except for banking. The economic future of North Carolina in the Anxious Age clearly will include tourism.

Last among the Other Basic Industries is farming. As farming has become more internationalized, and growth in North Carolina has pushed farmland to other uses, the relative contribution of farming to North Carolina's economy has dropped to under 1 percent.[10] Still, because farming produces essential products for life, and because technology like AI could have large impacts in reducing costs and increasing productivity in farming, its future significance in the state economy should not be ignored.[11]

Looking at the entirety of industries in table 7.1 reveals different shifting shares of relative impotence. The Big Three sectors continue to fade, the Big Five's importance has remained relatively stable, and some sectors in the Other Basic Industries have the potential for breakouts. The conclusion from table 7.1 is that there are suggestions of change in the future drivers of the North Carolina economy.

ACT 4: THE EMERGING NORTH CAROLINA ECONOMY

Table 7.2 shows how the relative importance of the Big Five, Big Three, and Other Basic Industries is expected to change during the Anxious Age. Rather than attempting to predict a specific numerical change, positive changes are indicated with a plus, negative changes are shown by a minus, and no change is designated by a zero. It is important to note that the forecasted changes are for production (GDP), not necessarily for employment. Indeed, as discussed in chapter 4, an impact of AI in some industries will be a smaller but more productive workforce, meaning that production can increase while employment declines.

Among the Big Five sectors, all except banking are expected to increase their relative importance to the state economy during the Anxious Age. Information technology, which includes AI, is certainly positioned to become more prominent in coming decades. Because North Carolina is considered one of the top technology states in the country and has many highly regarded universities, relatively low cost of living, and room to grow, it is likely to be a major part of the technology expansion based around AI.[12] Indeed, Apple has announced a $1 billion investment to be located in North Carolina's famous Research Triangle Park. Although the project has been delayed, Apple estimates that when completed it will generate three thousand jobs.[13]

The reasoning is the same for pharmaceuticals and other chemical-based products. The state ranks fourth in the number of bioscience firms, and the Triangle region is one of the nation's top locations for the industry.[14] The industry is expected to be a leader in growth and innovation in areas like precision medicine, digital health technologies, gene therapy, and advanced drugs.[15]

TABLE 7.2. Forecasted changes in the relative importance of industries to North Carolina during the Anxious Age.

Industry	Expected Change
Big Five industries	
Information technology	+
Pharmaceuticals and chemical products	+
Food processing	+
Transportation manufacturing	+
Banking	0
Total, Big Five industries	+
Big Three industries	
Tobacco products	–
Textiles and apparel	0
Furniture, paper, and lumber	+
Total, Big Three industries	0
Other basic industries	
Mining and quarrying	+
Military	0
Tourism	+
Farming	0
Total, other basic industries	+

With its links to North Carolina's poultry and hog meat industry, food processing should expand in future decades. As national and worldwide population growth slows, the expansion should be more modest than in the past. Yet support for food processing should come from an expected higher worldwide standard of living, which usually results in more meat consumption.[16]

The transportation manufacturing industry is expected to expand its portion of the state economy. As long as North Carolina continues to be favored by businesses, the aeronautical portion of the sector should continue growing at above-average rates. By contrast, the auto parts sector faces substantial uncertainty. Hurting it is the lure of lower-cost foreign producers. Conversely, the long-term use of tariffs could lead to greater local production. However, any decline in the parts component is expected to be more than offset by the expanding aeronautical component.

Among the Big Five industries, the greatest uncertainty exists about banking's future. First is the impact of AI on employment in banking. Many jobs in banking are certainly susceptible to replacement by AI. Hence, the trend is likely for a decline in workers in banking.

But a more impactful change could be the partial or even complete replacement of banks with an alternative form of money management. The most commonly mentioned substitute is cryptocurrency. With this model, money management is no longer a function of the government—particularly the Federal Reserve, which currently controls the supply of money. Instead, money management shifts to the private sector, where the supply of money is strictly controlled to avoid periods of inflation. While technically possible, most experts think banking will still continue, hence a "no change" prediction is applied.[17]

There is a possibility for banking's future to be very positive for North Carolina. This could happen if significant segments of the banking and financial industries sector leave the current top financial center, New York City, and relocate to Charlotte, the second-ranking financial center. There are precedents for such industry moves. Much of the auto manufacturing industry has left Detroit, mainly for locations in the South.[18] An estimated 20 percent of the film industry has moved out of Los Angeles.[19] Akron, Ohio, was once the center of tire making in the country, but now tire factories are in the South and West.[20] Some argue that high costs and quality-of-life issues have become major concerns and liabilities for New York City.[21] If that is accurate, some banking firms may consider moving to the second-biggest banking center, Charlotte. Collectively, the Big Five industries should expand and become more prominent in the North Carolina economy during the Anxious Age.

There are negative expectations for the Big Three industries, but with some sprinkles of optimism. The decline in the tobacco sector will likely persist. Smoking among adults has continued to fall and is now 75 percent lower than it was in the early 1950s.[22] Even more important for the future is the ongoing drop in smoking among teenagers.[23] As a result, the tobacco sector in North Carolina's economy will likely continue to shrink.

There is a slightly different outlook for another key part of the Big Three, the textiles and apparel sector. Some industry experts expect that AI will make US-based textiles and apparel producers more productive by improving efficiency and using fewer workers.[24] Less reliance on workers would reduce the advantage held by foreign companies that use less costly labor. However, since foreign producers can apply the same AI methods to increase efficiency, perhaps the best that can be expected from US textile and apparel companies is for them to hold their current position and stem the long-term decline. Any expansion in the industry will likely be in the luxury, or boutique, category.[25] Still, overall, at best there will be no change in the sector's economic share.

There's the same modest optimism for furniture production as there is for textiles and apparel. AI will increase the productivity of furniture factories in North Carolina, thereby allowing a reduction in the workforce.[26] The result will again be relatively lower costs of North Carolina–made furniture compared to foreign-made furniture, thereby slowing or even stopping the decline. Yet again, since AI efficiency can be applied worldwide, any competitive improvement for domestic firms will be modest, so the forecast is for no change in relative economic importance.

Paper usage is expected to decline due to greater digital usage, but packaging materials are forecasted to increase as a result of growth in deliveries of packages, and this will have offsetting impacts on the declining use of North Carolina lumber for paper.[27] But lumber is also used in the state's commercial and residential building. Since North Carolina is expected to add both households and businesses in the future, lumber production will climb at good rate from the construction of new structures. As a result, the combined lumber and paper sector of the Big Three is forecasted to modestly increase its share of the state economy in the Anxious Age. With forecasts for the individual Big Three sectors mixed, the prospect for the collective Big Three industry is rated as neutral.

The third industry category includes the unrelated sectors of mining/quarrying, the military, tourism, and farming. Each sector has its own outlook.

The future for North Carolina's mining and quarrying industry is very upbeat. From 2019 to 2023, mining and quarrying production in the state rose 24 percent.[28] Major reasons are increasing use of digital technology and the energy transition. One of the key ingredients for computer chips and numerous tech products is pure quartz, and pure silicon is a key element in pure quartz.[29] North Carolina is home to one of the largest pure silicon deposits in the world, at Spruce Pine in Mitchell County. The mine is responsible for between 70 percent to 90 percent of the world's pure quartz production.[30]

Lithium is a key component of batteries used in electric vehicles, and North Carolina is among the top states in the country with lithium deposits.[31] There is also a form of electric vehicle battery that uses phosphate, and North Carolina is among the top four states (along with Florida, Idaho, and Utah) with phosphate deposits.[32] As long as use of technology products and electric batteries continues expanding, mining and quarrying output in the state should grow.

Ft. Bragg is among the largest military bases in the country, and it is also the largest base in the world in terms of personnel.[33] Together with other military facilities in the state, the military contributes $14 billion annually to the state economy, as measured in 2023.[34] Although it is difficult to predict trends in military spending, as long as the country faces national security challenges, it is reasonable to expect the military installations in North Carolina to at least be sustained.

Over several decades, tourism spending in North Carolina has risen.[35] With a state that offers over three thousand miles of coastline, more than a million acres of national forests, 549 golf courses—the eighth highest among states—and large metropolitan areas with attractive venues, including major league sports, North Carolina has a variety of attractions for numerous types of leisure activities.[36] Assuming that future economic growth in both the nation and world generates increasing tourism volume, tourism should be a rising economic sector in the state.

Finally, farming can be considered the world's oldest industry. It is a very challenging industry, and competition is high, including between farmers in different countries. The industry is affected by factors beyond operators' control, especially the weather. Over recent decades, farming has moved away from single operators farming small acreage to much larger operators, often called "corporate farmers," operating massive acreage, including in North Carolina.[37]

In recent years there has been little change in the production value of agricultural output in North Carolina.[38] Part of the reason is an irony specific to farming. During good growing seasons, in which there is ample production, prices fall. During bad growing seasons, in which there is a shortfall in production, prices rise. Since revenues are a result of prices and output, the irony results in similar revenue over different kinds of growing years.

The conclusion is that farming will be a relatively stable component of the future North Carolina economy. As with many industries, AI could increase farm productivity, thereby improving farm profits. Challenges farmers will continue to face include environmental impacts of farming, competition for land in a state where the population is rising, and uncertain domestic and international policies, such as tariffs. The increased competition for land will motivate a new phase of farming, called "regenerative agriculture," which means increased emphasis on preserving the farmland and farming's ecosystem due to increased scarcity of unused land.[39]

Due to the strength of mining/quarrying and tourism, the Other Basic Industries are expected to increase their share of the North Carolina economy during the Anxious Age.

The analysis suggests that structural change in North Carolina's economy will not create a completely new leading set of industries, as in the past. Although the relative importance of the state's industries will change, all industries will undergo a transformation of varying degrees in the new North Carolina economy of the Anxious Age.

Finally, there are comments to make about two issues that emerged in 2025: the future of federal funding for public and educational projects, and tariffs. Both have the potential to affect the direction of North Carolina's future economy and the state's well-being.

In 2025 the new Trump administration announced plans to significantly reduce health and environmental funding, and this move has had a major impact on the National Institutes of Health, the EPA (Environmental Protection Agency), and universities. The reductions could be over $1 billion annually, impacting thousands of jobs.[40] But because these agencies and institutions contribute less than 0.5 percent to the state's economy, the aggregate direct economic impact will be minor.[41] The potential larger impact is a long-run reduction in health and environmental research findings that could lower the future quality of life in the state.

Increased tariffs were introduced by the Trump administration in 2025 as a tactic to reshore US manufacturing and lower the US trade deficit with other countries. Despite a Supreme Court ruling removing some of the tariffs, the administration added replacements that kept tariffs above pre-2025 levels.[42] However, what many don't understand is that a tariff, which is effectively a tax on an import, is paid *not* by the foreign exporter but by the US importing company. In 2025, the result was hundreds of billions of dollars in tariffs paid by US companies to the federal government. Most US companies compensate for the tariffs by reducing expenses—including labor—and raising the prices US consumers pay, resulting in a higher inflation rate. If tariffs are kept, the foreign markets for North Carolina pharmaceuticals, technology products, food products, and many other products could also be substantially reduced as foreign buyers retaliate by increasing tariffs on US-made exported products. As long as tariffs remain in place, there will be a question mark over any forecast for economic growth.

Geographic Shifts in the New North Carolina Economy

As the economy recovered from the pandemic from 2021 to 2024, North Carolina had an astonishing $42 billion of announced capital investments in the state, which are projected to add 72,000 permanent jobs to the state's workforce.[43] In both 2022 and 2023, CNBC ranked North Carolina first for business among all the states.[44] Examining the locations of the announced capital investments gives us indications of how North Carolina's economy might change geographically during the Anxious Age.

The following tables and maps in this chapter list and show the locations of the largest and potentially game-changing announced investments in the state from 2021 to 2024, defined as capital investments of at least $100 million.

Table 7.3 and map 7.1 show the announced major technology investments. There are several battery manufacturer investments and numerous semiconductor manufacturers. Also included is the electric vehicle manufacturer VinFast and the Albemarle lithium mine. These are included because EVs are a relatively new technology, and lithium is a key component of EV batteries. The leading investments are the $5 billion Wolfspeed semiconductor factory, the $4 billion VinFast automotive factory, the $1.4 billion Natron Energy battery manufacturer, the $1.3 billion Toyota battery factories, and the $1 billion Apple factory devoted to artificial intelligence.

There are three geographic implications of the announcements illustrated in map 7.1. The technology base that began in the Triangle region (Wake and Durham Counties) appears to be expanding westward along a corridor following US Route 64 to the Triad (Greensboro, Winston-Salem) region. Three of the largest investments—Wolfspeed, VinFast, and Toyota—are in this corridor. The corridor has three advantages: (1) Land is less costly there than in the Triangle; (2) the area is accessible to the cities of Raleigh, Durham, Greensboro, and Winston-Salem, each of which has major universities; and (3) the region has proximity to labor in counties—many of them relatively rural—both north and south of US 64.

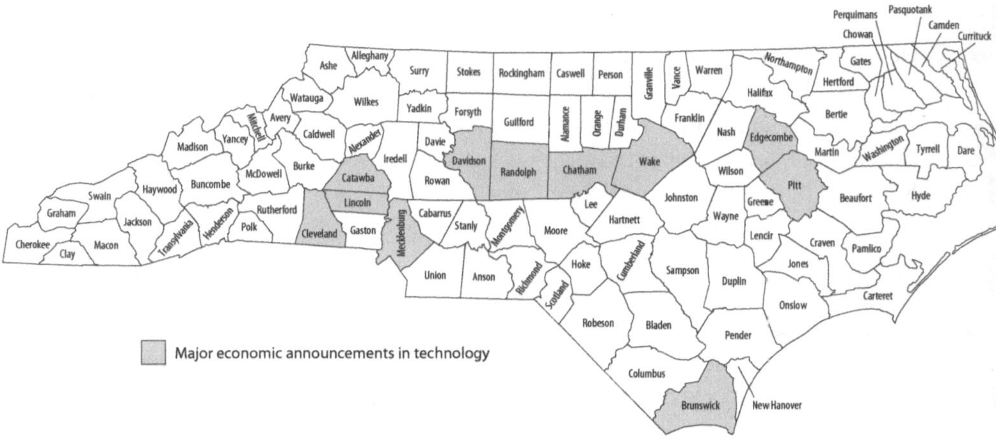

MAP 7.1. Locations of major economic announcements in technology, 2021–2024.

TABLE 7.3. Major economic announcements in North Carolina, 2021–2024: Technology.

Firm	Capital Investment	Jobs	Description	County
Toyota	$1.3 billon	1,750	Battery manufacturing	Randolph
Apple	$1.0 billion	3,000	Computer manufacturing	Wake
Wolfspeed	$5.0 billion	1,801	Semiconductor manufacturing	Chatham
VinFast	$4.0 billion	7,500	EV auto manufacturing	Chatham
Dai Nippon	$233 million	352	Battery manufacturing	Davidson
Forge Nano	$142 million	204	Semiconductor equipment	Wake
Epsilon	$650 million	500	Graphite in lithium batteries	Brunswick
Albemarle	$350 million	239	Lithium mining	Cleveland
Impact Data	$130 million	28	Data processing	Guilford
Natron Energy	$1.4 billion	1,062	Battery manufacturing	Edgecombe
Boviet Solar Tech	$294 million	908	Semiconductor manufacturing	Pitt
Compute North	$267 million	27	Data processing	Pitt
Corning Cable	$120 million	200	Fiber-optic cable manufacturing	Catawba
Albemarle Corp.	$200 million	205	STEM research	Mecklenburg
Green New Energy	$140 million	545	Plastic film & sheets	Lincoln
Siemens Energy	$149 million	559	Energy-efficient transformers	Mecklenburg

Source: Economic Development Partnership of North Carolina.

The second geographic implication is the technology investments in Edgecombe and Nash Counties, part of the Rocky Mount–Greenville region in Eastern North Carolina. Originally dependent on tobacco, the region has struggled in the new economy of the technological age. Yet the region has the benefits of lower costs, access to interstate highways, a short driving time to Raleigh (only an hour), and, in Greenville, a major UNC System university (East Carolina) with nearly thirty thousand students.

The three announced technology-related firms with over two thousand jobs are major achievements for the Rocky Mount region, and perhaps with more to come.

The third geographic implication is the announcement of major technology firms locating in areas near, but outside, the big technology regions, like the Triangle. Included are announcements in Catawba, Lincoln, Cleveland, and Brunswick Counties. The reopening of the lithium mine in rural Cleveland County will create economic benefits as well as environmental challenges in a multicounty region.[45] The Corning announcement for Catawba County is actually an addition to the technology sector that already exists in the county's major city, Hickory.[46] Likewise, the investment in Lincoln County is just south of Hickory. But the Epsilon firm's decision to come to coastal Brunswick County, a county primarily known for tourism and retirement, is the most surprising. Access to the Port of Wilmington, available power from the local nuclear power plant, and the willingness of the local community college to develop customized worker training programs were key elements in attracting the firm.[47] The success of such an unlikely group of counties attracting tech and tech-related firms suggests that the rules of business location may be different in the Anxious Age.

Table 7.4 and map 7.2 show the size and locations of the pharmaceutical-related announcements in North Carolina made in 2021–24. The three largest are a $4.1 billion investment by Novo Nordisk, a $2 billion investment by Fujifilm Biotech, and another investment by Fujifilm Biotech of $1.2 billion. Somewhat surprisingly, 30 percent (8 out of 23) of the announcements are in two counties in the Rocky Mount–Greenville region, Wilson and Pitt, which traditionally have not attracted pharmaceutical firms.

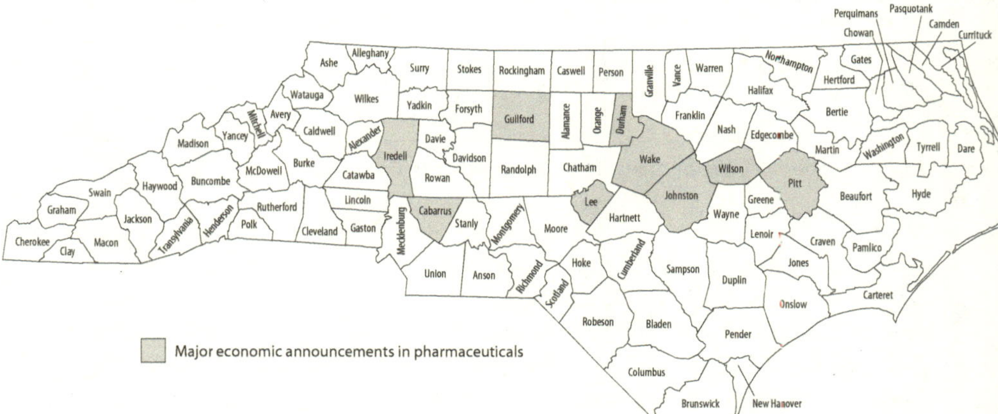

MAP 7.2. Locations of major economic announcements in pharmaceuticals, 2021–2024.

TABLE 7.4. Major economic announcements in North Carolina, 2021–2024: Pharmaceuticals.

Firm	Capital Investment	Jobs	Description	County
Jaguar Genes	$125 million	200	Biological product manufacturing	Durham
Procter & Gamble	$110 million	46	Inorganic chemical manufacturing	Guilford
Therma Fisher	$154 million	290	Lab instrument manufacturing	Pitt
Amgen	$554 million	355	Pharmaceutical manufacturing	Wake
Carsgen	$157 million	200	Biological research/ development	Durham
Invitae	$115 million	374	Medical laboratory	Wake
Abzena	$213 million	325	Biological product manufacturing	Lee
Fujifilm Biotech	$2.0 billion	725	Biological product manufacturing	Wake
Biogen	$200 million	90	Biological product manufacturing	Durham
Believer Meats	$123 million	100	Biotech research/develop.	Wilson
Fujifilm Science	$188 million	101	Pharmaceutical manufacturing	Wake
Novo Nordisk	$500 million	175	Pharmaceutical manufacturing	Johnston
BestCo	$177 million	394	Pharmaceutical manufacturing	Iredell
Eli Lilly	$939 million	589	Biological product manufacturing	Cabarrus
Pro Kidney	$485 million	330	Biological product manufacturing	Guilford
Eli Lilly	$450 million	100	Pharmaceutical manufacturing	Durham
Idexx Labs	$147 million	275	Medical instrument manufacturing	Wilson
NIPRO	$398 million	232	Medical instrument manufacturing	Pitt

(continued)

TABLE 7.4. *(continued)*

Firm	Capital Investment	Jobs	Description	County
Novo Nordisk	$4.1 billion	1,000	Pharmaceutical manufacturing	Johnston
Fujifilm Biotech	$1.2 billion	680	Bioproduct manufacturing	Johnston
Kyowa Hakko Kirin	$200 million	102	Pharmaceutical manufacturing	Lee
Reckitt	$146 million	289	Pharmaceutical manufacturing	Wilson
Janssen	$1.0 billion	420	Pharmaceutical manufacturing	Wilson

Source: Economic Development Partnership of North Carolina.

These findings again suggest that the eastern part of the state may finally be benefiting from investments by North Carolina's prominent economic sectors. Like the tech sector, pharmaceutical firms appear to be considering broader sites in the state, especially sites with lower costs.

Pharmaceutical announcements have continued for the major locations in the Triangle (Wake and Durham Counties), which have long been the strength of the pharmaceutical industry in the state. However, perhaps what is more interesting is the announced locations in other counties in the region. Almost $6 billion in investments was announced for Johnston County, adjacent to and just south of Wake County. Long a farming county, Johnston has the benefits of easy proximity to the Triangle counties, universities, and airport (Raleigh-Durham International Airport), especially with the completion of the outer-loop Interstate 540. It also has lower land costs compared to Wake and Durham Counties, and a fast-growing workforce. Lee County, just west of Johnston County, attracted two pharmaceutical firms.

There also were announcements for Cabarrus County, north of Charlotte; Guilford County, the home of Greensboro; and Iredell County, just west of Winston-Salem.

Table 7.5 and map 7.3 show the announcements and locations for warehousing and storage firms. The firms are concentrated in the central (Piedmont) part of the state, which contains most of the state's population. Locations are near the major metropolitan areas of the Triangle, Triad, and Charlotte.

TABLE 7.5. Major economic announcements in North Carolina, 2021–2024: Warehousing.

Firm	Capital Investment	Jobs	Description	County
Kroger	$139 million	722	Refrigerated storage	Mecklenburg
Newall Brands	$135 million	128	Warehousing	Gaston
Amazon	$100 million	500	Warehousing	Johnston
Macy's	$584 million	2800	Warehousing	Rowan
Amazon	$100 million	530	Warehousing	Cumberland
DHL Supply	$114 million	80	Warehousing	Rowan
Ross Stores	$491 million	852	Warehousing	Randolph

Source: Economic Development Partnership of North Carolina.

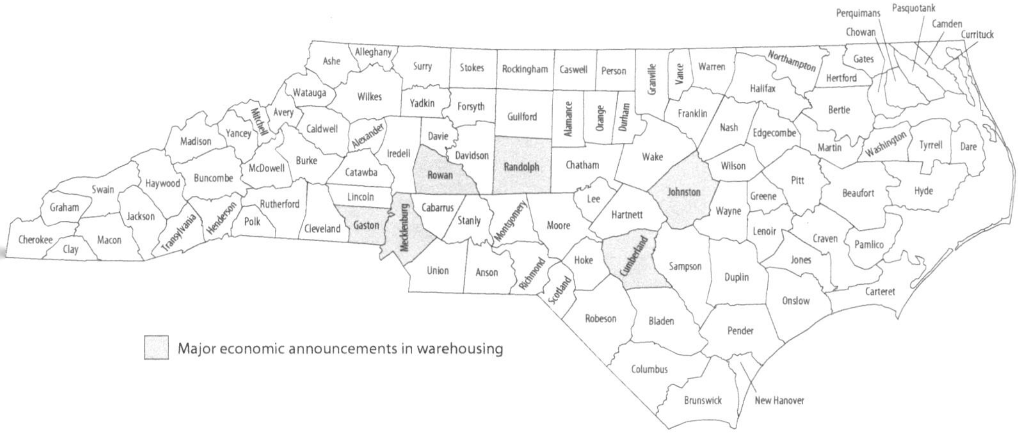

MAP 7.3. Locations of major economic announcements in warehousing, 2021–2024.

Last, the announcements for major manufacturing firms from 2021 to 2024 are given in table 7.6, and their geographic locations are shown in map 7.4.

Looking at table 7.6 shows a diverse group of manufacturing firms, from sawmills and animal food to paint and aircraft manufacturing. Except for confectionaries and animal food, the firms are engaged in manufacturing durable, or long-lasting, products instead of nondurable products, which have a short lifespan. The wide variety of products illustrates the attractiveness of North Carolina to a wide range of manufacturers.

TABLE 7.6. Major economic announcements in North Carolina, 2021–2024: Manufacturing.

Firm	Capital Investment	Jobs	Description	County
Ball Cap Red Bull	$132 million	633	Fabricated metal	Cabarrus
Roseburg	$200 million	137	Sawmills	Halifax
Rexam	$196 million	94	Metal cans	Forsyth
Do Good Foods	$100 million	100	Animal food	Johnston
CertainTeed Roofing	$121 million	37	Shingles	Granville
Nucor	$310 million	180	Rebar	Davidson
Weyerhaeuser	$100 million	0	Sawmills	Pitt
Bosch	$109 million	404	Tools	Lincoln
Semis Mobility	$220 million	506	Railroad stock	Davidson
Morinaga	$136 million	204	Confectionaries	Orange
American Titanium	$895 million	304	Metal rolling	Cumberland
Shott	$381 million	401	Flat glass	Wilson
Boom Supersonic	$500 million	1761	Aircraft manufacturing	Guilford
Sherwin-Williams	$324 million	183	Paint manufacturing	Iredell

Source: Economic Development Partnership of North Carolina.

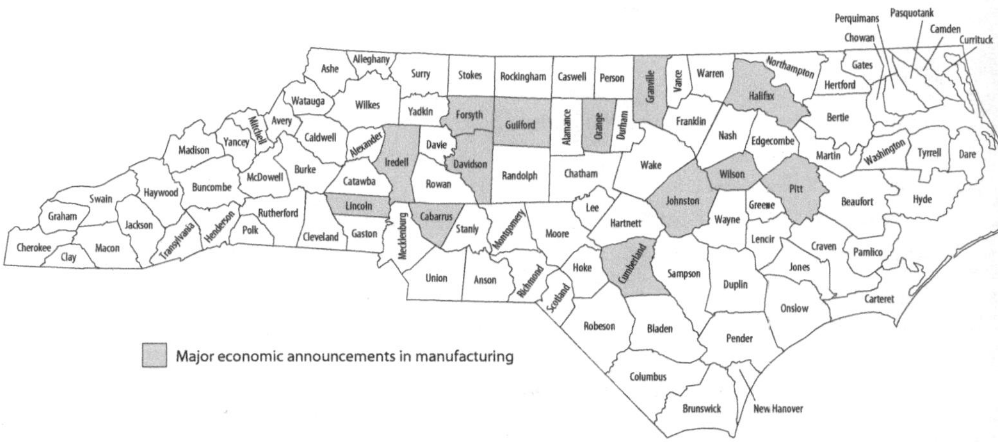

MAP 7.4. Locations of major economic announcements in manufacturing, 2021–2024.

Map 7.4 shows a wide geographic expanse for the major manufacturing announcements. Although the announcements don't include mountain and coastal counties, which is sensible due to the rugged terrain in the mountains and the sandy soil at the coast, the manufacturing announcements cover more counties than the announcements for technology, pharmaceuticals, and warehousing shown in maps 7.1, 7.2, and 7.3. Notably, one of the state's most rural counties—Halifax—attracted a $200 million investment.

There are several positive conclusions for North Carolina that can be derived from the examination of major firm announcements in the post-pandemic years. Business and job expansions have continued after the pandemic in a wide range of sectors. While the major metropolitan regions retain their attractiveness to businesses, costs may be motivating some firms to consider locations away from central cities, but still with good proximity. Johnston County in the Triangle region and several counties north and west of Charlotte are good examples. The analysis also suggests that major firms may be examining locations in smaller areas. The best example is the Rocky Mount–Greenville region: It is impressive that this region has attracted both technology and pharmaceutical firms. Perhaps the Anxious Age will see a "spreading of the wealth" across the state.

Strategies for Success

What has been North Carolina's formula for success, and will this formula need to be changed in the Anxious Age? Answering these questions will be a major task of public decision-makers during the next decades.

North Carolina has relied on a self-sustaining formula to generate economic growth in the twentieth and twenty-first centuries. The formula is based on low taxes, modest regulations, low business costs, and a careful use of financial incentives. Regarding taxes, the nonpartisan Tax Foundation ranked North Carolina as twenty-third lowest among the states in 2022, with an effective combined state and local tax rate of 9.9 percent.[48] The state ranks relatively lower on corporate income taxes than on individual income taxes.[49] The state's property tax rate, which funds local governments, places it in the lower third of states.[50] North Carolina has passed legislation to eliminate the corporate income tax by 2030 and to cut the individual income tax rate by 0.75 percentage points by 2026.[51]

The state also ranks relatively low for business regulations; almost two-thirds of the states have more significant regulations for businesses, especially small businesses.[52] North Carolina also has relatively low energy prices, as measured by electricity rates, and its overall cost of living is twentieth lowest among the states.[53]

Last, in the twenty-first century North Carolina developed an incentives program for attracting businesses to the state. North Carolina will consider reducing a newly locating firm's state taxes if it is estimated that the remaining taxes paid by the firm, plus the taxes paid by the firm's in-state suppliers and from the new worker incomes, is greater than the public costs—including the incentives—incurred by the state as a result of the new firm.[54] The state will continue the financial incentives as long as the firm meets established performance levels, usually based on employment. Firms that do not meet the performance levels will have their incentives reduced ("clawed back"). In numerous cases, firms have had their incentives contract cancelled.[55]

North Carolina has combined low taxes, low regulations, low costs, and incentives with an excellent location in the expanding South, a skilled workforce from the state's community colleges and universities, a pleasant climate, and numerous amenities such as outdoor activities at the state's beaches and mountains, and cheering for both college and professional sports. As more firms and out-of-state households move to North Carolina, the state's economic growth has become self-sustaining.

But will that situation continue in the Anxious Age? There are strong critiques of the strategy North Carolina has used to generate economic growth. Clearly, North Carolina has taken a "supply-side economics" approach to tax policy, based on the expectation that tax rate cuts will stimulate enough new economic growth to maintain or increase tax revenues. This approach has been a highly debated topic over decades; competing researchers have found evidence both supporting and refuting the theory.[56] Analysis specifically for North Carolina finds support for the notion that tax rate cuts can result in increased tax revenues, but only when the starting tax rate is at very high levels, such as double-digit rates.[57]

North Carolina has also been criticized for its level of worker protections. One analysis ranked North Carolina last on twenty-seven policies covering wages, worker protections, and the right to organize.[58] However, critics of those analyses make several counterarguments. First, data from the US Bureau of Labor Statistics show that a relatively small percentage of North Carolina workers (3.6 percent) earn at or below the national minimum wage; most of them are in the hospitality industry.[59] Second, as indicated earlier in the discussion of unions, workers in North Carolina can organize, but workers cannot be forced to join a union. The final counterargument: If worker conditions are so bad in the state, then why are individuals moving to North Carolina for jobs?[60] Of course, counter-critics reply that the standard of using the national minimum wage of $7.25, which hasn't been increased since 2009, is out of date. An alternative comparison to a more reasonable wage rate shows that 29 percent of North Carolina workers earn less than $17 an hour.[61]

Modifications may be coming to North Carolina's growth strategy. Concerns have been expressed that tax rate reductions have resulted in revenues too low to serve the needs of a continually growing state population.[62] If these concerns grow, it could cause some revisions in the state's supply-side strategy.

Also, as older generations decline in numbers and today's younger generations become more prominent, social issues will likely become more popular in the state. This is because surveys show that younger generations are more supportive of social change than older generations are.[63] Hence, it is logical to expect North Carolina to enact more worker protections in the Anxious Age. Also, North Carolina may lose the lure of low energy costs if energy prices are raised as a way of curtailing usage and lowering carbon dioxide emissions, or if they increase due to greater usage by AI. But although the fourth prong of the strategy—incentives to new businesses—has received criticism, the structure of the program is designed to be cost-beneficial to the state, and economic development generally receives bipartisan support, so the state incentives program will likely continue.[64]

North Carolina will certainly need to monitor other states' economic strategies and how they change in the Anxious Age. North Carolina is surrounded by other states that have been successful in economic development. In 2025, when North Carolina was ranked first in economic development by CNBC, Virginia, Georgia, Tennessee, and South Carolina all ranked in the top twenty, and all but South Carolina are also in the top ten.[65] These states have similar advantages to North Carolina, and the states have successfully used incentives and business recruitment programs to attract high-profile companies in a variety of sectors, including Toyota, Boeing, BMW, Volvo, Amazon, and Google. North Carolina will need to track these competing states and their progress. As a result, North Carolina should not rest on its laurels but should instead monitor the tactics and progress of nearby states and continually contrast their results to North Carolina's tactics and results. Also, North Carolina should watch how the competing states contend with the challenges of the Anxious Age, such as the issues of tax rates and adequate revenues, regulations, particularly regarding worker rights, and how the comparison between costs and environmental protection are balanced in the Anxious Age, a topic I will address in chapter 8.

Tactics for Success

A strategy is a broad-based plan for achieving a goal. A tactic is a specific action or step that will move toward that goal.

Supply-side economics, limited regulations, low business costs, and providing financial assistance to new firms that will have large positive impacts on the economy can be viewed as economic development strategies. Economic development tactics are ways of implementing those strategies. This section looks at three economic development tactics that may be applied during the Anxious Age. One tactic—megasites—has already been used. Another—corridor development—is in the process of being used. The third—remote work communities—is an idea that could be used.

Megasites are large tracts of land with improved infrastructure, including roads, landscape, and utilities like water and sewer, that make them ready for large business developments. The first megasite in North Carolina, and one of the first in the country, was developed in 1959 and marketed as the Research Triangle Park (RTP). Located in a central area adjacent to the major research universities of UNC–Chapel Hill, Duke, and North Carolina State, RTP has been enormously successful in attracting the technology, biotechnology, and pharmaceutical industries to the state. The RTP model has been copied by several other states. More recently, a megasite in the Triad region was used to motivate Toyota to build its $8 billion EV battery factory near Greensboro, which will be one of the largest in the world. Another megasite in Chatham County lured the VinFast vehicle factory, and a third megasite will be home to another battery factory in the Rocky Mount–Greenville area.[66]

There are two risks with the megasite tactic. The first is that the tactic might not attract enough firms to justify the public expenditure to make the site "shovel-ready." The second is that the focus on megasites and megafirms will detract resources and attention from encouraging smaller firms to locate in the state.[67]

The tactic of corridor development has long been used to stimulate economic development. The idea is to tie regions together with efficient transportation modes to generate economic development along the link as well as at the endpoints. The tactic has been used both internationally and in the United States. Frequently the transportation linkage is rail. Together with the federal government, North Carolina is in the process of analyzing plans and funding options for several rail corridor developments between cities in North Carolina and out-of-state cities such as Atlanta, Richmond, and Washington.[68]

Yet there is a second, often less expensive, application of the corridor development tactic. This is to again link two regions, but by a high-speed highway rather than by rail. US Route 64, which links the Triangle and Triad regions and along which a potential "renewable energy sector" is being developed, has been upgraded and will receive additional upgrades in the future.[69] Another section of US 64 between Raleigh and Rocky Mount has been approved for interstate upgrades, ultimately being part of new Interstate 87 from Raleigh to Norfolk.[70] The new technology and pharmaceutical firms in the Rocky Mount–Greenville region have already been noted, and interstate access to Raleigh on one side and Norfolk on the other will help encourage future development. In the Downeast region, US Route 70 is being upgraded to interstate quality between Raleigh and Morehead City on the coast. When complete, the highway will be Interstate 42.[71] Improved access along the new interstate will bring increased prosperity to small towns and rural residents that have lagged in economic growth compared to the rest of the state.

The new concept of remote work communities may be the economic development tactic that has the greatest impact during the Anxious Age. As discussed in chapter 2, remote work is likely a concept here to stay. The only question is what percentage of the workforce will be working remotely. With experts expecting a remote work percentage of over one-fourth as reasonable, the idea of communities built around remote work is both feasible and impactful.[72]

Remote work communities will bring many advantages for households. Commuting costs to the household budget and to the environment will be reduced. There will be less need for multiple vehicles in a household, resulting in lower vehicle payments.[73] For workers who completely eliminate work commuting, approximately 4.3 hours per week will be released per worker for use in other activities; for a worker who commutes two days weekly, 2.6 hours will be released.[74] If the newly available parental time is used to interact with children, recent studies show positive results for children's academic performance as well as mental health.[75] Studies also show that mental health can be improved by living in less dense areas compared to highly dense, urbanized locations.[76] Last, as documented in chapter 2, one of the largest potential advantages of remote living is lower shelter costs, especially if the job is in a high-priced city and the remote location is in an outlying area with lower real estate costs.[77]

A distinguishing feature of remote work communities will be their emphasis of "movement of things" instead of "movement of people." For most of our history, efficiently moving people for a variety of purposes—work, school, healthcare, shopping, entertainment—was the focus of new technology. Over the centuries the technology of moving people changed from walking, to using horsepower, and then to using motorized methods like trains, vehicles, and planes. Remote work communities will revolve around the idea of moving purposes to people. Hence, work, education, healthcare, and entertainment will be moved to households' residences, rather than moving the household to the purpose.

With remote work communities built around the idea of moving purposes to people, the first critical need of a remote work community will be easy and reliable access to high-speed internet in both private and public spaces. To take advantage of the expected use of drone delivery of packages in the Anxious Age, adequate space for the landing and take-off of drones will be essential. If the concept of 3D manufacturing of durable products like refrigerators and washing machines, which allows for those appliances to be customized and made on-site, becomes practical, space for this activity will be a standard part of residences.

Finally, with remote work communities constructed in areas with low-cost land, lot sizes in the communities will likely be larger than in cities and metropolitan regions. This will facilitate more outside activities, greater interaction with neighbors, and a greater appreciation of nature.

Remote work communities will not be a government-sponsored tactic like megasites and development corridors. Certainly, similar to current developments, there will be public permitting requirements and the need for some public infrastructure, including roads, schools, and other facilities funded through public revenues. Ultimately, however, remote work communities will appear when private developers determine that they are a profit-making venture. I predict this result will come sometime during the Anxious Age.

Summing Up

North Carolina has gone through several economic phases in its history. The first phase was the land-based economy, including farming, forestry, and mining. Second was the manufacturing phase of the Big Three—tobacco, textiles, and furniture/paper/lumber. Beginning in the late twentieth century, the expansion of international trade and health concerns about smoking prompted the decline of the Big Three. Fortunately, through the benefits of foresight, location, educational investments, favorable costs, and natural amenities, North Carolina was able to remake its economy around the new Big Five—information technology, pharmaceuticals, food processing, transportation manufacturing, and banking.

The economic and technology changes expected in the Anxious Age will have mixed impacts on North Carolina's industries. Most of the sectors in the Big Five will prosper, especially the information technology and pharmaceutical sectors. The questionable sector could be banking, especially if new forms of financial management for households are perfected.

Among the Big Three, tobacco—including growing and processing into tobacco products—will continue its decline as smoking drops in the population, especially among younger persons. Yet the productivity-enhancing results of applying AI to the textile/apparel and furniture sectors could provide some stability and make them more competitive with foreign producers.

The Anxious Age will likely see two economic sectors in North Carolina gain more prominence. One is mining and quarrying. North Carolina has major deposits of pure silicon, lithium, and phosphate, all minerals important to the production of electric batteries and many tech devices. A second up-and-coming industry will be tourism. Already important to the state's economy, North Carolina's beaches, mountains, golf courses, and exciting cities should increasingly attract more tourists as people look for escapes from the challenges of the Anxious Age.

An analysis of the announced major business investments in the initial four years after the pandemic suggests significant continuing expansion for technology, pharmaceuticals, and transportation, with modest growth for food processing and other manufacturing sectors. The new growth in transportation has moved away from parts to final products; examples include the VinFast EV auto plant and the Boom Supersonic aircraft production factory.

There have also been some locational shifts in economic growth within North Carolina. While the large metros still dominate the state economy, the increase in announcements for technology and pharmaceutical firms in the eastern micropolitan region of Rocky Mount–Greenville represent a significant geographic expansion of key industries to a region in need of economic growth. These moves could represent a turning point for wider geographic prosperity during the Anxious Age.

Two of North Carolina's recent strategies for economic growth—low taxes and limited regulations—have received widespread criticism. There will likely be combative debates about these two prongs for encouraging growth during the Anxious Age. The debates will be pushed by aging younger generations and possibly by businesses who align with more progressive viewpoints.

In terms of tactics for economic growth, North Carolina has had success using megasites, hence that tactic will likely continue in the upcoming decades of the Anxious Age. While the tactic of corridor development has primarily focused on rail linkages, a highway version is already being applied in North Carolina. The "renewable energy corridor" along US Route 64 between the Triangle and Triad is emerging as a potential new sector in North Carolina's economy. Similar highway corridor developments are in the process of being constructed between Raleigh and Rocky Mount and ultimately Norfolk, and from Raleigh to Morehead City. A new tactic taking advantage of the continuing popularity of working from home will be remote work communities, which could spread prosperity to rural areas during the Anxious Age.

North Carolina's economy will continue to transform, but in small steps and not big leaps, during the Anxious Age. What may be most noticed in the next decades is not what industries are growing, but where they are located. With greater flexibility of where both people and businesses are located, "widespread" may be the key descriptor of the Anxious Age—widespread jobs, widespread communities, and widespread prosperity.

This chapter's conclusions present some key questions for the state. As North Carolina's energy needs are expected to significantly increase with the expansion of AI to the entire economy, and with continued economic growth in the state, the question of how to meet these higher energy requirements will need to be addressed. Will the state be able to supply those energy needs and still meet goals for reducing adverse climate impacts? These crucial questions and others will be addressed in the next chapter.

8

MANAGING ENERGY USE AND THE CLIMATE IN THE ANXIOUS AGE

Modern economies have always been powered by energy. But the type of energy has changed over time. In the land-based economy of the eighteenth and early nineteenth centuries, power was generated by human physical effort; physical effort from animals, mainly mules and horses; and natural sources such as water. As the Industrial Revolution evolved in the late nineteenth and twentieth centuries, numerous inventions were created that increased humans' production and especially mobility, including the locomotive, automobile, and airplane. The new machines were mainly powered by fossil fuels like coal, oil, and later natural gas.

In the twentieth century, electricity became a major power source for many consumer-oriented inventions, including lighting, air-conditioning, and later computers and tech devices. However, electricity needed to be fueled by a primary source, and once again fossil fuels met the need. A non–fossil fuel source, nuclear power, became an additional primary source after World War II, but safety concerns and expense limited its application.

Like the nation, North Carolina moved through these energy transitions. The new inventions and power sources allowed agriculture to become more efficient, sparked the development of manufacturing in the state, facilitated the state's population growth, and helped create the cities and metropolitan regions that enhanced North Carolina's national and international reputation.

Pushed by population growth, income growth, and continuous inventions of new devices like the laptop computer and cell phone, the nation has been steadily consuming more energy. Greater energy consumption has contributed to higher living standards, more economic opportunities, and new industries.

Until very recently, most of the increase in energy usage was powered by fossil fuels. This circumstance has created what many regard as the issue of our lifetime, perhaps the issue of humanity's lifetime: climate change. Rising temperatures, greater weather extremes, and more severe weather are some of the conditions scientists have observed in the nation and throughout the world. North Carolina has also been susceptible to these conditions. For example, Hurricane Helene in 2024 could have a price tag as high as $50 billion in material damage and more than one hundred lost lives, and a significant share of these losses occurred in Western North Carolina.[1]

There is now a concerted effort to address climate change, including in North Carolina. Yet there are several challenging parts to this effort that the state will need to address during the Anxious Age. Included is the reality that power usage, mainly for electricity, will continue to expand as North Carolina's economy and population grow. A major part of increased electricity use will be from the implementation of AI into most parts of the economy, a result of AI's significant use of electricity for continual analysis of large amounts of data.

A second test of addressing climate change is ensuring reliability of power. An economy functions best when power is available when it is needed. To be reliable, power needs to be easily obtainable regardless of weather conditions or other variable factors, and the power needs to be delivered to users upon demand.

The third challenge is how to motivate both businesses and households to adopt climate-friendly behaviors and use climate-friendly products and services. To what degree, if any, should mandates and requirements be used to achieve these goals versus individual choice based on self-interest?

These are issues and questions that both the country and North Carolina will increasingly face as the Anxious Age progresses. They may actually be more of a challenge for North Carolina due to its rapidly growing and changing economy relative to the country.

There is one additional climate-related issue for North Carolina. As explained in earlier chapters, in addition to being a consumer of energy, North Carolina is becoming involved in the production of energy, specifically of renewable and climate-friendly energy and of products facilitating use of climate-friendly energy. North Carolina has over three thousand miles of Atlantic Ocean coastline (excluding inlets) that could be utilized for wind-generated power. The state also has over two hundred days of sunshine for producing solar power.[2] Furthermore, with the state in the process of developing a "renewable energy manufacturing corridor" for the production of computer chips, batteries for EVs, and EVs themselves, North Carolina could become a significant player in supplying products and technologies for the national energy transition. The state even has mines that include lithium, phosphate, and pure silicon, all minerals needed for renewable energy devices and components.

But as the state's renewable energy sector continues to expand, there are two important issues to address. First, given that the sector has been built in part due to federal financial assistance and state incentives, can the sector ultimately be sustained without governmental assistance, thereby becoming immune to the whims of shifting political agendas? Second, how can the state address some potential adverse environmental issues associated with some of the components of renewable energy?

Trends in Energy Usage and Environmental Impact

Graph 8.1 shows how North Carolina has performed on energy usage, both in the aggregate and per person (per capita), in recent years. It is clear from the graph that energy usage levels—both in aggregate (left *y*-axis) and per person (right *y*-axis) were impacted by the pandemic. Energy usage in the state significantly dropped between 2019 and 2020, obviously a consequence of the limitations and closures during 2020 curtailing commuting, travel, manufacturing, and other everyday economic activity. But by 2022 aggregate energy use was almost back to prepandemic highs. However, in

GRAPH 8.1. Trends in North Carolina annual total energy usage (left *y*-axis) and per capita energy usage (right *y*-axis), 2015–2023 (BTUs). Source: Energy Information Agency, US Department of Energy. BTU = British thermal unit.

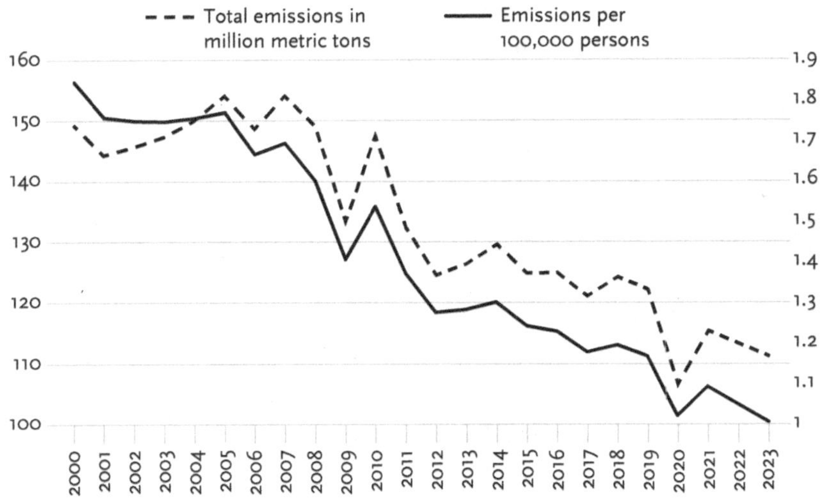

GRAPH 8.2. Trends in North Carolina annual total CO_2 emissions (left *y*-axis) and emissions per 100,000 population (right *y*-axis), 2000–2023 (in million metric tons). Source: Energy Information Agency, US Department of Energy; State Demographer of North Carolina.

2023 both measures resumed their drop, and the per capita measure was almost back to the low posted during the pandemic. The patterns are similar to those experienced for the entire country, but in 2023 the state's per capita usage was seventeenth lowest among the fifty states and DC.[3] The conclusion is, the data show that North Carolina is adjusting its energy usage behavior and is taking the climate challenge seriously.

Graph 8.2 shows North Carolina has significantly reduced its carbon footprint in the twenty-first century, both in total (left *y*-axis) and per hundred thousand people (right *y*-axis).[4] Tracking carbon dioxide (CO_2) emissions is important because the chemical compound has been found by experts to be the main contributor to atmospheric warming, which is related to changes in the climate.[5] The annual reductions have been significant. Comparing 2023 to 2000, total emissions were down 19 percent, and emissions per hundred thousand people declined 14 percent. Understandably, there was a large reduction from 2019 to 2020 due to the pandemic and consequent shutdowns in 2020, and hence a rebound between 2020 and 2021 as the economy reopened and recovered.

There are two main reasons for these trends. First is improvements in energy efficiency (see graph 8.1), which means that more outputs—lighting, heating/cooling, transportation, and so on—can be obtained per unit of

TABLE 8.1. Distribution of primary energy sources in North Carolina (percentage of total).

	2000	2015	2022
Coal	32	17	7
Natural gas	10	22	30
Petroleum	37	36	37
Nuclear	16	18	18
Renewables	5	7	8

Note: Percentage of total energy consumed (BTUs) for all uses from the source. All sources may not be produced in North Carolina. Source: Energy Information Agency, US Department of Energy, 2024.

energy. Many appliances, vehicles, lighting, and other machines are much more energy efficient today than in the past.[6] Much of this change has resulted from federal law and mandates.[7]

The second reason is the shift over time away from primary energy sources with high CO_2 emissions to sources with lower CO_2 emissions. Whereas energy efficiency mandates are nationwide, the mix of primary energy sources is state specific. Table 8.1 shows North Carolina's significant move away from higher-CO_2-emitting coal to lower-CO_2-emitting natural gas. Natural gas emits 50 percent less CO_2 per unit of energy than coal.[8] North Carolina has also increased its relative usage of nuclear-generated power, which has no direct CO_2 emissions, as well as renewable sources like wind and solar.[9] There has been relatively little change in the use of petroleum, most of which fuels vehicular transportation.

Energy Usage Forecasts

Before discussing the important issue of energy's role in environmental quality and climate change, we must examine forecasts of how much energy North Carolina will need in the Anxious Age.

Developing any forecast, but especially one of energy usage, must confront numerous future unknowns. For energy forecasts, there are two major unknowns. One is energy efficiency. As the machines that households and businesses use, most of which are energy powered, are able to generate more output per unit of energy, total energy usage can decline. Yet projecting energy efficiency can be very difficult.

The second unknown is energy uses that are not available now but will emerge in the future. The best current example is artificial intelligence.

Experts already observe current applications of AI using large amounts of electricity.[10] The challenge is that we don't know how fast AI will expand.

Accepting these reservations about energy forecasts, table 8.2 gives several forecasts for total energy usage in North Carolina for the years 2030 and 2050 using different assumptions. The forecasts depend on two factors: energy efficiency (usage per person); and the state's total population. Population forecasts for 2030 and 2050 are taken from the state demographer. Assumptions are made about energy efficiency.

The first forecast assumes that energy efficiency in North Carolina continues at 2022 levels. In this case, aggregate energy usage is totally driven by population. In 2030 there is an 11 percent increase in total energy usage compared to 2022, and in 2050 there is a 32 percent rise in total state energy usage compared to 2022. It is important to remember that total energy usage includes all forms of energy: both energy used directly, and energy used indirectly to produce a directly used source, such as electricity.

The increases are lower when continued energy efficiency improvements are assumed to occur in the future. The second forecast in table 8.2

TABLE 8.2. Predicted North Carolina total energy usage in 2030 and 2050 under different assumptions of future energy efficiency (millions of BTUs).

Assumption	2022 (actual)	2030	2050
2022 energy efficiency maintained	2,568,179	2,848,123	3,408,010
Annual energy efficiency improves at average rate from 2015 to 2022	2,568,179	2,679,300	2,814,000

Source: Energy Information Agency, US Department of Energy; NC State Demographer; author's calculations.

TABLE 8.3. Predicted North Carolina total energy usage in 2030 and 2050 under different assumptions of future energy efficiency and AI impacts (millions of BTUs).

Assumption	2022 (actual)	2030	2050
2022 energy efficiency maintained and AI impact included	2,568,179	2,990,529	3,748,811
Annual energy efficiency improves at average rate from 2015 to 2022 and AI impact included	2,568,179	2,813,265	3,095,400

Source: Author's calculations using data from table 8.2 and AI usage assumption from Goldman Sachs.

assumes that the pace of energy efficiency proceeds annually at the same rate as between 2015 and 2022. With this assumption, aggregate energy use in 2030 will be only 4 percent greater in 2030 than in 2022, and 10 percent greater in 2050 compared to 2022. These increases are substantially lower than those based on no efficiency gains.

However, table 8.3 shows there is a wild card in these forecasts: the card held by AI, likely the most significant technology of the Anxious Age. Because AI is based on continually analyzing very large volumes of data, it is a heavy user of power, mainly from electricity. Data centers devoted to AI are already being developed, and they will expand.[11] The expansion of data centers for AI is already occurring in North Carolina.[12] Since AI is in its infancy, estimates suggest that AI is currently using approximately 3 percent of total electricity usage.[13] But as AI becomes more widely accessed, forecasts suggest that it could use 8 percent of total electricity capacity by 2030, compared to 3 percent in 2022, resulting in a net increase of 5 percent of 2030 total usage forecasted in table 8.2.[14] There are no specific estimates of further net increases in electricity usage from AI in 2050, so an additional net increase of 5 percent—for a total of a 10 percent of 2050 total usage in table 8.2—is also applied for 2050 in table 8.3. It is important to recognize that these estimates are very tentative and that some forecasts suggest much larger growth in electricity usage by AI.[15]

The conclusion is North Carolina is on a clear track to use more energy in the Anxious Age due to population growth and new technology tools, even with improvements in energy efficiency. The only question is the size of the increase. There is also a corollary concern that the additional energy needs required by AI will boost energy costs and CO_2 emissions by as much as 25 percent and 30 percent, respectively.[16] These realities will make it challenging for North Carolina to achieve the two major climate and energy goals it has established—to achieve net-zero CO_2 emissions by 2050 and at the same time keep energy affordable.[17]

Energy Options in the Anxious Age

There are three paths North Carolina can pursue to achieve its climate goals in the Anxious Age, and all three will likely need to be used. The first is continuing to improve energy efficiency, but at a faster pace. All components of the climate environment will need to be included, such as residential, industrial, agricultural, and transportation, as well as all forms of energy. New technologies to reduce climate contamination in residential, industrial, agricultural, and transportation activities will be an important part of these efficiency gains. Interestingly, AI, which is creating part of the challenge of increased energy usage, may also be a major factor in improving energy efficiency.[18]

The second path is changing the mix of primary energy sources to reduce aggregated CO_2 emissions. We have already seen how North Carolina's shift from coal to natural gas has helped reduce CO_2 emissions per capita. The challenge for the Anxious Age will be further shifts to renewable and other sources and possibly to nuclear power.

The third path to meeting the state's climate goals is changing our lifestyles. Are there ways to reduce energy usage by altering our housing, transit, shopping, work, and other activities in ways that maintain our quality of life but reduce or eliminate deterioration of the climate? For example, could greater preferences for remote work as well as remote living be a pathway to this goal?

Turbocharging Energy Efficiency

There are several approaches that can be taken to improve energy efficiency and thereby reduce CO_2 emissions. One is to make the machines, devices, and structures using energy more efficient: for example, to increase the energy efficiency of factories, machines, appliances, vehicles, and so on. Traditionally the federal government has taken the lead in mandating efficiency improvements. Most states have deferred to the federal government regarding these initiatives; the exception is California, where stricter mandates have often been imposed.[19] Federal mandates can be politically contentious and subject to change. For example, many of the Biden administration energy initiatives have been significantly altered during the second Trump administration.[20]

Energy efficiency for structures is one initiative that has mainly been accomplished at the local level and sometimes at the state level. Energy efficiency for structures is important because homes and buildings account for 40 percent of total energy usage and 35 percent of CO_2 emissions.[21] North Carolina has statewide home energy efficiency requirements, which can periodically be updated.[22]

However, an important issue associated with increasing the energy requirements for structures is the cost, especially for residential units.[23] Stronger energy efficiency for structures usually increases costs for builders, who pass the costs on to homebuyers and renters. The higher costs could make the difference in whether some potential first-time homebuyers can purchase a home. Also, higher rents can force some income-constrained households to rent units much too small for their needs.

Over time, structures with better energy efficiency, and hence lower energy costs, can compensate for the greater up-front cost, but it may take time for this trade-off to occur. North Carolina could help with this timing issue by offering households low-cost loans to cover the higher price or higher rent of an energy-efficient structure. While the loans would eventually be repaid, loan payments to the state could be structured to begin only after sufficient savings on energy bills would have accumulated for the household.

Technological advances can also spur improvements in energy efficiency, and there are expectations that several key tech advances will occur during the Anxious Age. An important advance for North Carolina could be in controlling CO_2 emissions from farming.

Agriculture remains a key industry in the state, and within agriculture, hog farming has become a significant sector. Eight million hogs are raised annually in North Carolina for meat production, making North Carolina one of the leading hog-raising states in the country. Hog production is a leading source of income for the state's Downeast region.[24]

One agricultural problem is the emission of CO_2 from hog waste. It is estimated that the 77.5 million hogs in the US emit CO_2 at a rate equivalent to that from 646,000 passenger vehicles.[25] Fortunately, there are firms working on methods of reducing or eliminating these emissions.[26] Similar research is being conducted to address CO_2 emissions from methane produced by cattle, another significant part of the agricultural industry in North Carolina.[27]

One of the technologies with the potential to be perhaps the most important method of reducing CO_2 emissions in North Carolina, and in the whole nation, is carbon capture: that is, capturing CO_2 before it is emitted into the atmosphere, and then storing it, usually underground. An example is capturing the smoke from burning wood, which can release CO_2.[28] Some have proposed returning to wood burning to generate electricity, but capturing the smoke and piping it underground.[29] Researchers at North Carolina State University have been actively involved in developing the carbon capture technology.[30] Although this approach is promising, there are skeptics who question whether carbon capture can be a major answer to climate change. They argue that carbon capture is expensive, incomplete, not applicable to all forms of CO_2 emissions, and still unproven.[31] Even with these doubts, carbon capture could be one of many various approaches for dealing with climate change.

Last is the positive impact AI may have on addressing climate change, in addition to its role in improving energy efficiency. AI is already helping identify climate issues and point to solutions. For example, in North Carolina AI can identify and quantify the sources of CO_2 emissions, thereby helping to prioritize where action is most needed. AI also has a role in using the technology's ability to analyze massive amounts of data to predict climate-related disasters, such as hurricanes, severe storms, tornados, and flooding. Another proven use of AI is identifying the locations of waste in water bodies like lakes, rivers, and oceans, which is obviously the first step in their removal.[32]

Historically, technology has helped solve many of our greatest problems. Although technology will play a similar role in meeting the challenge of climate change, it will likely not be the only solution.

Remixing Our Primary Energy Sources

There are two major energy use categories in the economy. One is the use of energy to produce electricity for a variety of residential, commercial, and industrial final uses. Electricity accounts for 69 percent of total energy expended in a year in North Carolina. The second is the use of energy to generate power for transportation, which takes the remaining 31 percent of annual expended energy in the state.[33]

A variety of primary energy sources are used to generate electricity, including natural gas, coal, oil, hydro, solar, wind, and nuclear. Currently, the primary energy source behind transportation is oil, which is used to produce gasoline for most autos, diesel fuel for trucks, and jet fuel for airplanes. The environmental issues related to electricity generation and for the generation of power for transportation are considered separately.

One logical way to reduce CO_2 emissions is to shift more energy production to primary sources that are less polluting. However, in judging the environmental impacts of alternative primary energy sources, such as oil, natural gas, nuclear, and renewables, it is important to consider not only the CO_2 emissions during energy production but also the CO_2 footprint for any manufacturing, operational maintenance, and waste disposal associated with the fuel source.[34] The result is termed the "life-cycle carbon footprint."

Graph 8.3 shows the rankings of fuels by their life-cycle carbon footprint when all CO_2 impacts are included. Coal, oil, natural gas, biomass (energy derived from organic materials such as plants), and geothermal are the highest polluters, while solar, hydro, nuclear, and wind are the lowest.

The State of North Carolina and the state's largest electricity producer, Duke Energy, have developed plans for reducing CO_2 emissions and moving to net-zero carbon emissions by 2050. Their recommendations are remarkedly similar, but with a few key differences.[35] The top three primary energy sources of electricity generation are coal, nuclear, and natural gas,

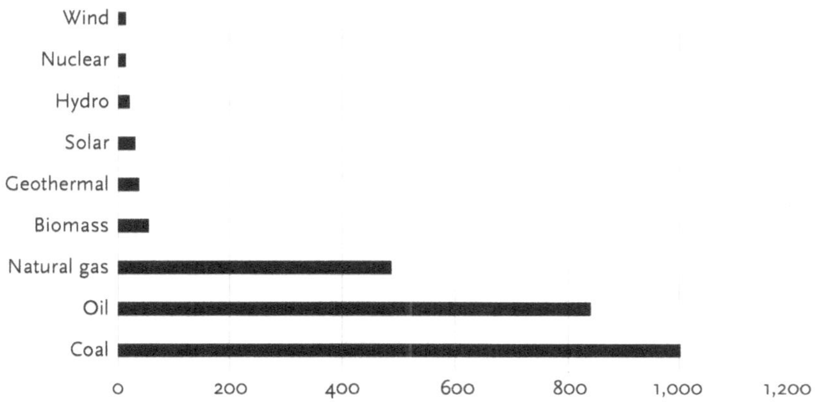

GRAPH 8.3. Life-cycle carbon footprint of alternative primary fuel sources for electricity generation (in grams of CO_2 emissions per kilowatt hour of electricity). Source: National Renewable Energy Laboratory.

which collectively account for 90 percent of production.[36] Both the state's and Duke Energy's plans recommend eliminating highly polluting coal as a primary source and replacing it with natural gas, nuclear power, and renewable sources. Both plans also recommend upgrading transmission lines and battery storage facilities to assist the expanded usage of renewable sources. The plans foresee a larger role for nuclear power, especially versions with a smaller physical footprint.

In terms of differences, the state plan recommends the creation of a North Carolina "green energy bank" for encouraging green energy power innovations. The Duke Energy plan recommends studying and possibly implementing a carbon capture system once such systems are developed. Among renewables, Duke Energy announced that it would not pursue using offshore wind projects for generating electricity, citing high costs.[37] Last, the Duke Energy plan expects natural gas to eventually be eliminated as a primary source and replaced with new sources such as hydrogen.

Graph 8.4 shows the path Duke Energy expects to use to reach net-zero CO_2 emissions in 2050. Coal will be phased out by 2035. Initially coal will be replaced by natural gas and renewables (wind, solar), but later natural gas will also decline in usage as the use of renewables expands even faster. Indeed, in 2050 Duke Energy's plan uses no natural gas for electricity generation. Reliance on existing nuclear power will continue, but in 2050 nuclear power will lag behind renewables and a category called "new technology" as the three power sources for electricity.

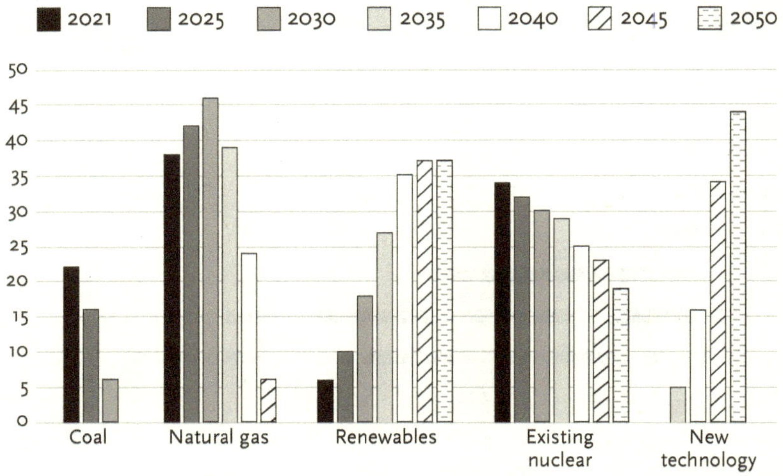

GRAPH 8.4. Duke Energy's forecasted primary energy mix for achieving net-zero CO_2 emissions in North Carolina in 2050 (% of total electric generation). Source: Duke Energy.

However, it should be noted that Duke Energy can make, and has made, adjustments to its primary energy mix, usually every two years, as it moves toward the 2050 goal.

In 2050, Duke Energy plans to derive over three-quarters (81 percent) of its electricity generation from just two sources, renewables and the "new technology" category. New technology includes several types of power sources, all of which either have zero or near-zero CO_2 emissions or prevent CO_2 from being released into the atmosphere. Most of the technologies are in the early stages of development, some are unproven, and others may not yet be cost effective. Examples include new modular nuclear reactors that leave less nuclear waste than current reactors; hydrogen energy, which has no carbon emissions; and the carbon capture concept, which prevents released CO_2 from reaching the atmosphere.

Since Duke Energy's zero-carbon plan for 2050 relies heavily on new and unproven technology, questions are raised about its feasibility for North Carolina, or, indeed, for any state. For these technologies to be successful in addressing climate challenge, they will have to both work and be affordable. The federal government has been promoting these initiatives.[38] Similarly, successful reliance on renewables—which are also key to meeting the 2050 goal—will rely on upgrades to energy storage and the electric grid. Energy storage is vital: Renewables can have periods of time when they are not generating electricity, such as when the sun isn't shining and the wind is not blowing, so the electric grid will need to be upgraded to integrate the new storage facilities into the electric generation and provision system. There will certainly be new costs from these improvements, potentially in the billions of dollars just in North Carolina.[39]

The dominant primary power source for transportation in North Carolina continues to be petroleum, accounting for 86 percent of the sector's power.[40] Although electric-powered vehicles are still in the single-digit range of drivers, sales of EVs have trended upward in the state, although not at a consistent pace.[41] If the electricity used to power EVs can be generated from primary sources that emit low levels of CO_2, then converting to EVs would significantly help in addressing the challenge of climate change.

At least this is the expectation. But as I pointed out earlier, with the concept of a life-cycle carbon footprint, it is important to consider all aspects of a primary power source's environmental impact (see graph 8.3). The same is the case for an activity that uses energy. A good example is transportation: While the operation of an EV may emit much less CO_2 into the atmosphere than gasoline-powered vehicles do, this comparison doesn't include CO_2 emissions that occur from mining and manufacturing the components of the EV, particularly the battery. Lithium mining alone is estimated to produce fifteen tons of CO_2 for every ton of lithium mined.[42] North Carolina is involved in this controversy because one lithium mine in the state was approved in 2024, and a second mine application is under review.[43] When the CO_2 impact of the most used battery for EVs—the lithium-ion battery—is included, research has shown that hybrid EVs produce 74 percent of the CO_2 per mile driven of a gas-powered vehicle, and full battery-powered EVs produce 57 percent of the CO_2 per mile of a gas-powered vehicle.[44] This obviously means that current-generation EVs are certainly not carbon free.

There are alternative battery options that are cleaner, including lithium-sulfur, sodium-ion, and radio frequency batteries, and ongoing research in North Carolina is furthering the search for functional options with acceptable costs.[45] Until the battery CO_2 emissions issue is solved, EVs will not be the total answer to transportation's contribution to climate change.

An associated question: To what degree have tax benefits encouraged people to purchase EVs, and if those tax credits are curtailed, as they were in 2025, will EV purchases be adversely impacted? The short answer is definitely yes, as surveys have shown that the tax incentives were important to EV buyers.[46] But there will remain other savings with EVs compared to gasoline vehicles, especially a significant reduction in fuel costs.[47] Consequently, it is very likely that EVs will remain as a viable option for transportation.

Lifestyle Changes: The Ultimate Climate Fix?

While shifts in the types of energy we use as well as the applications of that energy are crucial factors in addressing climate change, there is an associated viewpoint that an ultimate solution for climate change will occur only with lifestyle changes.[48] Such lifestyle changes include housing density, where we live, how we live, how we move, and even what we eat. If adopted, changes of this sort would mean new ways of living for North Carolinians in the Anxious Age.

With regard to housing density, ironically both higher-density and lower-density living could be part of a new climate-friendly lifestyle mix. Motivating households to live in more dense areas has long been recommended as a strategy for addressing climate change.[49] The idea is that higher densities reduce daily vehicular traffic and support public transportation, thereby reducing CO_2 emissions per capita. Indeed, the two largest cities in North Carolina—Charlotte and Raleigh—have adjusted their zoning to promote higher densities.[50] Even the famous industrial park—Research Triangle Park—now incorporates residential development in order to reduce work travel.[51]

Demographics and preferences may also lead to higher living densities. Compared to population averages, a higher percentage of older households live in lower-square-footage structures, including multifamily structures like apartments and condominiums.[52] North Carolina's aging population is consistent with future higher living densities. Also, with the declining birth rate, younger households are showing the greatest buying preferences for higher-density dwelling units compared to older-generation households.[53]

In chapter 2, I discussed the possibility of an increase in remote working and living during the Anxious Age. Remote living can be considered similar to a decrease in localized density, particularly in urbanized areas, as households move their residences away from jobs in dense metropolitan areas to residences in less populated areas while continuing to work remotely at their job. Daily commuting is eliminated, thereby reducing CO_2 emissions regardless of the mode of travel. Also, increases in the use of remote shopping, drone delivery, remote health, and remote education would result in additional decreases in carbon emissions.

Finally, with less daily commuting and with reductions in other types of road use, fewer highways would need to be built, thereby reducing the CO_2 emissions from the use of concrete for constructing roads. In total, it is estimated that the carbon footprint of a remote worker could be reduced by 54 percent just from the elimination of work commutes. For a hybrid worker going to the worksite one to three times weekly, the carbon footprint would decline by between 11 percent and 29 percent.[54] If reduced driving for other purposes (shopping, medical, education) is included, the reductions would be even higher.

Changes in what we eat is a lifestyle modification often recommended to address climate change. Specifically, the advice is to reduce or eliminate meat, particularly from cattle and hogs. Both animals emit significant amounts of methane, which when released combines with oxygen to form CO_2. Methane emissions from livestock account for 12 percent of annual CO_2 emissions.[55] As indicated earlier in this chapter, technology is being studied to eliminate or capture animal methane emissions, but the technology has not yet been perfected. But in the meantime, if hog and cattle production was ended until the technology for controlling methane emissions was developed, North Carolina farmers and related businesses would lose over $10 billion in annual revenue.[56]

Complementary Concerns

Related to energy is the infrastructure that complements it, such as roads and bridges carrying vehicles, the water necessary for utilities to operate, and the ports that move products both in and out of the state. As North Carolina expands in the Anxious Age, attention will need to be devoted to this basic infrastructure so the state can reach its capacity and not fall behind its competitors.

For roads, at best North Carolina starts in the middle. A 2025 measure of road quality using US Department of Transportation data ranks North Carolina nineteenth among all states and third among the immediate regional five states of Georgia, Tennessee, North Carolina, Virginia, and South Carolina, listed in order of their rankings.[57]

North Carolina looks better with regard to bridges. The latest rating for road bridge quality in 2022 shows that 45 percent of the state's bridges are of good quality, up from 39 percent in 2000. This is better than the national rating of 43 percent in 2022, down from 47 percent in 2000. Also, among the surrounding states, only Georgia had a better rating in 2022, and two of the states—Tennessee and South Carolina—saw their bridge quality rating drop between 2000 and 2022.[58]

Also, North Carolina received "C" marks for efficiency and sustainability of water resources in 2022, ranking twenty-first nationally among the states and ranking third in the regional five states of Virginia, Tennessee, North Carolina, South Carolina, and Georgia.[59]

North Carolina has long been criticized for its inadequate port capacity, which has led most shippers in the state to use out-of-state ports.[60]

However, in recent years, although port capacity has not expanded, the state has improved port efficiency at its main Wilmington port. Port efficiency refers to the time required for a ship to remain in the port to complete its workload. Due to operational investments recently made, in 2022 the Port of Wilmington ranked first in efficiency among all ports in North America, and it continues to set new annual volume records.[61]

While infrastructure improvements have been made in recent years, keeping infrastructure up to date with growth will be an ongoing challenge for the state during the Anxious Age. The biggest challenge will most likely be roads, especially as nongasoline vehicles such as EVs become more significant. In this case, alternatives to gas, including mileage fees, should be seriously considered as options to maintain the revenue flow needed for road expansion and maintenance.

Summing Up

North Carolina has made a pledge to confront the issue of climate change. Both North Carolina's political leadership as well as the state's largest energy producer have set a goal of net-zero CO_2 emissions in the state by 2050.

But, of course, the details of reaching that goal are important. While the state has made progress in reducing CO_2 emissions per capita, mainly by shifting away from higher-polluting coal as a primary energy source, forecasts of continued population and economic growth in North Carolina will increase total energy usage. There is also the potential for additional carbon emissions from higher electricity usage forecasted from the expanding use of artificial intelligence in the economy.

Like most states, there are three paths for North Carolina to follow to reach its net-zero CO_2 goal in 2050. One is to pursue greater energy efficiencies, such as developing factories, appliances, vehicles, and other machines that use less energy per unit of output, thereby achieving more miles traveled per gallon of gasoline for vehicles, improving cooling capacity per watt of electricity used by air conditioners, and similar examples for other activities. As in the past, some of these improvements will be done by government mandate—usually the federal government—whereas others will be motivated by individual firms seeking to expand their sales by producing and selling environmentally friendly products. Improving the energy efficiency of structures has traditionally been a local and state issue, so North Carolina could consider altering building codes to achieve higher energy efficiencies in construction. However, because more energy-efficient structures currently require greater costs, some public financing assistance may be required for such an initiative.

Changing the mix of primary energy sources has been a major path to addressing climate change, including in North Carolina. The state has already significantly reduced its use of high-polluting coal and increased its use of natural gas and renewables. The state's major electricity producer has outlined a plan to reach net-zero CO_2 emissions in 2050 by totally eliminating the use of coal, reducing that of natural gas, increasing that of renewables, and continuing the reliance on nuclear power, plus generating electricity from new sources such as hydrogen and small nuclear plants. The concern with the plan is that many of the new sources are not yet ready for use and hence are still speculative. Critics argue that Duke Energy's plan should include much more reliance on renewables, with greater complementary investments in battery storage and transmission.[62] Controversy has already occurred after Duke Energy announced the cancellation of offshore wind power operations due to costs. Still, billions of dollars will likely need to be spent in upgrading transmission lines and energy storage for renewables.[63] With nuclear power an important part of North Carolina's energy plan for the foreseeable future, debate will also continue over its expense, its safety, and the disposal of radioactive waste.[64] The concern over radioactive waste disposal could be removed if initial success in converting nuclear waste to fuel becomes fully successfully.[65]

The conversion of energy usage in transportation has been slow; the percentage of drivers using electric vehicles is still in single digits. Cost, EV reliability, the availability of charging stations, and the CO_2 implications of battery production are still issues to be addressed. Therefore, while the goal of an energy transition is apparent, how it will evolve in the Anxious Age is still undecided.

The final leg of the clean energy plan is changes in how we live. A traditional suggestion has been higher-density living, where services such as restaurants, stores, schools, and hospitals are clustered close to residential developments, reducing personal travel and encouraging reliance on public transportation for any needed travel. Demographic trends of smaller households and aging households would support a move to higher densities.

Another lifestyle change supportive of the environment is the idea of remote living, discussed in chapter 2. Based on remote working and linked with remote shopping, remote education, and remote healthcare, this lifestyle could reduce a typical household's annual CO_2 emissions by close to half.

North Carolina has another role in addressing climate change apart from averting human and environmental damage from the warming of the planet. The state now has a developing business sector focused on producing computer chips, batteries, and electric vehicles, all key pieces in the transition to an environmentally friendly society. But many of these investments were developed with federal and state financial assistance.[66] If the public financial assistance is curtailed, the question is whether the businesses will be able to continue. To be sustainable, the products produced by the firms will have to be desired by consumers, affordable, and easily operated and maintained. Costs will need to fall, batteries will need to be more efficient and lasting, charging stations will have to be plentiful, and supply chains will need to be more environmentally friendly.

It will likely take all three approaches—greater energy efficiency, use of more climate-friendly energy power sources, and lifestyle changes—for North Carolina to attain its net-zero carbon goal in 2050. Achieving the goal will also not be easy due to potential conflicts with other goals. For example, solar power panels are often placed in rural areas and are usually termed "solar farms." Farmers choose to use their land for solar panels instead of for animal or crop uses due to better financial returns. Yet this land usage shift adds to the concern over shrinking farmland for food purposes. There can also be conflicts when the solar-generated power is transmitted outside the rural community, and especially when the landowner lives outside the area.[67]

A final issue is whether the energy conversion is dependent on significant government financial assistance and, without that assistance, the conversion will end. Interestingly, after the reductions of federal help announced in 2025, there is already evidence that the conversion will continue. In late 2025, Ford revealed the development and future production of a new low-cost EV model.[68] Also, analysis shows that the costs of nonsubsidized solar power and onshore wind power have significantly fallen in recent years and remain competitive with traditional energy sources. Indeed, some argue that the removal of government financial support will prompt more innovation and cost-effectiveness from the producers.[69] It is also important to remember that states can provide their own clean-energy subsidies, even if the federal government does not.

Although the goal of net-zero CO_2 emissions in North Carolina by 2050 has been established, how and when it will be reached will be one of the most important, yet most uncertain, stories of the Anxious Age.

9

NORTH CAROLINA'S POSITION IN THE NATION AND WORLD DURING THE ANXIOUS AGE

As North Carolina's population and economy have grown at rates faster than the nation's, the state has seen its role expand in both the nation and world. In 2025, North Carolina ranked ninth in population, behind California, Texas, Florida, New York, Pennsylvania, Illinois, Ohio, and Georgia.[1] The population ranking was up one place from 1990 and up three places since 1970.[2] From 1997 to 2024, total economic production in North Carolina increased 94 percent, compared to 88 percent for the nation.[3] Even in the fast-growing Southeast—which includes North Carolina—the state beat the region 42 percent to 31 percent in population growth as well as 94 percent to 87 percent in economic production growth during the 1997–2023 period.[4]

Importantly, North Carolina's growing prominence is not expected to stop. Population forecasts for all states indicate that North Carolina will rise to the eighth-most-populous state in 2030 and to the seventh-most-populous state in 2050.[5] North Carolina is forecasted to have the twelfth-fastest population growth rate among the fifty states between 2020 and 2050.[6] While forecasts are not available for economic production, it would be expected that North Carolina's economy will expand in tandem with its population.

With a larger relative population, North Carolina will likely have a greater prominence in the country during the Anxious Age, perhaps similar to states like California, New York, and Texas today. However, while this elevated prominence will have positive impacts, some negative impacts could also occur.

The purpose of this chapter is fourfold. First, I analyze North Carolina's rise in prominence during recent decades and identify factors that have led to the state's attractiveness. Second, I identify the expected welcome impacts on North Carolina's people, economy, and quality of life from its increased status in the nation and the world. These impacts will be anticipated by studying the effects of rapid growth that has already occurred in North Carolina, as well as rapid growth in other states. The third objective of the chapter is to identify the opposite side of the growth coin—how rapid growth can present adverse impacts and challenges, and to pinpoint exactly what these challenges may be. Again, the experiences of various states—including North Carolina—with rapid growth will be the guide for this analysis. The final goal is to present a strategy for North Carolina to follow in order to maximize the positive results from growth while at the same time minimizing the negative results from growth. If successful, this strategy will allow North Carolina to prosper in all facets of life as the state sees its role and impacts rise during the Anxious Age.

Tracking North Carolina's Rise Entering the Anxious Age

As documented, growth has not been new to North Carolina. The state's growth has been outpacing other states for several decades. As noted in chapter 1, North Carolina's population growth has stemmed from two important factors: in-migration of households from other states, and immigration from foreign countries, especially in recent years. These trends, which began in the 1970s, are shared by other Southern states. Analysts attribute the shift of population, particularly from Northern states to Southern states, to costs and lifestyle.[7] In the late twentieth and early twenty-first centuries, the cost of living has been higher in Northern states than in most Southern states, especially North Carolina.

Graph 9.1 shows the advantage North Carolina has had in its cost of living compared to the nation and other states. The values in the figure are an index measuring the state's cost of living relative to the national cost of living for the years spanning 2008 to 2022. For example, the number 112 for California in 2022 means that California's cost of living in 2022 was 12 percent higher than the national cost of living in 2022. By contrast, the value of 94 for North Carolina in 2022 indicates that the state's cost of living was 6 percent lower than the nation's in 2022.

Besides North Carolina, the states shown in the figure are the top ten states for household in-migration to North Carolina in 2023 (Florida, Virginia, South Carolina, New York, California, Georgia, Texas, Maryland, Pennsylvania, and New Jersey).[8] Among these states, North Carolina consistently has the second-lowest cost of living; only South Carolina is less costly. In 2022 the state's cost of living was 17 percent lower than Califor-

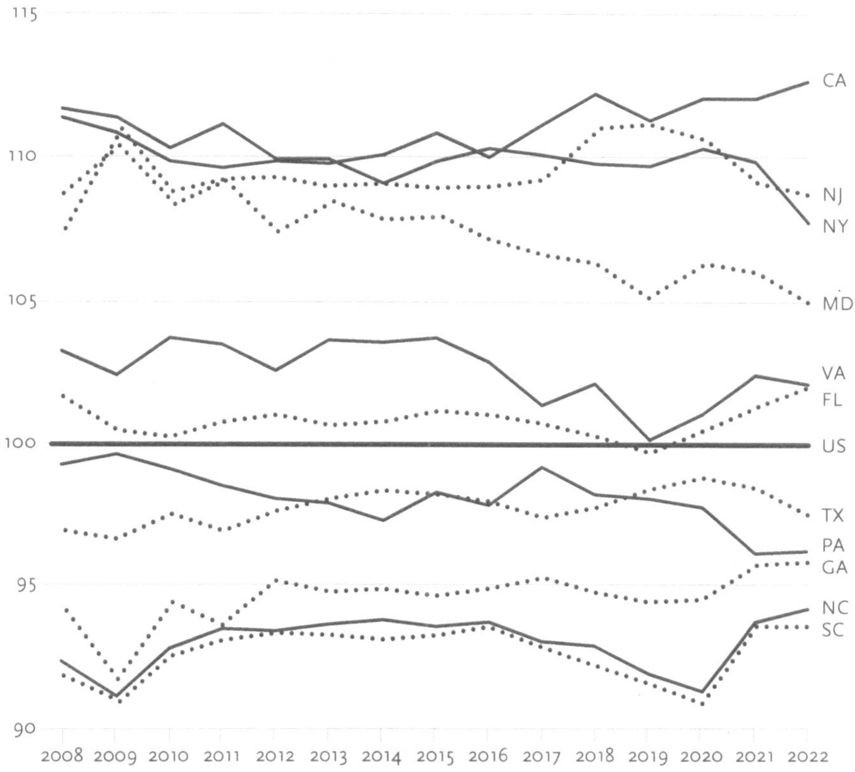

GRAPH 9.1. Relative cost of living in the US, North Carolina, and selected states, 2008–2022 (national cost-of-living index equals 100 in each year). Source: US Bureau of Economic Analysis.

nia's and 13 percent less than New York's. However, there has been some erosion in North Carolina's cost advantage in recent years. In 2008, the state ranked sixteenth lowest in the cost of living among the fifty states and the District of Columbia. In 2022, the state had the twenty-third lowest cost of living among the fifty states and the District of Columbia.[9]

Table 9.1 shows that North Carolina's cost advantage extends to its metropolitan regions, where most of the state's growth has occurred in the last five decades. The numbers under years 2008 and 2022 show the percentage reduction in the cost of living from the national level to the designated metropolitan level in North Carolina. All the numbers are negative, meaning a lower cost of living in the state's metro areas. The largest reductions are in the smaller metros like Greenville, Rocky Mount, and Goldsboro. The numbers in the column labeled "difference" are the change in the metro's

TABLE 9.1. Cost-of-living differences (by percentage) between the nation and designated North Carolina metropolitan areas in 2008 and 2022.

Metro	2008	2022	Difference[a]
Asheville	−7	−5	+2 pts.
Burlington	−7	−8	−1 pt.
Charlotte	−5	−3	+2 pts.
Fayetteville	−9	−9	0 pts.
Goldsboro	−10	−10	0 pts.
Greensboro	−9	−7	+2 pts.
Greenville	−10	−12	−2 pts.
New Bern	−13	−9	+4 pts.
Raleigh	−3	−2	+1pts.
Rocky Mount	−11	−12	−1 pts.
Winston-Salem	−8	−8	0 pts.

Source: US Bureau of Economic Analysis.

[a] Positive value means that metro's cost of living relative to the nation decreased between 2008 and 2022; negative value means that metro's cost of living relative to the nation increased between 2008 and 2022.

cost-of-living discount relative to the national cost of living from 2008 to 2022. A negative value means the discount became larger, while a positive number indicates the discount became smaller. Five metros—Asheville, Charlotte, Greensboro, New Bern, and Raleigh—have positive changes, meaning their cost-of-living discount has narrowed in the twenty-first century. Charlotte, Greensboro, and Raleigh are the top three metros that have been growing rapidly, thereby putting greater upward pressure on land and housing costs. Asheville and New Bern are tourist and retirement centers that have also experienced large gains in population, resulting in similar price-inflating pressures on land and housing costs.

By contrast, three smaller metros—Burlington, Greenville, and Rocky Mount—widened their cost-of-living advantage in the early twenty-first century. This may make them more attractive for economic development in the future. Indeed, chapter 7 documented several major investment announcements for these areas thus far in the twenty-first century.

Although North Carolina's lower costs may be attractive both to businesses and households, couldn't the state's lower worker wages also be a

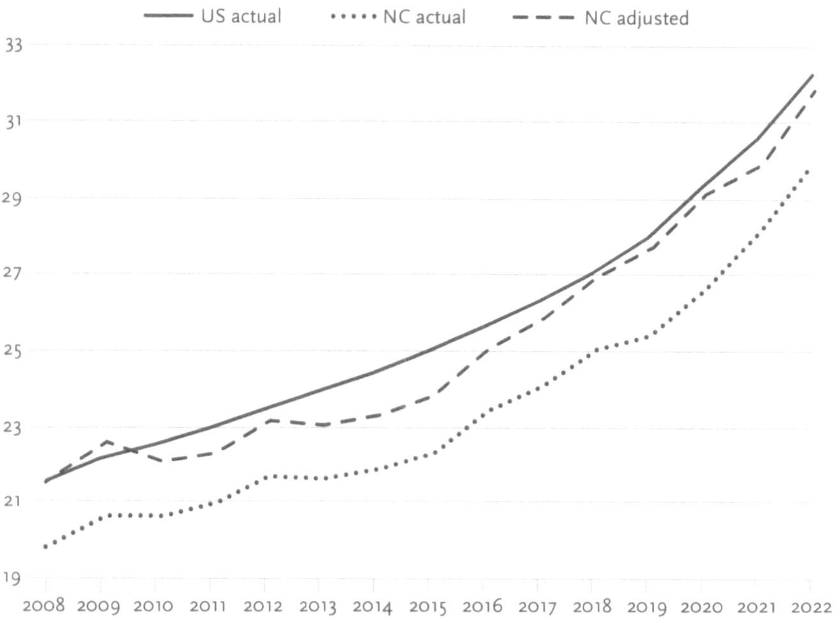

GRAPH 9.2. Average hourly wage rate in the US and North Carolina after adjusting for cost-of-living differences, 2008–2022 (in dollars). Source: US Bureau of Economic Analysis; author's calculations.

deterrent to workers and families moving to the state? Indeed, in 2024 North Carolina's average wage rate (pay per hour) was 7 percent less than the national average.[10]

The question is directly answered by adjusting North Carolina's wage rates by the state's lower cost of living and then comparing the resulting cost-of-living-adjusted wage rate to the national wage rate. Graph 9.2 shows the recent path of average wage rates (pay per hour) for workers in the nation and in North Carolina. Two wage rates are shown for North Carolina—one without adjusting for the lower cost of living in the state (labeled "NC actual"), and the second after adjusting for the lower cost of living in the state (labeled "NC adjusted").

Comparing the actual US average wage rate to the North Carolina actual wage rate, North Carolina's rate is always less. For example, in 2022 North Carolina's average wage rate is $2.31 less than the national average wage rate. However, what matters to workers is the purchasing power of their earnings, meaning what they can buy with what they earn. When the North Carolina average wage rate in 2022 is adjusted to account for the state's lower cost of living in that year, the state's wage rate is only 47 cents less than the national rate, much closer than the $1.17 deficit for North Carolina compared to the nation in 2014. Hence, the trend in the last two decades has been for the state's cost-of-living-adjusted wage rate to move closer to the national rate.

The conclusion is that when North Carolina's lower cost of living is included, the state's average wage rate is very close to the national average wage rate, thereby implying that lower wages are not a major deterrent to motivating households to move to North Carolina.

We should recognize, however, that North Carolina's costs are not the lowest among the state's immediate neighbors. Looking at the five states of Virginia, North Carolina, Georgia, Tennessee, and South Carolina, the latest data show that North Carolina is directly in the middle on the overall cost of living. Ranking the states from lowest to highest cost of living, the comparison is Tennessee with the lowest cost, followed by South Carolina, North Carolina, Georgia, and Virginia.[11] The implication is that North Carolina must regard its neighbors Tennessee and South Carolina as important competitors.

A second factor behind North Carolina's success in luring households to the state has been lifestyle. Especially compared to Northern states, North Carolina has a more moderate climate (most importantly in the winter), less crowding in its cities, and easy access to natural amenities such as mountains, the ocean, lakes, and public forests.[12]

Yet will these advantages deteriorate during the Anxious Age, thereby resulting in slowing population and declining economic growth in North Carolina? The state's cost advantages in its largest metropolitan areas have already been dropping (see table 9.1). Densities in cities have jumped, causing home prices in the state's largest metros to rise faster than the national average.[13] In recent decades the benefit of North Carolina's mild winters has been countered by hotter summers.[14] Also, climate change, in the form of more frequent and intense storms, may be putting the state at a disadvantage compared to states that are not in the pathway of hurricanes and tornados.[15] Hurricane Helene in 2024 showed that severe storms can impact not only the North Carolina coast but even the state's mountains.

Hence, the question increasingly faced by North Carolinians and their leaders during the Anxious Age will be the balance between the benefits of growth and the costs of growth. Are there initiatives the state should consider using to guide this balance, helping to maximize the benefits and minimize the costs? Or should the state allow the trends to continue unabated, and let the results determine the future path of the state during the Anxious Age? Before these questions can be answered, more details regarding the pluses and minuses of growth need to be examined.

The Benefits of Growth

States have usually sought growth and applauded growth when it occurs, simply because growth brings many benefits and advantages. Businesses moving to a state create more jobs and often provide opportunities for higher rates of pay to workers. This is one reason that numerous states—including North Carolina—offer financial incentives to attract businesses. Faster growth sometimes leads to more prosperity for regions of the state that have lagged economically. As documented in chapter 7, North Carolina has already witnessed in the years immediately after the pandemic the spread of economic growth in the state to numerous regions that have been behind in advancing their economies.

Economic growth provides benefits for consumers. As a state's population and economy grow, more businesses, especially those with national reputations, are likely to seek locations in the state, thereby providing consumers with opportunities they would not have had without the growth. Some businesses require a very large population base due to their high cost and limited operation time. Professional sports is an excellent example. North Carolina's strong population growth in recent decades has attracted three pro teams, each in a different national league—the Carolina Panthers in the National Football League, the Carolina Hornets in the National Basketball Association, and the Carolina Hurricanes in the National Hockey League.

Population and economic growth allow states to develop greater international connections. By 2024, the number of internationally based firms with a presence in North Carolina had increased to 1,700, employing over 300,000 workers.[16] Similarly, the number of nonstop international flights from North Carolina's largest airports—Charlotte Douglas International and Raleigh-Durham International—increased from zero in 1970 to forty-seven in 2024.[17] These connections promote international ties and opportunities for the state's businesses and residences; they also show the growing importance of the state in the international economy.

A larger state economy obviously allows a state to collect and utilize greater public resources, mainly in the form of taxes: The state can collect a larger amount of tax revenues even without increasing the tax rate because the state tax base has been increased. While a large portion of the increased tax revenue from growth is needed because the population is larger, there are also some projects with high initial costs (economists call them "fixed costs") that are independent of the population. Transportation, including roads and light rail transit, is an excellent example. The cost of providing transit, such as a two-lane highway between two geographic locations, is the same regardless of the population at the two points.

As a state grows in size and importance, its national political clout increases. Between 1970 and 2024 North Carolina gained three members in the US House of Representatives, increasing their number from eleven to fourteen.[18] The state gained the same number in the US Electoral College, which elects the president and vice president. During the 2024 presidential election, North Carolina was one of the most-visited states by the presidential campaigns. Among the seven so-called swing states (Arizona, Georgia, Michigan, Nevada, North Carolina, Pennsylvania, and Wisconsin), North Carolina was the third-most-visited state, behind only Pennsylvania and Michigan.[19]

Last, greater population and economic size bring greater diversity of people, products, culture, ideas, experiences, and background—elements that make for a thriving society with widespread opportunities.

The Challenges of Growth

The challenges of growth are based on the simple notion that "more" not only creates more good results but also can generate more bad results. More people and businesses likely mean more waste, more pollution, more traffic congestion, more commuting time, more land being converted from agricultural uses to development, and more space being taken for additional concrete, asphalt, structures, and waste dumps.

Many prices are also impacted by growth, and not in a good way. The more people trying to crowd into cities and suburbs, where most of the jobs are located, the higher land prices become, thereby resulting in higher home prices and rents. Converting farmland to subdivisions has the potential to increase food prices unless farm productivity increases.[20] Open space has been found to support mental health.[21] Less open space could lead to more mental health issues, which in turn increases use of the healthcare system and potentially increases both healthcare prices and health insurance prices.

Table 9.2 quantifies some of these adverse impacts from growth by comparing recent changes in several of the factors adversely impacted by growth in North Carolina and the nation. Although it still has a lower cost of living than the nation, North Carolina's cost of living has risen faster than the nation's cost of living in recent years.[22]

TABLE 9.2. Cost increases in North Carolina and the US for factors impacted by growth.

Factor and Time Period	North Carolina	US
Cost of living, 2010–22	30.1%	29.0%
Commuting time, 2010–22	7.3%	6.3%
Farmland acreage, 2012–22[a]	−3.4%	−2.2%
Amenity-adjusted house price, 2010–22[b]	123.4%	108%

[a] Data not available for 2010 to 2022; [b] Comparison is available only for Charlotte and the US.

Sources: US Bureau of Economic Analysis; US Census Bureau; US Department of Agriculture; Federal Reserve Bank of St. Louis.

Average commuting time has also increased faster, and farmland in the state has disappeared at a greater rate in North Carolina than in the nation. Amenity-adjusted home prices only compare homes with similar amenities, such as square footage, size of garages, and lot size. Although data are available only for Charlotte, the difference in the price gain from 2010 to 2022 between Charlotte and the nation is considerable. These results confirm that faster growth in North Carolina has come at the expense of some higher important costs.

A Strategy for Addressing the Pros and Cons of Growth During the Anxious Age

Over the decades I have heard many North Carolinians say the state should close its borders and stop people from moving here from other states and other countries. My guess is that most were not serious, but even their joking recommendation showed a frustration with some of the negative effects of growth. And, of course, if such an action was implemented, all the benefits from growth would also be lost.

Any situation where benefits and costs emerge has a simple solution: Make the benefits pay for the costs, hopefully leaving a net benefit. This is the recommended approach for North Carolina's growth during the Anxious Age.

Some of this strategy is already built in. Energy forecasts assume a growing state, with plans in place for moving to net-zero CO_2 emissions by 2050 (see chapter 8) even as more electricity output is produced. Although these plans will likely be altered several times in the coming decades, the assumptions of population and economic growth are already included.

Likewise, the increased public services required by an expanding state can rely on funding generated by existing taxes levied on both new households and new businesses. Debates may occur about the needed level of public services for all residents, but there is an automatic process for collecting additional public funds when growth occurs.

There is one question that may need to be addressed when state financial incentives are used to attract new businesses. Currently the model used to evaluate incentives considers added state spending when new businesses and workers are attracted to the state. The incentives are granted only if expected new revenues resulting from the firm moving to the state exceed the expected new state public expenditures as a result of the move. However, local (county and municipal) expenditures, including for public safety, teacher salary supplements, and possibly new construction for facilities like school buildings, are often not included. State leaders may want to consider automatically including these local costs in the calculations by making incentives packages also contingent on new *local* revenues exceeding new *local* expenditures.

The costs of growth manifested in favored locations by rising prices of land and housing can be mitigated by new forms of residential developments and building methods. One is remote-working residential developments (see chapter 2). A second is developments on the periphery of the metro area and served by rapid mass transit, such as light rail or dedicated bus lanes. A third is considering simplifying building regulations and even authorizing the use of lower-cost factory-built housing to construct more housing with a lower price tag.[23]

Losing open space may be the most difficult cost to contain. In our market system, land uses go to the highest bidder. If farmland is more valuable when used as a subdivision, then the use will likely shift from farming to housing. However, if food prices rise sufficiently higher as a result, the forthcoming higher profitability of farming may slow similar future shifts.

One alternative option is for the public sector to become involved. If open space—either in the form of a farm or simply idle use—is deemed to provide benefits to the population that can't be replaced, then some form of public subsidy or support for specified open spaces may be recommended. This is similar to the justification for public support of parks.

Summing Up

In recent decades, North Carolina has been one of the fastest-growing states in the nation. This trend is likely to continue during the Anxious Age. With both population and economic growth come many benefits, including more jobs and economic opportunities—many paying higher salaries—a wider range of stores and shops for consumers, more international connections, additional public revenues, added political clout at the national level, and greater societal diversity.

Yet at the same time, growth can create numerous adverse consequences: more waste and pollution, additional traffic congestion, reductions in open space, and upward pressures on prices, particularly for land and housing.

The challenge for North Carolina is to balance the expected benefits and costs of growth during the Anxious Age. The best strategy is one ensuring that the monetary returns from growth are sufficient to cover the monetary costs from growth. One challenge is that often the monetary costs from growth don't have an obvious price tag. Examples are the costs from growth generating more pollution, and the adverse impacts of reduced open space on human well-being. More work should be devoted to quantifying these costs.

Addressing the benefits and costs of future growth in North Carolina will require advanced planning, a recognition that the consequences of growth are double sided, and careful communication explaining that those who benefit from growth should realize they will be responsible for addressing the costs of growth. As North Carolina's population and economy become bigger and more prominent nationally in the Anxious Age, the benefits and costs of growth will receive greater focus and debate.

10

NORTH CAROLINA IN 2050

North Carolina has a long history of change and development. From a farming state in the seventeenth and eighteenth centuries to a manufacturing-dominated area in the nineteenth and twentieth centuries to today being a nationally recognized state in the leading sectors of technology, pharmaceuticals, and finance, change has been a way of life for "the Old North State." Along the journey, North Carolina's residents and workers have seen their economic opportunities and collective prosperity improve. Today North Carolina is considered one of the most dynamic, innovative, and competitive states in the country.[1]

Yet the journey has not always been easy, and the next destination has not yet been determined. With each transformation has occurred major disruptions to places, people, and businesses. For example, in the farming era of the seventeenth and eighteenth centuries, rural counties were the most prosperous. In the technology age they have been the least prosperous. As mechanization came to the farm in the manufacturing period, thousands of households left rural regions and resettled in cities where new manufacturing factories were booming. These former farm families had their way of life totally transformed by leaving wide-open rural spaces for the dense and noisy cities. Later, the shift from manufacturing to technology expanded the income gap between non-college-educated workers and college-educated workers from a crack to a cavern.

The emergence of artificial intelligence will open new paths for businesses to create and operate alternative ways of working and living, and to reshape commercial boundaries and expectations. The result will be a combination of imagination and anxiety in the perception of North Carolina's future. When 2050 is reached, will the trends and transitions experienced during the Anxious Age make North Carolina a better state? This chapter explores that question.

We can already see the Anxious Age as a time period of new ways, new perceptions, and new anticipations. It is a period of breaking with the past and creating a new future, much like the "Roaring '20s" of the early twentieth century and the rebellious but transformative 1960s and 1970s of the mid- and late twentieth century. Just as in these earlier evolutions, the hope is that the final result will be an improvement for our collective lives.

But the future is still unknown, and hence we are anxious, maybe even more anxious due to the scope of the expected changes. While the major new technology of the period, AI, is an extension of the technology age we have already been experiencing, the potential power and game-changing capacities of AI leave many of us questioning what the future will hold.

As in the nation as a whole, there are several issues North Carolinians continue to be anxious about for the future. Among them are prosperity, income inequality, jobs, the affordability of housing, the affordability of healthcare, and the cost of climate-friendly energy. Based on the analysis and conclusions from the earlier chapters, how will these issues be impacted as North Carolina moves through the Anxious Age? The following sections look at the future of each of these issues individually.

The Future of Prosperity

To be prosperous means to be thriving. Since prosperity and thriving are open to numerous definitions, measuring prosperity is highly subjective. Obviously, prosperity can be captured by financial measures. But it can also be indicated by measures of happiness and nonmonetary factors affecting well-being. There has been a long debate over the issue of measuring prosperity at both the national and international levels. The common measure of prosperity is real gross domestic product (real GDP), which measures the monetary value of aggregate production in a country or region after adjusting for price changes, which doesn't change the quantity produced. Real GDP is used in most countries and is available for US states. But some countries, including France and Bhutan, have created gross domestic happiness (GDH) measures.[2] Bhutan's GDH includes wealth and income measures, but also metrics for ecology, the environment, education, and charity.

Here, the traditional financial prosperity measure of real GDP will be used, followed by separate indicators of well-being for North Carolina. For each, past trends of the indicators are shown along with projections of how the indicators might change in North Carolina during the Anxious Age.

The solid line in graph 10.1 shows the recent trend in North Carolina's

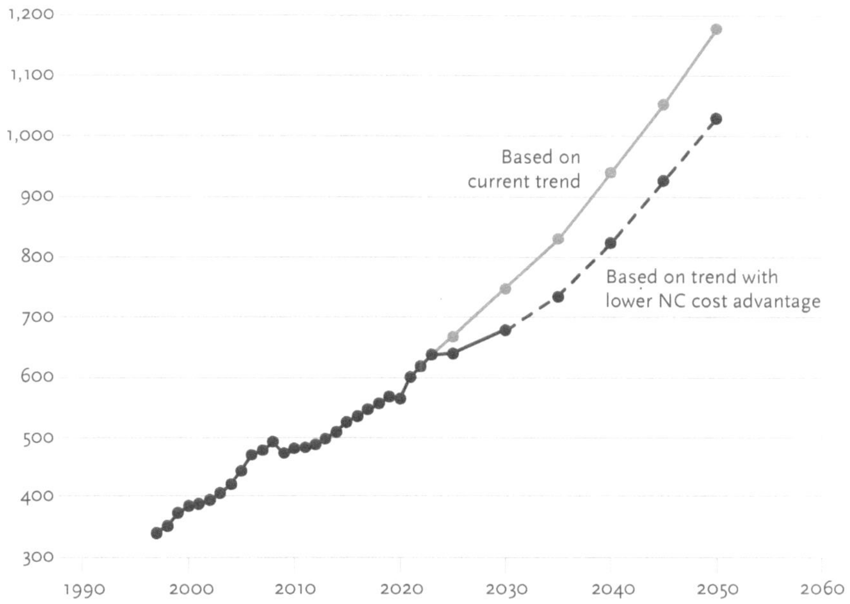

GRAPH 10.1. Past and projected alternative trends of prosperity in North Carolina as measured by real gross domestic product (in billions of dollars; actual numbers to 2024 and forecasts after 2024). Source: US Bureau of Economic Analysis; author's calculations based on Andres and Ignacio.

real GDP, together with projections to 2050. As the figure shows, real GDP has increased and is projected to continue increasing through the Anxious Age if past trends continue There are two factors behind the forecast of rising financial prosperity for the state. One is continued population growth, and the second is ongoing attractiveness of North Carolina to businesses.

However, as discussed in chapter 9, if the costs of growth rise in North Carolina in the Anxious Age, prosperity will still increase, but likely at a slower pace as both businesses and households consider alternative states with better cost advantages. An alternative forecast for prosperity in the state is also shown in graph 10.1 using the assumption that North Carolina's advantage in the cost of living will narrow in coming decades.[3] In 2050, the graph shows that the less optimistic growth path will be $148 billion under the forecast that assumes the past trend continues. The less optimistic prosperity forecast should warn North Carolina to monitor the costs of growth and to consider actions and policies outlined in chapter 9 to offset growth's adverse consequences during the Anxious Age.

The Future of Income Inequality

How financial prosperity is shared has been a major issue in North Carolina for several decades, and it will continue to be an issue during the Anxious Age. Graphs 10.2 and 10.3 show the trends of two measures of income inequality in recent decades in the state.

Graph 10.2 shows how the earnings of medium-income and low-income households have compared to the earnings of high-income households. The graph makes it clear that the earnings of both medium- and lower-earning households relative to the earnings of high-income earners in the state have declined over the last three decades.[4]

However, there was a slight break in these trends during the pandemic and the immediate years afterward. The downward trend continued for medium-income workers, although at a slower pace. For low-income workers, the trend reversed and increased slightly. The reason is likely the labor shortage occurring for many businesses hiring lower-wage workers during that time period, as documented in chapter 3. Businesses increased worker earnings in order to attract individuals to the open positions.

Graph 10.3 shows trends in the comparative sizes of the three income groups during the same time period. Graph 10.3 shows the long-run trends in the percentages of workers in the three income groups. The share of medium-income workers declined over the entire time period, and the downward trend actually accelerated during the pandemic and postpandemic years. The share of high-income workers has slowly risen during the three decades, with some acceleration after the pandemic. Perhaps the most interesting trend has been for low-income workers. Until the pandemic there was a slight but steady increase in the percentage of low-paying jobs. During the pandemic there was a sharp decline, then followed by a sharp increase in the initial postpandemic years. The increase likely occurred because many of the jobs held by lower-income workers, such as in food and accommodations, were the last to be filled. But in the most recent period there has been some reduction in the percentage of lower-paying jobs.

Overall comparing the years from 1997 to 2023, in 2023 the percentage of high-earning jobs was at its highest, the percentage of medium-earning jobs was at its lowest, and the percentage of low-earning jobs was only slightly below its peak in 2022. Hence, for North Carolina, the "middle-class glue" between high-income earners and low-income earners has eroded.

The initial conclusion is that North Carolina will continue to have a challenge in sharing prosperity. However, as discussed in chapter 5, some

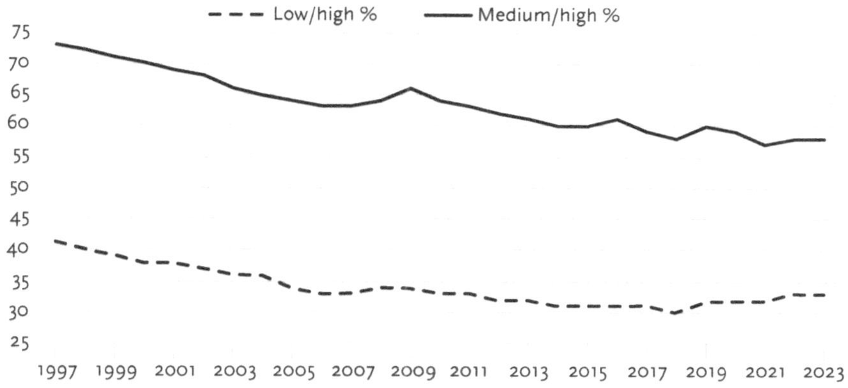

GRAPH 10.2. Medium and low earnings as a percentage of high earnings in North Carolina. Source: US Bureau of Economic Analysis; author's calculations.

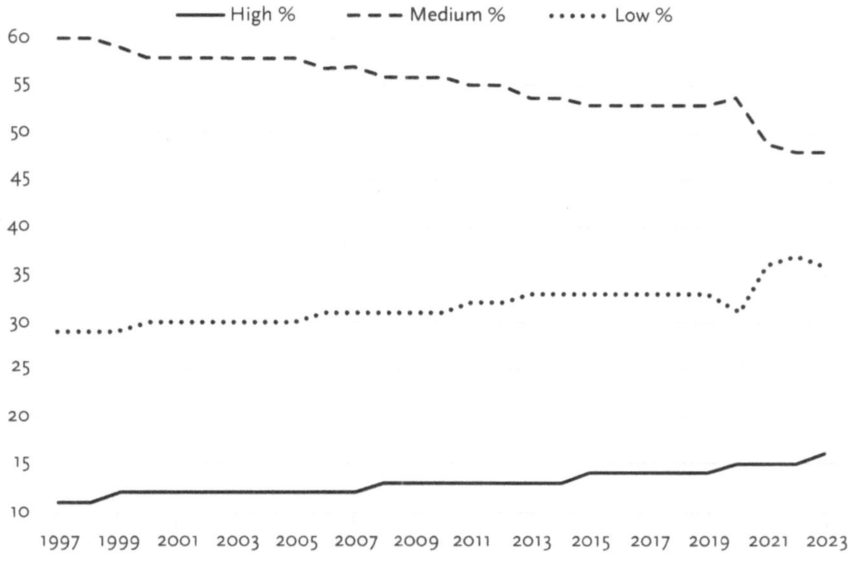

GRAPH 10.3. Percentages of high-, medium-, and low-earnings employment of total employment in North Carolina, by year. Source: US Bureau of Economic Analysis; author's calculations.

experts think AI may improve prosperity sharing, as AI both reallocates tasks and alters the value of tasks during the Anxious Age. Technological changes in the past, such as farm and factory automation and the development of computers for data analysis, displaced workers with lower levels of education while increasing the value of higher-educated workers. It might be expected that AI will do the same thing. Since AI is another high-level technological advance, the immediate conclusion may be that the value of less educated workers will decline and the value of higher-educated workers will increase, thereby further widening income inequality.

Actually, as discussed in chapter 4, some analysts conclude that the exact opposite will happen. Several experts think AI has the potential to narrow, and not expand, income inequality. For example, David Autor argues that the essence of AI is making access to information and analysis more widespread.[5] No longer will it be only experts with high-level training who will have the ability to find and use technical information and analysis needed to address and solve problems. Physician assistants will be able to do more of the work of medical doctors. Legal aides will replace bar-certified lawyers in a greater number of client cases. College teaching assistants can use AI-generated summaries and explanations of the latest research findings in almost every subject. As a result, the gap between the financial value of top trained experts and lesser-trained assistants will shrink; the value of the former will fall, and that of the latter will rise. The implication, Autor suggests, will be less income inequality, manifested both by the narrowing of earnings differences, as well as by a reduction in the numbers of higher-earning workers and an increase in the numbers of medium- and lower-earning workers.

Researchers at the International Organisation for Economic Co-operation and Development have actually found some empirical evidence of AI reducing income inequality.[6] Using data from several countries, including the United States, the findings indicate that wage inequality fell more in occupations most exposed to AI. These occupations were legal professionals, managers, and engineers. The researchers concluded that AI made work productivity more similar between workers with different educational and training backgrounds, a conclusion much like what Autor hypothesized. Since wage rates are primarily based on what a worker contributes to the company during a given time period (i.e., productivity), greater similarity in productivity leads to more similarity in wage rates.

Of course, there are contrary views too. One prediction argues that the initial impacts of AI will be to benefit higher-trained and higher-income workers and hurt lower-trained and lower-income workers. Yet as AI expands, more workers of all income levels will be replaced.[7] Indeed, some analysts still see worker replacement at all levels as the biggest and most challenging impact of AI.[8]

If the first set of analyses is correct, then there will be a downward trend in income inequality in North Carolina as AI is increasingly applied in the economy of the Anxious Age. The relative earnings of higher-educated workers will decline while the relative earnings of lower-educated workers will increase. This result would be a sharp change from the past.

Consequently, it may not take public income transfers, labor unions, or a higher minimum wage to share more of the prosperity in North Carolina. During the Anxious Age, reduced income inequality may naturally occur as the labor market is reshaped by artificial intelligence. Yet if the contrary set of analyses occurs, income inequality may not decline, and indeed could increase, so public policies may be needed to share prosperity.

Unfortunately, these contrasting forecasts imply that income inequality in North Carolina could be either higher or lower in 2050. This conundrum is just another example of the unpredictability of the Anxious Age.

The Cost of Living

The most important component of the cost of living is housing, both of owner-occupied and rental units. If, as expected, North Carolina grows in population during the Anxious Age at a rate faster than the nation as a whole, then housing costs will continue to rise faster here than in the nation. Indeed, some already argue that an "affordable housing crisis" currently exists in the state. An analysis sponsored by the North Carolina Chamber of Commerce estimated North Carolina needs over 440,000 for-sale units and over 322,000 rental units to be built in the state to close the affordability gap.[9] Doing so would require an estimated expenditure of $260 billion.[10]

The discussion in chapter 2 showed there are two ways for North Carolina to moderate the future increase in housing costs. One is to increase the supply of housing, and the second is to locate housing in regions where land is less costly. Making zoning codes and housing codes less restrictive are the most direct ways to motivate the private sector to develop more housing units. Encouraging housing development on the fringes of metropolitan areas, where land is less expensive, is a viable approach to moderating housing prices as long as relatively easy transit to major employment centers is available.

Perhaps the most transformative solution to housing costs is the previously discussed idea of remote work communities. Several analysts suggest that AI could encourage remote work.[11] With AI providing workers with easy and fast access to massive amounts of information available with just a few clicks on the keyboard, separation from the office will be easier. AI should also enable easier communication and collaboration between multiple remote workers. With a significant number of companies likely to cut workforces as a result of AI, workers who don't require expensive office space may be given priority for retention. New technologies that support remote living, including drone delivery, cyberlearning, and remote healthcare, can address perceived disadvantages of the lifestyle. The expansion of remote work communities in regions with significantly lower land costs could be one of the major factors slowing the rise of housing prices during the Anxious Age, thereby resulting in greater housing affordability in 2050.

In fact, companies may also prompt the dispersal of households to more remote areas with lower housing costs by choosing to make the same move themselves. AI as well as modern technology make proximity less important for communication and collaboration. As chapter 7 showed, such a dispersal may already be underway in the state, as companies are being attracted to smaller cities and rural areas with lower land costs.

Some argue another solution to high housing prices is to ban the recent phenomenon of large corporations owning dwellings. Critics claim that such ownership has increased housing prices.[12] Yet academic research reveals a more complicated impact. Corporate ownership appears to be a disadvantage for homeownership by increasing the price of dwellings. However, when corporations convert the homes to rental units, the supply of rental units increases, particularly in neighborhoods with few rental units. As a result, rents decline. Consequently, the evidence suggests that while homeowners may lose from corporate ownership, renters could win.[13]

Prior to the pandemic, food prices were one of the positives in the cost of living. In the decade before the pandemic, food prices rose at less than 2 percent each year. But from 2020 to 2023, food prices jumped 5.5 percent annually. However, by 2024 food price inflation had moderated to again under 2 percent.[14] Barring a catastrophic event like another pandemic, a virus decimating animal populations, or a major international war, food price inflation should continue to be modest. In fact, food price inflation could be even more moderate during the Anxious Age as a result of efficiencies AI can introduce into the food supply system. For example, AI may be able to help farmers get better weather forecasts, improved analysis of irrigation needs, and more accurate identifications of pest threats.[15] These improvements should increase the productivity of farming—meaning more farm output per acre—and thereby offset some of the negatives resulting from the reduction of farmland.

Efficiency improvements in healthcare should also be forthcoming from AI during the Anxious Age. Faster and more accurate diagnoses, the use of remote healthcare appointments, and more efficient healthcare practitioners, resulting in smaller staffs, can work together to contain healthcare costs.

However, many economists assert that another essential part of moderating healthcare costs will be increased competition in the healthcare market.[16] Research suggests that the consolidation of healthcare practices and hospitals into large networks has supported rising healthcare costs.[17] Competition can also be limited by requiring state approval for a healthcare practice to purchase major new equipment. The approval is called a "certificate of need," and in practice it allows competitors to block important purchases, such as modern equipment, by a healthcare practice striving to become more attractive to patients. The continuation of North Carolina's certificate of need is currently being reviewed by state courts.[18]

An ongoing major consumer price of concern is energy, and it may be the most challenging price issue during the Anxious Age. From 2000 to 2024, the retail price of electricity in North Carolina jumped 34 percent, 60 percent faster than average prices, and the increase may not slow during the Anxious Age.[19] As with any price, the level of the price is a race between supply and demand. With the state economy expected to expand and AI sure to be widely implemented during the Anxious Age, as shown in chapter 8, it is a good bet that the demand for energy will rise, especially for electricity. Certainly, conservation methods can be promoted, lifestyle changes can be recommended, and advances in technology can be developed to make many energy uses more efficient and cleaner. Still, the strong likelihood is that North Carolina will need more energy in the future. Hence, the major question is whether the supply of energy will keep up with the need for energy in the state. If not, energy prices will rise beyond the average inflation rate.

Jobs

I've left the most challenging issue for quality of life—in my opinion—for North Carolina during the Anxious Age to last, and this is the question of jobs and job training. Changes in the types of jobs and the training required for jobs is not unusual. During a four-decade span from the 1980s to the 2020s, the North Carolina labor market shifted from manufacturing to digital technology. Necessary training for many of the new jobs changed from having either no degree or a high school degree to needing a college degree.

Over the decades of the Anxious Age, we will see another major shift in the labor market. AI will destroy many jobs, create new jobs, and restructure still more. It is still uncertain how these changes will evolve. What is more certain is that educational programs will need to be remade at the high school, community college, and four-year college levels to successfully accommodate the changes and to transition the workforce to the realities of an AI-dominated economy. Short-term training and retraining, including by businesses, will become a larger part of the broader education system. Long-term, flexible state financial support used at the discretion of the individual will be required to replace financial support targeted to specific educational providers. This change will be controversial, which will add to the challenge of impending job disruption during the Anxious Age. Still, the remaking of education will permit North Carolina's labor force to successfully shift to the AI-led economy. If this retrofitting of education successfully happens, then the state's job market in 2050 will serve both workers and employers.

I believe North Carolina can successfully address the challenges expected in the upcoming decades. As I have documented, North Carolina has a long history of experiencing change, especially in the state economy. The state has had several generations of forward-looking leaders who have guided North Carolina through multiple remakings of its economy. I hope the same will be the case for current and future generations of leaders, both in the private and public sectors.

But the first step in addressing change is to realize that it is happening and will continue to happen. Documenting this message has been a major goal of *North Carolina in the Anxious Age.* Two complementary goals have been to show the impacts of the change and how the change can be addressed to preserve—and hopefully expand—prosperity for the state's population.

North Carolina has tremendous assets, especially in its people. The state has reset itself several times, and it is now embarking on a new remake during the Anxious Age. While disappointments will occur during the new journey, I am confident the "next North Carolina" during the Anxious Age will be an improvement.

In 2050, we will likely see the results of the transformed North Carolina that occurred during the Anxious Age. I hope achieving this transformation will have resulted in spreading prosperity and success among people and among regions. If this book can help the state achieve that goal, then my reason for writing it will have been fulfilled.

Summing Up

Predicting the future is always difficult, no matter the outcome one is trying to foresee. In the case of a state like North Carolina, predicting where it will be decades ahead is full of both excitement and uncertainty. This may be particularly true for the Anxious Age, as the emerging AI technology is likely to have transformative impacts on all aspects of society.

There are four specific factors determining the success of North Carolina through the Anxious Age. One is relative costs in the state and the impact of North Carolina's aggregate prosperity. A reason North Carolina has been attractive to both households and businesses is its lower costs. Yet as the state has moved upward in the rankings of states' population, its advantage in lower costs has narrowed. While North Carolina's cost advantage won't disappear and people and jobs will still be added in the state during the Anxious Age, some potential prosperity will be lost.

The second factor is income inequality. As in most other states, the sharing of prosperity has been an issue in North Carolina. Earnings of higher-income households have increased faster than earnings of middle-income and lower-income households, albeit with some slowdown during recent years. At the same time, the number of higher-income households has been increasing faster than the numbers of middle-income and lower-income households.

Third are the trends in individual costs important to the average household, including housing, food, and energy costs. There are challenges in North Carolina for keeping each of these costs affordable. Housing prices face upward pressure as increased numbers of households compete for limited land, particularly in the favored metropolitan areas of the state. Food prices can be adversely impacted by the ongoing reduction of farmland in the state. Energy prices could continue rising as energy usage grows and uncertainty over energy sources and quantities persists.

The last key factor is the job market. With the expansion of AI into almost all occupations during the Anxious Age, we are looking at likely the greatest upheaval and transformation of the labor market since the movement from farm to factory.

The book has offered ideas for addressing each of these four questions which will largely determine what North Carolina will look like in 2050. These ideas include spreading growth across the state to reduce cost pressures in metropolitan areas, reducing regulations on construction, moving ahead with new "clean" energy sources such as modular nuclear stations and hydrogen, infusing more competition in healthcare, promoting farm efficiency, publicly assisting the preservation of open spaces, and reshaping education for tomorrow's workforce.

North Carolina is a beautiful, resourceful, and forward-thinking state that does not back down from challenges. The Anxious Age presents a mix of opportunities and challenges. I expect North Carolina will both use the opportunities and address the challenges to keep the state the envy of the nation and the world.

11

AN AGENDA FOR THE ANXIOUS AGE

This chapter collects and presents numerous suggestions and warnings made throughout the book for addressing issues and challenges faced by North Carolina in the Anxious Age. The suggestions and warnings are most useful for public and private leaders in North Carolina, but should also be of interest to anyone living in the state during the Anxious Age.

1. Encourage consideration of remote residential and business development to geographically spread the wealth in the state. Consider appropriate zoning changes to allow for remote development, as well as to facilitate safe drone delivery when the technology is developed.
2. Consider the use of AI tutors in K–12 education.
3. Remake higher education to accommodate changing skills and evolving occupations occurring with the emergence of AI.
4. With nearly five hundred thousand North Carolina workers estimated to lose their jobs as a result of AI, recognize that some workers will be negatively impacted by AI and will need special financial assistance until they are reskilled.
5. Consider a modest tax on AI usage to fund the financial assistance of workers displaced by AI.
6. Refocus state support for higher education by providing individual educational vouchers to be used over the lifetime of a work career.
7. Promote on-the-job training and private task training as appropriate options for higher education.
8. Recognize that new energy sources, such as mini–nuclear plants and hydrogen, and new energy techniques, like carbon capture, will be needed to meet the state's dual goals of energy adequacy and clean energy, and provide appropriate authorizations.

9. Increase public support of open spaces, including farmland, to sustain agricultural production and promote mental health.
10. Because housing is a major contributor to carbon emissions, develop a state loan program for households to purchase or rent energy-efficient dwellings.
11. Support policies to encourage growth of the housing supply, including less-restrictive zoning and use of lower-cost, prefabricated housing components.
12. Recognize that supporting competition among healthcare providers puts downward pressure on healthcare prices, and support policies that facilitate competition, such as removing certificates of need and being cautious about state approval—through the attorney general—of hospital mergers.
13. Augment North Carolina's program for evaluating financial incentives to businesses to include local costs and benefits.
14. Recognize that growth brings both positive and negative effects. Approaches are needed to address negative impacts of growth both for the quality of life and for keeping North Carolina attractive for investors. Consider using revenues derived from the positive effects of growth, such as additional tax revenue, to fund programs that address the negative impacts of growth.

ACKNOWLEDGMENTS

Once again, as with my previous books about the North Carolina economy, I thank the tens of thousands of individuals from all professions and all of the state's regions who have attended my presentations and challenged me with questions about the state's economy and future. You have motivated me to continue to think, study, and analyze the Old North State.

For this book, special thanks is owned to the Director of the Economic Development Partnership of North Carolina, Chris Chung, and his colleague, Alyssa Brown Moseley, for rapid assembly of key data used in the book. Chris and his staff are busy recruiting businesses that improve the quality of life of North Carolinians. Taking the time to fulfill my request was extraordinary. A big thanks is also owed to Professor Hamilton Lombard of the University of Virginia for providing me with his data on the recent movement of households in North Carolina. Professor Lombard saved me hours of work and provided me with key insights about the data.

The professionals at the University of North Carolina Press are once again to be thanked for guiding this book to publication. Among this group, Lucas Church, who initially approved the project, and Madge Duffey, who constructed the maps, deserve special thanks. Of course, project editor Matthew Somoroff kept the project on time and in the correct direction!

Then, of course, I thank Mary, my wife. Mary is always the first person I seek for reaction to ideas, and she always has well-reasoned responses. She also honored the implied do-not-disturb message of the closed sliding doors to my office when I was diligently at work on the book. I wish I could say the same for Buddy the cat, who would use his strong paws to wedge an opening between the doors, followed by a jump to my desk to see what I was doing!

NOTES

Preface

1. The comparison is for 1920 to 1970 and for 1970 to 2020. US Census Bureau, Decennial Census of Population and Housing.
2. This figure includes individuals age twenty-five years and over with an associate degree, bachelor's, master's, professional degree, and PhD between 1970 and 2020. The percentages of educational attainment above a high school degree for the population age twenty-five and over increased 423 percent in North Carolina compared to 386 percent in the nation, US Census Bureau, Educational Attainment.
3. US Census Bureau, Decennial Census of Population and Housing, 1970 and 2020.
4. José María Barrero, Nicholas Bloom, and Steven J. Davis, "The Evolution of Work from Home," *Journal of Economic Perspectives* 37, no. 4 (2023): 23–50, https://doi.org/10.1257/jep.37.4.23; "What's the Status of Remote Work in 2025," *Oyster*, January 1, 2025, https://www.oysterhr.com/.
5. "This Is the Number 1 State for Working from Home, According to WalletHub," *Job Advisor*, April 11, 2024, https://www.jobadvisor.link/2024/04/this-is-no-1-state-for-working-from.html; Jodi Glusco, "Triangle Ranks #2 Nationwide for Remote Work; Durham-Chapel Hill Also in Top 10," *WRAL TechWire*, March 4, 2024, https://wraltechwire.com/2024/03/04/triangle-ranks-2-nationwide-for-remote-work-durham-chapel-hill-also-in-top-10/?amp=1.
6. "Office Vacancy Rates," Colliers and Lee and Associates; "Charlotte and Raleigh Marketbeats," Cushman and Wakefield, January 1, 2025, www.colliers.com.
7. Elaina Athans, "Another Business Closing in Downtown Raleigh as DRA Works to Revitalize 'Mass Exodus," April 15, 2024; "NC Trend: Uptown Charlotte Ponders Public Support for Developers of Vacant Uptown Buildings," *Business North Carolina*, March 30, 2024, https://www.businessnc.com.
8. "Downtown Recovery Rankings," University of Toronto, School of Cities, October 16, 2023, https://schoolofcities.toronto.ca; Jatrissa Wooten, "Raleigh Looks to Bring New Businesses, More People Downtown," *Spectrum News*, April 4, 2024; PurplePlanet7, "Will There Ever Be Any Retail/Shopping in Uptown Charlotte?," Reddit, January 2025, https://www.reddit.com/r/Charlotte/comments/1i51thi/will_there_ever_be_any_retailshopping_in_uptown/.
9. David P. Goldman, *How America Can Lose the Fourth Industrial Revolution* (Claremont Provocations Monograph Series, 2021). The First Industrial Revolution was based on steam power, the second began with the creation of electricity, and the third was the digital revolution from computers. The AI-created Fourth Industrial Revolution involves enhanced machine learning and analysis.
10. "COVID-19 Increased the Use of AI. Here's Why It's Here to Stay," World Economic Forum, February 24, 2021, https://www.weforum.org/stories/2021/02/covid-19-increased-use-of-ai-here-s-why-its-here-to-stay/.

11. Heather Stringer, “Mental Health Care Is in High Demand. Psychologists Are Leveraging Tech and Peers to Meet the Need,” *Monitor on Psychology*, January/February 2024, https://www.apa.org/monitor/2024/01/trends-pathways-access-mental-health-care.

Chapter 1: The New Demography

1. US Census Bureau, Decennial Census of Population and Housing, 1970, 1980.
2. US Census Bureau, Decennial Census of Population and Housing, 1970, 2020.
3. “Births: Data for North Carolina,” March of Dimes, January 2024. The decline in Black birth rates is particularly evident for teenage mothers; see Tia Thacker, Ashley Jackson, and Bianka Reese, “Swimming Upstream: Addressing Racial Disparities in Teen Births in North Carolina,” *North Carolina Medical Journal* 83, no. 4 (2022): 249–52. A key reason for the disparity is the continuing and widening gap in infant deaths for Black people and white people; the Black death rate is much higher, “New Data Show Black Infants Are Dying at Rates Three Times Higher than White Infants,” NC Department of Health and Human Services, March 6, 2025, www.ncdhhs.gov.
4. NC State Demographer, “Who Migrates to N.C.?,” OSBM (Office of State Budget and Management), December 6, 2023, www.osbm.nc.gov. Not surprisingly, in the time period from 2015 to 2023, the highest number of deaths was in 2021 (118,040), the year after the COVID outbreak. Since then, annual deaths have moderated but were still higher than in the previous decade.
5. NC State Demographer, “Who Migrates to N.C.?”
6. US Census, “State to State Migration Flows,” tables for 2011 and 2023, www.census.gov.
7. NC State Demographer, “Where Do NC Newcomers Hail From?,” OSBM, November 2023, www.osbm.nc.gov.
8. Joe Robison, “Carolina in Our Minds,” *Buddha Weekly*, December 2023, https://www.buddhaweekly.com.
9. Simone Jasper, “People Flocked to These Cities in 2023,” *Raleigh News and Observer*, January 3, 2024.
10. Thomas Bollyky, Isabella Turilli, and Emma Castro, “Judging How US States Performed in the COVID-19 Pandemic Depends on the Metric,” Council on Foreign Relations, July 2023, https://www.cfr.org/articles/judging-how-us-states-performed-covid-19-pandemic-depends-metric; Phil Kerpen, Stephen Moore, and Casey Mulligan, “A Final Report on the States’ Response to COVID-19,” National Bureau of Economic Research, April 2022, https://www.nber.org/papers/w29928.
11. Michael Macing, “State Migration Rates: Net Totals, 2002–2016,” *Governing*, July 2016, www.governing.com.
12. Maggie Foley and Florentina Angjellari-Dajci, “Net-Migration Determinants,” *Journal of Regional Analysis and Policy* 45, no. 1 (2015): 30–35.
13. Konrad Putzier and Rachel Louise Ensign, “America’s Defining Mobility Is Stalling,” *Wall Street Journal*, August 16, 2025.
14. US Census Bureau.
15. The NC counties that became younger were Alamance, Cabarrus, Camden, Cleveland, Currituck, Davidson, Davie, Forsyth, Franklin, Gaston, Graham, Greene, Henderson, Hoke, Johnston, Jones, Lenoir, Nash, New Hanover,

Orange, Pender, Randolph, Richmond, Robeson, Sampson, Scotland, Stanley, Stokes, Surry, Tyrell, Vance, Wayne, and Yadkin.

16. "Population Growth, 2040–2050," OSBM, 2024.
17. "Population Growth, 2040–2050," OSBM, 2024.
18. CBO (Congressional Budget Office), "The Demographic Outlook: 2025–2055," January 2025, https://www.cbo.gov/publication/60875.
19. The state demographer predicts deaths will exceed births in North Carolina in both the 2040 decade (2040–50) and the 2050 decade (2050–60). NC State Demographer, "County State/State Population Projections, 2040–2060," OSBM.
20. Congressional Budget Office (CBO), "Demographic Outlook."
21. CBO, "Demographic Outlook"; Nick Pipitone, "The New #1: Will These Be the Most Populated States in 2100?," *MoveBuddha*, September 26, 2024, https://www.movebuddha.com/blog/most-populated-states-2100/.
22. Priyom Bose, "How Did the COVID-19 Pandemic Impact Childbearing Rates," *News Medical*, August 21, 2023, https://www.news-medical.net/news/20230821/How-did-the-COVID-19-pandemic-impact-childbearing-rates-in-the-United-States.aspx.
23. CBO, "Demographic Outlook."
24. CBO, "Demographic Outlook."
25. Based on applying the CBO forecasts to North Carolina's average annual immigration numbers for 2015–23.
26. "Migration Between States," Policy Circle, 2024, https://www.thepolicycircle.org/minibrief/migration-between-states/.

Chapter 2: The New Economic Geography

1. "History of Urban and Rural Areas," US Census Bureau, https://www.census.gov/about/history/historical-censuses-and-surveys/census-programs-surveys/geography/urban-and-rural-areas.html.
2. Rebecca Tippett, "NC in Focus: When Did We Transition to Majority Urban?," *Carolina Demography*, February 25, 2016, https://carolinademography.cpc.unc.edu/2016/02/25/nc-in-focus-when-did-we-transition-to-majority-urban/.
3. Nathan Dollar, "How Does the New 'Urban Area' Definition Affect North Carolina?," *Carolina Demography*, May 25, 2023, https://carolinademography.cpc.unc.edu/2023/05/25/how-does-the-new-urban-area-definition-affect-north-carolina/.
4. "Regional Data: Gross Domestic Product," US Bureau of Economic Analysis, bea.gov.
5. Richard McGahey, "Can the Urban-Rural Divide Be Reversed?," *Forbes*, December 4, 2020.
6. Continued growth in urbanization was the author's primary forecast in *North Carolina Beyond the Connected Age* (University of North Carolina Press, 2017), 18.
7. Sam Wasson, "Gen Z Bucks Moving Trends by Heading to Major Cities as Other Generations Leave," *Today's Homeowner*, April 11, 2024, https://todayshomeowner.com/moving/guides/moving-by-generation/.
8. Stanford University, "Golf, Rent, and Commutes: 7 Impacts of Working from Home," *Stanford Reports*, March 13, 2023, https://news.stanford.edu/stories/2023/03/7-things-know-working-home.

9. Stanford University, "Golf, Rent, and Commutes."
10. Shelly Buckman, Jose Maria Barrero, Nickolas Bloom, and Steven Davis, "Measuring Work from Home," Becker-Friedman Institute for Economic Policy Research, University of Chicago, February 15, 2025; Nicholas Bloom, Steven Davis, Jose Barrero, Kevin Foster, Brent Meyer, and Emil Mihaylov, "US Executives Expect Work from Home Is Here to Stay," Stanford Institute for Economic Research Policy, March 2025, https://siepr.stanford.edu/publications/policy-brief/us-executives-predict-work-home-here-stay.
11. Katie Peralta Soloff, "Remote Work Dominates in North Carolina," *Axios Charlotte*, November 17, 2024 https://www.axios.com/local/charlotte/2024/11/17/remote-work-dominates-in-north-carolina; David Rouse, Ben Hitchings, and Anita Brown-Graham, "Workplace/Workforce Disruption in North Carolina," *NCImpact*, June 2024, https://ncimpact.sog.unc.edu/2024/06/workplace-workforce-disruption-in-north-carolina/.
12. Michael L. Walden, *Re-Launch: How Families Can Be Renewed and the American Dream Revived in the New Independent Lifestyle of the Post-Pandemic Economy* (Defiance Press, 2021).
13. "Census Bureau Estimates Show Average One-Way Travel Time to Work Rises to All-Time High," US Census Bureau, March 18, 2021. Of course, remote work varies by occupation. It is highest among professional jobs, in health care, as well as in real estate. Louise Sheiner, David Wessel, and Elijah Asdourian, "The US Labor Market Post-COVID: What's Changed, and What Hasn't?," Brookings Hutchins Center, March 22, 2024, https://www.brookings.edu/articles/the-us-labor-market-post-covid-whats-changed-and-what-hasnt/. Average commuting time is expected to increase in the future. Anne Marie Chaker, "America's Commute to Work Is Getting Longer and Longer," *Wall Street Journal*, June 5, 2024.
14. "Urban, Suburban, and Rural Home Prices in the US," Zillow, February 10, 2016; with prices updated to 2023 using Peyton Whitney and Alexander Herman, "Rural Areas Saw Disproportionate Home Price Growth During the Pandemic," Harvard University, Joint Center for Housing Studies, May 16, 2024, https://www.jchs.harvard.edu/blog/rural-areas-saw-disproportionate-home-price-growth-during-pandemic.
15. Christine Rosen, *The Extinction of Experience* (W. W. Norton, 2024).
16. David A. Spenser, "Marshall's Economics at Work: An Assessment," *Cambridge Journal of Economics* 49, no. 3 (2025): 505–25.
17. John Purcell, "Remote Work and the Collaboration Conundrum," *Forbes*, February 23, 2024.
18. Nicholas Bloom, Ruobing Han, and James Liang, "Hybrid Working from Home Improves Retention Without Damaging Performance," *Nature*, June 12, 2024.
19. Gleb Tsipursky, "The AI Revolution Transforming Hybrid and Remote Work and the Return to the Office," *Forbes*, May 9, 2023.
20. Matt Beane, "Gen AI Is Coming for Remote Workers," *Harvard Business Review*, July 22, 2024.
21. Jason Reginato, Christina Locopo, Darren Geeter, and Tala Hadavi, "Here's Why Retail Outlets Haven't Recovered," *CNBC*, July 18, 2024.
22. "Quarterly Retail E-Commerce Sales, 2015–2024," US Census Bureau; "51 Economic Statistics in 2025," Sellers Commerce, June 19, 2025.
23. "E-Commerce as a Percentage of Total Retail Sales Worldwide from 2021 to

2027," *Statista*, February 2024, https://www.statista.com/statistics/484400/ecommerce-share-total-retail-sales/.
24. "Virtual Fitting Room Making Shopping a Breeze," *Debutify*, March 12, 2024, https://debutify.com/blog/virtual-fitting-rooms.
25. Suzanne Kapner, "COVID-19 Rewrites the Rules of Shopping: What Is Next?," *Wall Street Journal*, March 12, 2021.
26. Haydon Fleming, "A Breakdown of Last-Mile Delivery Costs and How to Reduce Them," *Dropoff*, February 6, 2023 https://www.dropoff.com/blog/last-mile-delivery-costs-breakdown-and-how-to-reduce-them/.
27. Andrea Cornell, Saria Mahan, and Robin Riedel, "Commercial Drone Deliveries Are Demonstrating Continued Momentum in 2023," McKinsey and Company, October 23, 2023 https://www.mckinsey.com/industries/aerospace-and-defense/our-insights/future-air-mobility-blog/commercial-drone-deliveries-are-demonstrating-continued-momentum-in-2023.
28. "The Transformative Impact of Drones and Automated Technologies on Logistics," Park University, May 2, 2024 https://www.park.edu/blog/the-transformative-impact-of-drones-and-automated-technologies-on-logistics/.
29. Cornell, Mahan, and Riedel, "Commercial Drone Deliveries."
30. NC Governor Roy Cooper, "NC Awards $80 Million to Give More North Carolinians High-Speed Internet Access, Governor Cooper Announces" (press release), July 6, 2023.
31. "North Carolina Broadband Map," National Institute on Minority Health and Health Disparities, 2021.
32. "Here's How Starlink Satellites Are Getting Western NC Back Online," *WRAL News*, October 3, 2024.
33. Andreas Riveria, "Satellite Internet Statistics," Satellite Internet Com, April 1, 2024.
34. "Number of Fixed Broadband Subscribers in the United States from 2010 to 2023 by Quarter," *Statista*, 2025, https://www.statista.com/statistics/217938/number-of-us-broadband-internet-subscribers/.
35. Hamilton Lombard, "As Remote Work Persists, Migration Sure Continues in 2023 for Rural America," *StatChat*, May 9, 2024, https://www.coopercenter.org/research/remote-work-persists-migration-continues-rural-america; Michael Sasso, "Record Wave of Americans Fled Cities," *Bloomberg*, May 7, 2024, https://www.bloomberg.com/news/articles/2024-05-07/record-wave-of-americans-fled-big-cities-for-small-ones-in-2023; and John Cromartie, "Net Migration Spurs Renewed Growth in Rural Areas of the United States," *Amber Waves*, Economic Research Service, US Department of Agriculture, February 22, 2024, https://www.ers.usda.gov/amber-waves/2024/february/net-migration-spurs-renewed-growth-in-rural-areas-of-the-united-states.
36. Charlotte is the major city in the Charlotte-Concord-Gastonia Metropolitan Statistical Area; Raleigh is the major city in the Triangle Metropolitan Area, which also includes Durham and Chapel Hill; and Greensboro is a main city in the Piedmont Triad Metropolitan area, along with Winston-Salem and High Point.
37. National Center for Health Statistics, "COVID Death Rates in Urban and Rural Areas," NCHS Data Brief No. 447, October 2022, https://www.cdc.gov/nchs/products/databriefs/db447.htm.
38. Kimberly Lowe-MacAuley, "What Is Extreme Commuting?," *FlexJobs*, November 1, 2023.

39. Raleigh-Durham, Charlotte, and Piedmont Triad are all international airports.
40. A typical household could reduce their monthly expenses by an average of 22 percent by moving from urban areas to rural areas. Data are from Walden, *Re-Launch*.

Chapter 3: The New Workforce

1. "Chart Book: Tracking the Recovery from the Pandemic Recession," Center on Budget Policy and Priorities, Washington, DC, April 3, 2024, https://www.cbpp.org/research/economy/tracking-the-recovery-from-the-pandemic-recession.
2. Stephanie Ferguson Melhorn, "Understanding America's Labor Shortage: The Most Impacted Industries," US Chamber of Commerce, December 13, 2024, https://www.uschamber.com/workforce/understanding-americas-labor-shortage-the-most-impacted-industries.
3. US Bureau of Labor Statistics, State and Area Employment, Hours, and Earnings, https://www.bls.gov/help/one_screen/sa.htm.
4. Michelle Long and Matthew Rae, "Employers Strengthen Paid Leave Benefits During the COVID-19 Pandemic: Findings from the 2021 Employer Health Benefits Survey," *Women's Health Policy*, November 11, 2021; NC Office of State Human Resources, 2024 Compensation and Benefits Report, https://oshr.nc.gov/2024%20Compensation%20and%20Benefits%20Report.
5. "Labor Unions and the US Economy," US Treasury Department, July 11, 2024.
6. Sampada Kapoor, "The Labor Union Spike," *Business Law Today*, July 21, 2022, https://businesslawtoday.org/2022/07/us-labor-union-spike/.
7. Randy Capps, Michael Fix, Jeffrey Passel, Jason Ost, and Dan Perez-Lopez, "A Profile of the Low-Wage Immigrant Workforce," *Urban Institute*, November 2003, https://www.urban.org/sites/default/files/publication/59111/310880-A-Profile-of-the-Low-Wage-Immigrant-Workforce.PDF.
8. Max Zahn, "The Four-Day Workweek Is Gaining Momentum. Could the US Adapt It Nationwide?," *ABC News*, June 1, 2023.
9. North Carolina is ranked the least union-friendly state based on the rate of union membership and the four-year change in union membership. If only the union membership rate is considered, North Carolina is ranked second worst behind South Carolina. Jeff White, "States with Strongest Unions," *Smartasset*, November 16, 2022, https://smartasset.com/data-studies/states-with-the-strongest-unions-2022.
10. Dvorkin Maximiliano and Maggie Isaacson, "Retirements Surge for Older Workers During COVID-19," Federal Reserve Bank of St. Louis, December 20, 2021, https://www.stlouisfed.org/on-the-economy/2021/december/retirements-surge-older-workers-covid19; Jack Favilukis and Glen Li, "The Great Resignation Was Caused by the COVID-19 Housing Boom," UBC Sauder, June 26, 2023, https://www.sauder.ubc.ca/news/insights/great-resignation-was-caused-covid-19-housing-boom-study.
11. Melhorn, "Understanding America's Labor Shortage."
12. "One Big Beautiful Bill Law Summary," Association of State and Territorial Officers, July 9, 2025, https://www.astho.org/advocacy/federal-government-affairs/leg-alerts/2025/one-big-beautiful-bill-law-summary/.

13. Hubert Janicki, "From Great Resignation to Great Reshuffling," US Census Bureau, May 13, 2024, https://www.census.gov/library/stories/2024/05/great-reshuffling.html.
14. Emma Goldberg, "All of Those Quitters? They're at Work," *New York Times*, May 13, 2022.
15. Felix Richter, "The Great Resignation Is Over: Quits Return to Pre-COVID Levels," *Statista*, January 8, 2024, https://www.voronoiapp.com/economy/The-Great-Resignation-Is-Over-Quits-Return-to-Pre-Covid-Level-480; "Understanding Young Worker Motivations During the Great Resignation," Annie E. Casey Foundation, June 7, 2023, https://www.aecf.org/blog/understanding-young-worker-motivations-during-the-great-resignation.
16. Bruno Venditti, "The US Industries That Rely Most on Illegal Immigration," *Visual Capitalist*, November 23, 2024, https://www.visualcapitalist.com/the-u-s-industries-that-rely-most-on-illegal-immigration/.
17. Chloe East, "The Labor Market Impact of Deportations," Brookings, September 18, 2024, https://www.brookings.edu/articles/the-labor-market-impact-of-deportations/.
18. US Bureau of Labor Statistics, State and Area Employment, Hours, and Earnings, https://www.bls.gov/help/one_screen/sa.htm.
19. US Bureau of Labor Statistics, State and Area Employment, Hours, and Earnings, https://www.bls.gov/help/one_screen/sa.htm.
20. Reuse Gurchiek, "Report: Pandemic Drives Workers' Desires to Learn New Job Skills," Society for Human Resource Management, June 16, 2021, https://www.shrm.org/topics-tools/news/organizational-employee-development/report-pandemic-drives-workers-desire-to-learn-new-job-skills.
21. David Autor, Arindrajit Dube, and Annie McGrew, "The Unexpected Compression: Competition at Work in the Low Wage Labor Market," Working Paper No. 31010, National Bureau of Economic Research, May 1, 2023, https://www.nber.org/papers/w31010.
22. "The First McDonald's Where You Are Served by Robot," *Newsweek*, December 22, 2022.
23. NC State Demographer, "Population Projections by Age," OSBM, 2024.
24. Ronni Sandroff, "History and Impact of Labor Unions in the U.S.," *Investopedia*, updated March 25, 2026, https://www.investopedia.com/financial-edge/0113/the-history-of-unions-in-the-united-states.aspx.
25. "Work in the Late 19th Century," US Library of Congress, https://www.loc.gov/classroom-materials/united-states-history-primary-source-timeline/rise-of-industrial-america-1876-1900/work-in-late-19th-century/.
26. Massimiliano Cali, "Trading Away from Conflict," World Bank Group, 2015, https://www.worldbank.org/content/dam/Worldbank/document/Trade/Trading%20Away%20from%20Conflict.pdf.
27. "China Member Information," World Trade Organization, December 2001, https://www.wto.org.
28. Richard Carver, "NC Job Losses Tied to China Trade," *Winston-Salem Journal*, July 30, 2008.
29. US Bureau of Labor Statistics, State and Area Employment, Hours, and Earnings, https://www.bls.gov/help/one_screen/sa.htm.

30. Carver, "NC Job Losses Tied to China Trade."
31. Ken Green, "Why Organized Labor Struggles in the South," *UnionTrack*, March 25, 2024, https://blog.uniontrack.com/labor-american-south.
32. Sophie Hollis, "Textile Workers and Labor Movements," *DigitalNC*, https://www.digitalnc.org/primary-source-sets/textile-workers-labor-movements/.
33. "Right to Work," AFL-CIO, https://aflcio.org/issues/right-work.
34. Kabir Dasgupta and Zofsha Merchant, "Understanding Workers' Financial Well-Being in States with Right-to-Work Laws," Board of Governors of the Federal Reserve, September 8, 2023, https://www.federalreserve.gov/econres/notes/feds-notes/understanding-workers-financial-wellbeing-in-states-with-right-to-work-laws-accessible-20230908.htm.
35. Christos Andreas Makridis, "Do Right-to-Work Laws Work? Evidence on Individuals' Well-Being and Economic Sentiment," *Journal of Law and Economics* 62, no. 4 (2019): 713–45.
36. Green, "Why Organized Labor Struggles in the South."
37. Dillion Roberts, "Unionization in the South: Economic Development Implications," Camoin Associates, June 3, 2024, camoinassociates.com/resources/unionization-in-the-south/; Christos Doucouliagos and Patrice Laroche, "What Do Unions Do to Productivity? A Meta Analysis," *Industrial Relations* 42, no. 4 (2003): 650–691.
38. Kate Bahn and Joe Peek, "How Unions Can Increase Firm Productivity and Strengthen Economic Growth," WorkRise, September 6, 2023, https://workrisenetwork.org/working-knowledge/how-unions-can-increase-firm-productivity-and-strengthen-economic-growth; Doucouliagos and Laroche, "What Do Unions Do to Productivity?"
39. US Bureau of Labor Statistics, State and Area Employment, Hours, and Earnings, https://www.bls.gov/help/one_screen/sa.htm.
40. "Americans' Views on Labor Unions," Pew Research Center, February 1, 2024.
41. Megan Brenen, "Democratic Party Still Seen as Better for Union Members," September 9, 2024, Gallup, https://news.gallup.com/poll/650147/democratic-party-seen-better-union-members.aspx.
42. Kevin Hardy, "As a Key Labor Union Pushes into the South, Red States Push Back," *Stateline*, May 20, 2024, https://stateline.org/2024/05/20/as-a-key-labor-union-pushes-into-the-south-red-states-push-back/. Countering this objective is the reality that a vote to unionize an Amazon warehouse in North Carolina in early 2024 failed significantly; see Brian Gordon and Korie Dean, "Triangle Amazon Workers Overwhelmingly Vote Against Unionizing in Historic Election," *Raleigh News and Observer*, February 16, 2025.
43. "Big Labor Gamble—Push to Unionize Every US Auto Plant," *New York Times*, March 2, 2024.
44. Ramishah Maruf, "Amazon Workers at North Carolina Warehouse Vote Against Unionizing," *CNN*, February 15, 2025. In 2025, there was also legislation introduced in the North Carolina General Assembly to modify and relax the right-to-work statute in North Carolina. Donald Bryson, *Locke Notes*, March 12, 2025, https://www.johnlocke.org.
45. See Arthur Okun, *Equality and Efficiency: The Big Tradeoff* (Brookings Institution Press, 2015); and Milton Friedman and Rose Friedman, *Free to Choose* (Mariner Books Classic, 1990).

46. US Bureau of Labor Statistics, State and Area Employment, Hours, and Earnings, https://www.bls.gov/help/one_screen/sa.htm.
47. For personal stories about working in the gig economy, see Sarah Kessler, *Gigged: The Gig Economy, the End of the Job, and the Future of Work* (Random House Business Books, 2018).
48. "Best States for Gig Workers," Agents Only, September 20, 2023, https://www.agentsonly.com/blog/best-states-for-gig-workers.
49. Andre Dua, Kweitin Ellingrud, Bryan Hancock, Ryan Luby, Ann Nadgavkar, and Sarah Pemberton, "Freelance, Side Hustles, and Gigs: Many More Americans Have Become Independent Workers," McKinsey and Company, Washington, DC, August 22, 2022; "Understanding Labor Unions in the Gig Economy," Union Coded, May 1, 2024, https://unioncoded.com/labor-unions-in-the-gig-economy/.
50. Green, "Why Organized Labor Struggles in the South."
51. Sophia Lee, "The History and Evolution of the 40 Hour Workweek," *Culture Amp*, https://www.cultureamp.com/blog/40-hour-work-week.
52. Lee, "History and Evolution."
53. Tom Hasher, "Henry Ford Invented the 40-Hour Work Week," *Legends Report*, June 27, 2016.
54. Rachel Looker, "Sanders to Introduce Bill Shortening Workweek to Four Days," *USA Today*, March 13, 2024.
55. Leah Sarnoff, "Does a Four Day Workweek Work? Companies Share Results After Two Years," *ABC News*, March 1, 2024.
56. Nick Sweet, "Why a Four Day Workweek Might Be Better for Your Physical and Mental Health," *Health*, March 3, 2023; Douglas Broom, "Four Day Workweek in Spain Leads to Healthier Workers, Less Pollution," World Economic Forum, October 25, 2023, https://www.weforum.org/stories/2023/10/surprising-benefits-four-day-week/.
57. "Shorter Workweek: Pros and Cons for Worker Productivity," Maryville University, October 10, 2022, https://online.maryville.edu/blog/shorter-work-week-pros-cons/.
58. Benjamin Laker, "The Hidden Costs of the 4-Day Workweek and Its True Impact, *Forbes*, October 3, 2024, https://www.forbes.com/sites/benjaminlaker/2024/10/03/the-hidden-costs-of-the-4-day-workweek-and-its-true-impact/.

Chapter 4: The World with AI

1. Brent Glass, *The Textile Industry in North Carolina: A History*, Division of Archives and History, NC Department of Cultural Resources, 1992, https://www.srchives.ncdcr.gov.
2. Alex Irwin-Hunt, "From Tobacco to Tech: North Carolina Triangle's Renaissance," FDI Intelligence, February 2, 2024, LinkedIn, https://www.linkedin.com/posts/ajih_from-tobacco-to-tech-north-carolina-triangle-activity-7165686539253899264-fRwp/.
3. "Industry Insights: Financial Services in the Charlotte Region," Charlotte Regional Business Alliance, February 25, 2021, https://charlotteregion.com/do-business-here/industries-and-major-employers/financial-services/.
4. Institute for Transportation Research and Education, "Economic Contribution

of Rail in North Carolina," North Carolina State University, August 11, 2023, https://www.itre.ncsu.edu.

5. US Census Bureau and US Bureau of Labor Statistics. Classifications for cognitive and routine occupations are from Maximiliano Dvorkin and Hannah Shell, "The Growing Skill Divide in the US Labor Market," *On the Economy*, Federal Reserve Bank of St. Louis, May 18, 2017, https://fraser.stlouisfed.org/title/economy-9397/growing-skill-divide-us-labor-market-686581. The author updated the figures to 2023 using the same methodology and BLS data.
6. Emily Thomas, "North Carolina Sees Increase in Adult Educational Attainment," *EdNC*, February 25, 2024, https://www.ednc.org/north-carolina-sees-increase-in-adult-educational-attainment/.
7. IBM Global Adoption Index, Enterprise Report, IBM, November 23, 2023.
8. Rebecca Hinds, "How to Decode the Very Mixed Reactions to AI in the Workplace," *Reworked*, November 27, 2023 https://www.reworked.co/digital-workplace/how-to-decode-the-very-mixed-reactions-to-ai-in-the-workplace/.
9. Anil Ananthaswamy, *Why Machines Learn: The Elegant Math Behind Modern AI* (Random House, 2024).
10. Mara Hvistendahl, "Can AI Escape Our Control and Destroy Us?," *Popular Science*, May 29, 2019.
11. Vivek Singh, "Machine's Consciousness: Can AI Develop Self-Awareness?," *Information Week*, July 4, 2025, https://www.informationweek.com/machine-learning-ai/the-machine-s-consciousness-can-ai-develop-self-awareness-.
12. Daron Acemoglu, "The Simple Macroeconomics of AI," Working Paper No. 32487, National Bureau of Economic Research, May 2024.
13. David Deming, Christopher Ong, and Lawrence Summers, "Pace of Labor Market Change Has Accelerated Technological Disruption in the Labor Market," Working Paper No. 3323, National Bureau of Economic Research, January 2025.
14. "New Jobs Created with AI in the Workplace," Resources for Employers, US Department of Labor, June 2023, https://www.dol.gov/agencies/whd/employers.
15. "Generative AI Could Raise Global GDP by 7 Percent," Goldman Sachs, 2023, https://www.goldmansachs.com/insights/articles/generative-ai-could-raise-global-gdp-by-7-percent; Michael Chui, Eric Hazan, Roger Roberts, Alex Singla, Kate Smaje, Alex Sukharevsky, Lareina Lee, and Rodney Zemmel, "The Economic Potential of Regenerative AI: The Next Productivity Frontiers," McKinsey and Company, June 14, 2023, https://www.mckinsey.com/~/media/mckinsey/business%20functions/mckinsey%20digital/our%20insights/the%20economic%20potential%20of%20generative%20ai%20the%20next%20productivity%20frontier/the-economic-potential-of-generative-ai-the-next-productivity-frontier.pdf; Acemoglu, "Simple Macroeconomics of AI."
16. "What Is the Impact of Mobile Telephony on Economic Growth?," Deloitte, November 2012; "How AC Changed the World," *BBC News*, June 5, 2017, https://www.bbc.com/news/business-39735802.
17. Noah Smith, "Stop Pretending You Know What AI Does to the Economy," *Noahpinion* (blog), July 20, 2025, https://www.noahpinion.blog/p/stop-pretending-you-know-what-ai.
18. William Halal, Jonathan Kolber, and Owen Davies, "Forecasts of AI and Future Jobs in 2030: Muddling Through Likely, with Two Alternative Scenarios," *Journal of Futures Studies* 12, no. 2 (2016): 83–96.

19. Jack Kelly, "Goldman Sachs Predicts 300 Million Jobs Could Be Replaced by AI by 2030," *Forbes*, March 31, 2023.
20. Eric Hazan, Anu Madgavkar, Michael Chui, Sven Smit, Dana Maor, Gurneet Singh Dandona, and Roland Huyghues-Despointes, "A New Future of Work: The Race to Deploy AI and Raise Skills in Europe and Beyond," McKinsey Global, May 2024, https://www.mckinsey.com/mgi/our-research/a-new-future-of-work-the-race-to-deploy-ai-and-raise-skills-in-europe-and-beyond.
21. Angus Fletcher, *Primal Knowledge* (Avery, 2025).
22. Fletcher, *Primal Knowledge.*
23. "US State by State AI Legislative Snapshot," Bryan Cave Leighton Paisner (BCLP), 2025, https://www.bclplaw.com/en-US/events-insights-news/us-state-by-state-artificial-intelligence-legislation-snapshot.html.
24. Adrien Book, "Should AI Be Regulated? The Arguments For and Against," WeAreDevelopers, November 19, 2024, https://www.wearedevelopers.com/en/magazine/271/eu-ai-regulation-artificial-intelligence-regulations.
25. House Bill 591, North Carolina General Assembly, 2023–24 session.
26. Congressional Research Service, "Automation, Worker Training, and Federal Tax Policy," May 27, 2022, https://www.congress.gov/crs_external_products/IF/PDF/IF12124/IF12124.1.pdf.

Chapter 5: Education and the Evolution of Tasks

1. "National Assessment of Educational Progress," Report CED 2010-468, National Center for Educational Statistics, US Department of Education.
2. "The Nation's Report Card, State Profiles, 2024," US Department of Education, https://www.nationsreportcard.gov/profiles/stateprofile?sfj=NP&chort=1&sub=MAT&sj=&st=MN&year=2024R3.
3. "Nation's Report Card, State Profiles, 2024."
4. "National Assessment of Educational Progress."
5. "National Assessment of Educational Progress." In the comparisons of white and Black students and white and Hispanic students on reading and math performance in fourth and eighth grades, in only one case—for white and Hispanic eighth-graders—did the performance gap between the two groups narrow from 2019 to 2024.
6. Megan Kuhfeld, Jim Soland, Karyn Lewis, and Emily Morton, "The Pandemic Has Had Devastating Impacts on Learning. What Will It Take to Help Students Catch Up?," *Brookings*, March 3, 2022, https://www.brookings.edu/articles/the-pandemic-has-had-devastating-impacts-on-learning-what-will-it-take-to-help-students-catch-up/.
7. Mebane Rash, "New Interactive Map Shows How Learning Loss and Academic Recovery Varied by District in N.C.," *EducationNC*, January 31, 2024, https://www.ednc.org/01-31-2024-new-interactive-map-shows-how-learning-loss-and-academic-recovery-varied-by-district-in-nc/; Santiago Pinto, "The Pandemic's Effects on Children's Education," Economic Brief No. 23-29, Federal Reserve Bank of Richmond, August 2023, https://www.richmondfed.org/publications/research/economic_brief/2023/eb_23-29.
8. James Farrell, "Pandemic Recovery: Where Are North Carolina's Students Lagging?," WFAE 90.7, December 9, 2024.

9. "Chronic Absenteeism," myFutureNC, 2025, https://dashboard.myfuturenc.org/college-and-career-access/chronic-absenteeism/.
10. There was not complete data for all states to allow rankings for twelfth-graders. Assessments for states are done every two years with the "National Assessment of Educational Progress."
11. "Cohort 4-Year Graduation Rates," NC Department of Public Instruction, 2023, https://www.dpi.nc.gov/districts-schools/accountability-and-testing/school-accountability-and-reporting/cohort-graduation-rates. Economically disadvantaged students are defined as those enrolled in the school lunch program or possessing other characteristics that may impede their learning. "Economically Disadvantaged Students Data Collection," NC Department of Public Instruction, June 22, 2023, https://www.dpi.nc.gov/documents/economically-disadvantaged-data-collection/open.
12. National Center for Educational Statistics, using data for 2017–2018, the latest available, https:// www.nces.ed.gov.
13. Danielle Farrie and Robert Kim, "Making the Grade: How Fair Is School Funding in Your State," Education Law Center, 2024. State and local spending on vouchers, private schools, and public schools are excluded, and correspondingly the per pupil calculations exclude students not in public schools, https://www.elc-pa.org.
14. "Regional Price Parities," US Bureau of Economic Analysis.
15. Farrie and Kim, "Making the Grade."
16. "North Carolina's State of Educational Attainment Report," myFutureNC, February 20, 2025, available at https://www.myfuturenc.org/2025-state-of-educational-attainment/.
17. Rebecca Tippett, "In-Migration Plays a Large Role in NC's Rising Educational Attainment," *Demography North Carolina*, March 13, 2019, https://carolinademography.cpc.unc.edu/2019/03/13/in-migration-plays-large-role-in-ncs-rising-educational-attainment/.
18. "NCSU On-Line and Distance Education," NC State University, 2024, https://online-distance.ncsu.edu/.
19. Jessica Bryant, "Pandemic Learning Loss: How COVID-19 Academically Impacted College Students," *Best Colleges*, April 8, 2024, https://www.bestcolleges.com/research/pandemic-learning-loss/.
20. Melissa Buelow, James Wirth, and Jennifer Kowalsky, "Poorer Decision-Making Among College Students During the COVID-19 Pandemic: Evidence for 'Pandemic Brain,'" *Journal of American College Health* 72, no. 9 (2024): 3621–31, https://doi.org/10.1080/07448481.2023.2186129.
21. Vasilki Yotside, Erini-Kohstahtina Nokolatou, Elias Kouskovtas, and Georgios Kougiovmtzis, "Mental Distress and Well Being of University Students and the COVID-19 Pandemic: Findings from an Integrated Intervention or Psychology Trainees," *Frontiers in Psychology*, July 13, 2023, https://www.frontiersin.org/journals/psychology/articles/10.3389/fpsyg.2023.1171225/full.
22. Hannah Lee, "COVID Four Years Later: Social, Academic, and Mental Impacts on Students," *The Trail*, December 1, 2023, https://trail.pugetsound.edu/?p=18528.
23. "National Assessment of Educational Progress."

24. State Higher Education Executive Officers Association, *State Higher Education Finance, Fiscal Year 2023*, May 24, 2024, https://www/sheeo.org.
25. Melanie Hanson, "Student Loan Debt by State," *Education Data Initiative*, May 13, 2024, https://educationdata.org/student-loan-debt-by-state.
26. Liang Zhang, Xiangmin Lu, and Yitong Hu, "Degrees of Return: Estimating Internal Rates of Return for College Majors Using Quantile Regression," *America Educational Research Journal*, March 11, 2024, https://doi.org/10.3102/00028312241231512; "Historical Average Stock Market Returns for S&P 500," *TradeThatSwing*, June 28, 2024, https://www.tradethatswing.com.
27. Zhang, Lu, and Hu, "Degrees of Return."
28. Zhang, Lu, and Hu, "Degrees of Return."
29. "University of North Carolina System Evolution of University Programs," Deloitte and Burning Glass, February 2024, http;//cbe.ncsu.edu.
30. Preston Cooper, "Does College Pay Off? A Comprehensive Return on Investment Analysis," Foundation for Research on Equal Opportunity, May 8, 2024, https://freopp.org/whitepapers/does-college-pay-off-a-comprehensive-return-on-investment-analysis/; Jason Wingard, *The College Devaluation Crisis* (Stanford University Press, 2022).
31. "National Assessment of Educational Progress."
32. Ben Unglesbee, "Enrollment Woes Hit Both Private and Public Colleges in 2023, S&P Reports," *Highereddive*, July 19, 2024, https://www.highereddive.com/news/enrollment-woes-private-public-colleges-2023-sp/721810/.
33. "National Assessment of Educational Progress."
34. "2024 Fall Enrollment," UNC System, November 2024; "NC Community Colleges See Highest Enrollment," NC Community Colleges, March 15, 2024.
35. Jesse Homan, "Seeing Past the Enrollment Cliff of 2025," *Education Dynamics*, April 4, 2024, https://www.educationdynamics.com/enrollment-cliff-2025/.
36. Sara Weissman, "Why Would-Be Students Aren't Choosing College," *Inside Higher Ed*, September 28, 2022, https://www.insidehighered.com/news/2022/09/29/new-study-explores-why-people-drop-out-or-dont-enroll.
37. Richard Fry, "Fewer Young Men Are in College, Especially at 4-Year Schools," Pew Research Center, December 18, 2023; Te-Ping Chen, "He Skipped College. He's on His Way to $175,000 a Year," *Wall Street Journal*, August 3, 2024.
38. Jeffrey Jones, " US Confidence in Higher Education Now Closely Divided," *Gallup News*, July 8, 2024.
39. Jason Wingard, "Companies Are Hiring Fewer College Grads—So Why Bother with School?," *Forbes*, April 30, 2024.
40. Brian Rosenberg, *Whatever It Is, I'm Against It: Resistance to Change in Higher Education* (Harvard University Press, 2023).
41. Daniel Susskind, *A World Without Work* (Picador, 2020).
42. Edward Felten, Manav Raj, and Robert Seamans, "Occupational, Industry, and Geographic Exposure to Artificial Intelligence: A Novel Dataset and Its Potential Uses," *Strategic Management Journal* 42, no. 12 (2021): 2195–2217, https://doi.org/10.1002/smj.3286.
43. Andrew Green, "Artificial Intelligence and the Changing Demand for Skills in the Labour Market," *OECD [Organisation for Economic Co-operation and Development] Artificial Intelligence Papers*, no. 14 (April 2024); Christian Keller,

Mark Cus Babic, Akash Utsav, Ana Paula, Jesus Assis, and Brian Goehring, "AI Revolution: Productivity Boom and Beyond," Barclays and IMB, Impact Series, no. 12, January 11, 2024.

44. Keller et al. "AI Revolution."
45. Felten, Raj, and Seamans, "Occupational, Industry, and Geographic Exposure to Artificial Intelligence."
46. Bhargs Sriathsan, Mark Sorel, Hrjita Bhan, Pankaj Sachdeva, Rankaj Sachdeva, Haripreet Batra, Raman Sharma, Rishi Gupta, and Surbhi Choudhary, "AI Power: Expanding Data Center Capacity to Meet Growing Demand," McKinsey and Company, October 29, 2024.
47. John Lenio, "The Mystery Impact of Data Centers on Local Economies Revealed," *Area Development*, 2015, https://www.areadevelopment.com/data-centers/Data-Centers-Q1-2015/impact-of-data-center-development-locally-2262766.shtml; Rich Miller, "The Economics of Data Center Staffing," *Data Center Knowledge*, January 18, 2008, https://www.datacenterknowledge.com/data-center-career-development/the-economics-of-data-center-staffing.
48. Jonathan Heathcote, Fabrizio Perri, Giovanni Violante, and Lichen Zhang, "More Unequal We Stand? Inequality Dynamics in the US, 1967–2021," *Review of Economic Dynamics* 50 (2023): 235–66; Michael L. Walden, "Economic Growth and Income Distribution in North Carolina and Introduction of the NC-Growth and NC-Share Indices," Department of Agricultural and Resource Economics, NC State University, November 2021.
49. David Bloom, Klaus Prettner, Jamal Saadaui, and Mario Vervete, "The Expansion of AI Will Likely Shrink Earnings Inequality," Center for Economic Policy Research, October 18, 2024, https://cepr.org/voxeu/columns/expansion-ai-will-likely-shrink-earnings-inequality; Anton Korinek and Joseph E. Stiglitz, "Artificial Intelligence and Its Implications for Income Distribution and Unemployment," Working Paper No. 24174, National Bureau of Economic Research, January 2018, https://www.nber.org/papers/w24174; Ajay Agrawal, Joshua Gans, and Avi Goldfarb, eds., *The Economics of Artificial Intelligence* (University of Chicago Press, 2019).

Chapter 6: Restructuring Education in the Anxious Age

1. "Rising Education Inequality Revealed: Here's Where North Carolina Ranks on Most and Least Educated States List," *WTVD-AP*, January 16, 2023, https://abc11.com/post/education-inequality-gap-test-scores-math-reading-nc/12710020/.
2. Michael L. Walden, *North Carolina Beyond the Connected Age* (University of North Carolina Press, 2017).
3. "Types of Learning Styles—The Definitive Guide," Bay Atlantic University, Washington, DC, https://bau.edu.
4. Salman Khan, *Brave New Words: How AI Will Revolutionize Education (and Why That's a Good Thing)* (Viking, 2024).
5. James Robert, *AI in Education* (MadTown Publishing, 2024).
6. Nicholas Lanum, "Texas Private School's Use of 'AI Tutor' Rocket Student Test Scores to Top 2% in the Country," *Fox News*, March 22, 2025; Martin E. Simone, Federico Tiberti, Wuarola Mosuro, Fedrico Manolio, Maria Barron, and Eliot

Dikoru, "From Chalkboards to Chatbots: Transforming Learning in Nigeria, One Prompt at a Time," *World Bank Logs,* January 9, 2025, https://blogs.worldbank.org/en/education/From-chalkboards-to-chatbots-Transforming-learning-in-Nigeria.

7. Daniel Susskind, *A World Without Work* (Picador, 2020).
8. "Bricklaying Robots: Building the Future of Construction," HowToRobot, September 5, 2024, https://howtorobot.com/expert-insight/bricklaying-robots-building-future-construction.
9. Kathleen Delaski, *Who Needs College Anymore?* (Harvard University Press, 2025).
10. Andrew Gardner, "How NC Community Colleges Are Transforming Workplace Development," *Constructing the Carolinas,* March 25, 2024, https://constructingthecarolinas.com.
11. Sam Curry, "Why AI Can (and Should) Lead to a Renaissance in the Humanities," *VentureBeat,* February 24, 2024, https://venturebeat.com/ai/why-ai-can-and-should-lead-to-a-renaissance-in-the-humanities.
12. Genevieve Carlton, "2024 On-Line Learning Statistics," *Forbes Advisor,* May 17, 2023.
13. Michael D. Smith, *The Abundant University: Remaking Higher Education for a Digital World* (MIT Press, 2023).
14. Bryan Caplan, *The Case Against Education* (Princeton University Press, 2019).
15. Isabelle Bousquette, "Colleges Come to Terms with the Use of Artificial Intelligence Technology," *Wall Street Journal,* August 27, 2024.
16. Anne Manning, "Professor Tailored AI Tutor to Physics Course. Engagement Doubled," *Harvard Gazette,* September 5, 2024; Tyler Cowen and Alex Tabarrok, "The Industrial Organization of Online Education," *American Economic Review: Papers and Proceedings* 104, no. 5 (2014): 519–22.
17. M. D. Smith, *Abundant University.*
18. "National Assessment of Educational Progress," Report CED 2010-468, National Center for Educational Statistics, US Department of Education, https://www.nces.ed.gov.
19. Hannah Vinueza McClellan, "General Assembly Overrides Veto and Adds Additional Funds for Vouchers," *EdNC,* November 20, 2024, https://www.ednc.org/general-assembly-overrides-veto-of-the-mini-budget-adds-additional-funds-for-vouchers/.
20. Louis Sosres, "Alternative Post Education Providers: Mapping the Ecosystem," *Educause Review,* April 12, 2023; Delaski, *Who Needs College Anymore?*
21. "College Enrollment and Work Activity of Recent High School and College Graduates Summary," Bureau of Labor Statistics, April 23, 2024, https://bls.gov. However, the college enrollment rate of North Carolina high school graduates is much lower, at 38 percent in 2022. "Percentage of North Carolinians Aged 18–24 Enrolled in a Postsecondary Institution," myFutureNC, 2023, https://dashboard.myfuturenc.org/college-and-career-access/postsecondary-enrollment-rate/.
22. Alek Sandar Dimovski, "Eye Opening Statistics About the State of Career Changes in 2023," GoRomotely, March 7, 2023, https://gemote.com.
23. Susskind, *World Without Work.*
24. John Maynard Keynes, "Economic Possibilities for Our Grandchildren," in *Essays in Persuasion* (Harcourt Brace, 1932).

25. Research shows that a potential downside of a guaranteed income is the disincentive for recipients to look for work. Eva Vivalt, Elizabeth Rhodes, Alexander Bartik, David Broockman, and Sarah Miller, "The Employment Effects of a Guaranteed Income: Experimental Evidence from Two US States," Working Paper No. 32719, National Bureau of Economic Research, July 2024.

Chapter 7: Another New North Carolina in the Anxious Age?

1. Hugh Talmage Lefler and Albert Ray Newsome, *North Carolina: The History of a Southern State* (University of North Carolina Press, 1973), chap. 6.
2. Lefler and Newsome, *North Carolina*.
3. William Powell, "What's in a Name? Why We're All Called Tarheels" (1982), *Carolina Alumni*, https://alumni.unc.edu/whats-in-a-name-why-were-all-called-tar-heels/, accessed December 1, 2025.
4. Lefler and Newsome, *North Carolina*.
5. Michael L. Walden, *North Carolina in the Connected Age: Challenges and Opportunities in a Globalizing Economy* (University of North Carolina Press, 2008), 42.
6. US Bureau of Labor Statistics, State and Area Employment, Hours, and Earnings, https://www.bls.gov/help/one_screen/sa.htm.
7. "About the City of Charlotte," University of North Carolina Charlotte, 2025, https://www.charlotte.edu/about/.
8. Walden, *North Carolina in the Connected Age*, 7.
9. Tom Gerken, "Bill Gates: AI Is the Most Important Tech Advance in Decades," *BBC*, March 21, 2023.
10. The farming (or agriculture) measure only includes the raising of livestock and the growing of crops.
11. William Boston, "Meet the Fully Autonomous Farm," *Wall Street Journal*, July 31, 2025. "Agribusiness" activities, which include the processing, delivery, and retailing of farm products on their way to final users, are not included in the farming numbers in table 7.1.
12. "Top US States and Cities for Tech Jobs in 2024," *Goodwin Recruiting*, May 27, 2024, https://www.goodwinrecruiting.com/blog/top-u-s-states-and-cities-for-tech-jobs-in-2024; Cecilla Seiter and Brenna Swanston, "The Best and Worst States for Technology Careers, *Forbes*, February 26, 2024; US Bureau of Labor Statistics, State and Area Employment, Hours, and Earnings, https://www.bls.gov/help/one_screen/sa.htm.
13. Jason DeBruyn, "Apple Plans $1 Billion Investment and 3,000 Jobs in Research Triangle Park," *WUNC Radio*, April 26, 2021; Brian Gordon, "Apple Pauses Planned RTP Campus as Tech Giant Seeks to Push Back North Carolina Agreement," *Durham Herald Sun*, June 24, 2024.
14. Peter Pellerito, "The US Biosciences Industry in the States," Council of State Biosciences Association, June 2023, https://www.bio.org/csba; Jimmy Mooney, "Top 10 Pharmaceutical Hubs in the USA," Proclinical, March 15, 2016, https://www.proclinical.com/blogs/2016-3/top-10-pharmaceutical-hubs-in-the-usa.
15. Turkowski Przemyslaw, "What Will the Life Sciences Industry Look Like in 2025?," *Netguru*, November 11, 2024, https://www.netguru.com/blog/life-sciences-industry.

16. "Looking to 2060: A Global Vision of Future Economic Growth," Organisation for Economic and Co-operation and Development, November 7, 2012, available at https://docs.dpaq.de/2141-oecd-report_2060.pdf.
17. Chris Skinner, "Most Banks Will Disappear, Parts One and Two," *Chris Skinner Blog*, March 2 and 3, 2023, https://thefinanser.com/2023/03/most-banks-will-disappear.
18. "The Collapse of the Auto Industry in Detroit," Reddit, 2013, https://www.reddit.com/r/explainlikeimfive/comments/1lzfwm/eli5_the_collapse_of_the_auto_industry_in_detroit/.
19. "Production Is Fleeing Los Angeles: How Poor Policies Push Producers Away," *FilmTake*, November 19, 2024, https://www.filmtake.com/production/production-is-fleeing-los-angeles-how-poor-policies-push-producers-away/.
20. "Exodus from Akron's Sign of the Times," *Modern Tire Dealer*, August 1, 1994
21. Barbara Russo-Lennon, "More Money, More Problems: NYC (New York City) Is the Worst City in America for Living Comfortably, New Study Shows," *AMNY*, April 2, 2024, https://www.amny.com/news/nyc-ranks-low-living-comfortably-income-study/.
22. Jeffrey Jones, "Cigarette Smoking Rate in US Ties 80 Year Low," *Gallup News*, August 13, 2024.
23. Gisele Galoustian, "Dramatic Decline in Cigarette Use Among US Teens over Three Decades," Florida State University, January 10, 2024.
24. Yimiao Wu, "How AI Is Leading the Textile Industry to a New Lease on Life?," Arts, Management, and Technology Laboratory at Carnegie Mellon University, January 1, 2024; Todd Morgan, "The Year of Transformation: How AI Will Define the Textile Industry in 2025," LinkedIn, January 6, 2025, https://www.linkedin.com/pulse/year-transformation-how-ai-redefine-textile-industry-2025-todd-morgan-gtj3e/?trackingId=LXuvgJzUReWroOVkUUiNQw%3D%3D.
25. "LG Textile Expanding in Clinton," *Business North Carolina Daily Digest*, August 6, 2025, http://www.businessnc.com.
26. "What AI Can Do for the Furniture Industry?," *Interzum Magazine*, November 26, 2024.
27. Shraddha Wankhade, "Latest Global Pulp, Paper, and Packaging Market Size, Forecast and Share Surpass US $421.5 Bn by 2032 at 5.6% CAGR," LinkedIn, March 1, 2024, https://www.linkedin.com/pulse/latest-global-pulp-paper-packaging-market-size-share-surpass-ovsyf/?trackingId=VSH1tIxoQz%2B36XzHsULkTw%3D%3D.
28. US Bureau of Labor Statistics, "Productivity and Artificial Intelligence."
29. "What Is Silicon and How Is It Used for Microchips?," LAM Research, November 16, 2023, http://www.lamresearch.com.
30. Ed Conway, "What's Happening at Spruce Pine?," *Material World*, October 1, 2024; Tom Snyder, "Complex Pivotal Global Semiconductor Supply Chain Runs Through Western North Carolina," *WRAL News*, February 28, 2025.
31. Ann Almerini, "Lithium Mines in the United States: Where It Stands Today?," *Solar Reviews*, December 2024, https://www.solarreviews.com/blog/lithium-mining-in-the-united-states.
32. US Geological Service, "Annual NLCD Assessment: Phosphate Mining and Land Cover Change," December 12, 2024, https://www.usgs.gov/centers/eros/news/annual-nlcd-assessment-phosphate-mining-and-land-cover-change.

33. Subhadra Srivastnava, "Top 7 Largest Military Bases in the World, You Won't Believe How Big They Really Are," WION, November 7, 2025, https://www.wionews.com/photos/top-7-largest-military-bases-in-the-world-you-won-t-believe-how-big-they-really-are-1762523084441.
34. NC Department of Environmental Quality, "NC Mineral Resources, An Overview," https://www.deq.nc.gov/about/divisions/energy-mineral-land-resources/north-carolina-geological-survey/mineral-resources/mineral-resources-faq.
35. NC Department of Commerce, "NC Breaks Tourism Spending Record in 2023," August 13, 2024.
36. "Facts About NC Beaches," VisitNC.com; "National Forests in North Carolina," *Carolina Outdoor Guide*, https://www.carolinaoutdoorguide.com; "Golf Courses by State," *World Population Review*, 2024, https://www.worldpopulationreview.com.
37. "Farms and Farmland," US Department of Agriculture, March 2024; Obed Quaicoe, Fafanyo Asieh, Anthony Baffoe-Bonnie, and John N. Ng'ombe, "Small Farms in North Carolina, United States: Analyzing Firm and Operator Characteristics in the Pursuit of Economic Resilience and Sustainability," *Applied Economic Perspectives and Policy* 46, no. 1 (2024): 13–31.
38. *Britannica*, "North Carolina: Land," https://www.britannica.com/place/North-Carolina-state#ref78496
39. Uma Vanka, *The Future Is Big* (Business Expert Press, 2024).
40. "Researchers Warn Proposed NIH Cuts Could Cost NC's Research Triangle over $1 Billion Economically," WUNC Radio, August 20, 2025.
41. US Bureau of Economic Analysis, "Annual Gross Domestic Product by State."
42. Penn-Wharton Budget Model, University of Pennsylvania, "Effective Tariff Rates and Revenues," February 3, 2026, https://budgetmodel.wharton.upenn.edu/p/2026-02-03-effective-tariff-rates-and-revenues-updated-february-3-2026/.
43. "Why NC: Top Reasons to Do Business Here," Economic Development Partnership of North Carolina, 2025, https://www.edpnc.com.
44. CNBC, "Top States for Business in America in 2025," June 10, 2025, https://www.cnbc.com.
45. Kristin Stowe, "The Economic and Environmental Impacts of Reopening the Carolina Lithium Belt," *Journal of Regional Analysis and Policy* 52, no. 2 (2023): 30–38.
46. Ramenda Cyrus, "The Small Town That's Connecting America," *American Prospect*, August 9, 2023, https://prospect.org/2023/08/09/2023-08-09-hickory-small-town-connecting-america/.
47. Emma Dill and Cece Nunn, "How Brunswick Nabbed a $650 M, 500 Employee Plant Deal," *Wilmington Biz*, December 14, 2023.
48. Erica York and Jared Walczak, "State and Local Tax Burdens, 2022," *Tax Foundation*, April 7, 2022. The statistic is measured as state and local taxes collected as a percentage of income.
49. York and Walczak, "State and Local Tax Burdens, 2022."
50. Jim Probasco and Mia Taylor, "Property Tax Rates by State: What to Expect in Your Area?," *Bankrate*, May 29, 2024, https://www.bankrate.com.
51. "Corporate Rate Set to Go to 0% in 2030," Poole Thought Leadership, August 1, 2023, https://poole.ncsu.edu/thought-leadership/.
52. Wayne Winegarden, "North Carolina Ranks 31 in Small Business Regulation Index," Pacific Research Institute, July 8, 2015, https://pacificresearch.com.

53. In September 2024, North Carolina's average rate per kilowatt hour was tenth lowest among the states. "Electricity Rates for September 2024," Electric Choice, https://www.powertochoose.org.
54. The author wrote the program the state uses to calculate the net revenues estimated to be received by North Carolina. Included in the calculations are "multiplier effects" from the location of a new firm. In addition to the benefits from employment, new salaries, and tax payment directly from the new firms, multiplier effects account for similar benefits from in-state suppliers to the new firms that experience an increase in sales as well as to retailers who gain sales due to additional income to workers.
55. Theresa Opeka, "Three More Incentives Deals Fall Through," *Carolina Journal*, February 28, 2024, www.carolinajournal.com/three-more-nc-incentive-deals-fall-through/.
56. William Gale, Aaron Krupkin, and Kim Rueben, "The States Try Supply Side Tax Cuts," *Milken Institute Review*, October 19, 2015, https://www.milkenreview.org/articles/trends-3?IssueID=8.
57. Michael L. Walden, "Dynamic Revenue Curves for North Carolina Taxes," *Public Budgeting and Finance* 23, no. 4 (2003): 49–64.
58. "Best and Worst States to Work 2024: DC, California Top the List, While North Carolina, Mississippi, Lag Behind," Oxfam, August 29, 2024, https://www.oxfamamerica.org/press/best-and-worst-states-to-work-2024-dc-california-top-the-list-while-north-carolina-mississippi-lag-far-behind/.
59. US Bureau of Labor Statistics, "Minimum Wage Workers in North Carolina," 2016.
60. David Larson, "Is NC the Worst State for Workers? Hardly," *Carolina Journal*, September 20, 2024, https://www.carolinajournal.com/opinion/is-nc-best-state-for-business-but-worst-for-workers-hardly/.
61. Ashley Mahoney, "NC's High Rate of Low-Wage Workers," *Axios Charlotte*, July 24, 2024, https://www.axios.com/local/charlotte/2024/07/23/n-c-s-high-rate-of-low-wage-workers. To keep up with price inflation from 2009 to 2025, the North Carolina minimum wage would need to be raised from $7.25 an hour to $11.32 an hour (author's calculations using data from the US Bureau of Labor Statistics).
62. Alexandra Sirota, "Taxes Are One Way We Deliver a Better North Carolina," North Carolina Budget and Tax Center, April 15, 2024, https://ncbudget.org/taxday2024/.
63. Kim Parker, Nikki Graf, and Ruth Igielnik, "Generation Z Looks a Lot Like Millennials on Key Social and Political Issues," Pew Research Center, January 17, 2019, https://www.pewresearch.org/social-trends/wp-content/uploads/sites/3/2019/01/Generations-full-report_FINAL_1.18.pdf.
64. Paige Terryberry, "Economic Development Incentives: Are They Worth It?," Locke Foundation, February 10, 2023.
65. "America's Top States for Business, 2025," *CNBC*, November 10, 2025.
66. "Governor Cooper Promises 1,000 New Jobs in Edgecombe County as Natron Energy Selects the Kingsboro Megasite," NC Office of the Governor, August 15, 2024, https://governor.nc.gov/news/press-releases/2024/08/15/governor-cooper-announces-1000-new-jobs-edgecombe-county-natron-energy-selects-kingsboro-megasite; "Governor Cooper Announces VinFast Automotive Selects North Carolina for Electric Vehicle Assembly Plant," NC Office of the

Governor, March 29, 2022, https://governor.nc.gov/news/press-releases/2022/03/29/governor-cooper-announces-vinfast-automotive-selects-north-carolina-electric-vehicle-assembly-plant; "Toyota Announces New $8 Billion Investment at Greensboro-Randolph Megasite," Greensboro City News, October 31, 2023, https://www.greensboro-nc.gov/Home/Components/News/News/18727/36.

67. Courtney Dunbar, "The Risks and Realities of Megasite Mania: Navigating the Mid-Tier Client Landscape," *Area Development*, second quarter 2024, https://www.areadevelopment.com/corporate-site-selection-factors/q2-2024/the-risks-and-realities-of-megasite-mania-navigating-the-mid-tier-client-landscape.shtml.
68. "Corridor Identification and Development," NC Department of Transportation, May 2024.
69. "US 64 Improvements in Apex and Cary," NC Department of Transportation, May 30, 2024.
70. Bruce Siceloff, "US 64 Will Become Interstate 495 Between Raleigh and Rocky Mount," *Raleigh News and Observer*, December 13, 2013; Bob Adams, "Highways Connect Eastern NC to the Future," *Greenville Daily Reflector*, March 29, 2020.
71. "US 70 Corridor Improvements," NC Department of Transportation, January 3, 2024.
72. "The Rise of Remote Work in Rural Areas," Center on Rural Innovation and Rural Innovation Strategies, October 2021, https://ruralinnovation.us/resources/reports/the-rise-of-remote-work-in-rural-america/.
73. "National Household Travel Survey," US Department of Transportation, 2022.
74. "Commuting / Journey to Work," 2023 American Community Survey, US Census Bureau.
75. Li D and Xi Guo, "The Effect of Time Parents Spend with Children and Children's Well Being," *Frontiers in Psychology*, April 14, 2023, https://doi.org/10.3389/psyg/2023.1096128.
76. Andre Worneck and Danilo Silva, "Population Density, Depressive Symptoms, and Suicidal Thoughts," *Brazilian Journal of Psychiatry* 42, no. 1 (2020): 105–6.
77. Michael L. Walden, *Re-Launch: How Families Can Be Renewed and the American Dream Revived in the New Independent Lifestyle of the Post-Pandemic Economy* (Defiance Press, 2021).

Chapter 8: Managing Energy Use and Climate Change in the Anxious Age

1. "Final Estimated Damages for Hurricane Helene to Be Between $30.5 Billion and $47.5 Billion," CoreLogic, October 4, 2024, https://www.cotality.com/press-releases/corelogic-final-estimated-damages-for-hurricane-helene-to-be-between-30-5-billion-and-47-5-billion.
2. "What Is North Carolina's Year-Round Climate Like?," *WRAL News*, October 10, 2023, https://www.wral.com/story/what-is-nc-climate-year-round/21062002/.
3. "Consumption of Primary Energy per Capita in the US, 1950–2022," *Statista*, 2024; "Total Energy Consumption in the US from 1975–2022," *Statista*, 2024; "Leading States in Energy Consumption per Capita in the US in 2022," *Statista*, October 2, 2024.

4. The measure is expressed per 100,000 persons due to the very small numbers when expressed per person.
5. Rebecca Lindsey, "Climate Change: Atmospheric Carbon Dioxide," National Oceanic and Atmospheric Administration, April 9, 2024; Lora Shinn, "Energy Efficiency: The Clean Facts," Natural Resources Defense Council, September 20, 2023, https://www.nrdc.org/stories/energy-efficiency-clean-facts.
6. The EPA estimates that overall energy efficiency has improved by 42 percent between 2003 and 2022. "Energy Efficiency," Environmental Protection Agency, November 11, 2024, https://www.epa.gov.
7. "Federal Laws and Legislation," American Council for an Energy Efficient Economy, June 22, 2021, https://www.aceee.org.
8. "Carbon Dioxide Emissions Coefficients," US Energy Information Administration, US Department of Energy, September 18, 2024, https://www.epa.gov.
9. Although nuclear reactors do not produce CO_2 emissions while operating, the mining and refining processes for uranium ore and the making of reactor fuel can produce air pollutants. There is also the issue of safely disposing of radioactive wastes created by the operation of the nuclear reactor. "Nuclear Power Reactors Do Not Produce Direct Carbon Dioxide Emissions," Energy Information Administration, US Department of Energy, November 7, 2022, https://www.eia.gov/energyexplained/nuclear/nuclear-power-and-the-environment.php.
10. Lauren Leffer, "The AI Boom Could Use a Shocking Amount of Electricity," *Scientific American*, October 13, 2023.
11. Louise Matsakis, "The Data Center Boom Is Warping the US Economy," *Wired*, November 5, 2025, https://www.wired.com/story/data-center-ai-boom-us-economy-jobs/.
12. "North Carolina Data Center Construction Jumps 15X as Cloud and Artificial Intelligence Providers Drive Demand," CBRE (Coldwell Banker Richard Ellis), August 22, 2024, https://www.cbre.com/press-releases/north-carolina-data-center-construction-jumps-15x-as-cloud-and-artificial-intelligence-providers.
13. James Vincent, "How Much Electricity Does AI Consume," *The Verge*, February 2, 2024, https://www.theverge.com/24066646/ai-electricity-energy-watts-generative-consumption.
14. "AI Is Poised to Drive 160% Increase in Data Center Power Demand," Goldman Sachs Research, May 14, 2024, https://www.goldmansachs.com/insights/articles/AI-poised-to-drive-160-increase-in-power-demand; Vincent, "How Much Electricity Does AI Consume."
15. "Data Center Capacity Demands Will Strengthen in 2025," Moody's, January 14, 2025, https://www.moodys.com/web/en/us/insights/credit-risk/outlooks/data-centers-2025.html.
16. Michael Blackhurst and Paulina Jaramillo, "Data Center Growth Will Increase Electricity 8% Nationally and as Much as 25% in Some Regional Markets," Carnegie Mellon University, 2025, https://www.cmu.edu/work-that-matters/energy-innovation/data-center-growth-could-increase-electricity-bills.
17. "Clean Energy Plan," NC Department of Environmental Quality, October 2019, https://www.deq.nc.gov. The term "carbon neutral" means that the amount of CO_2 emitted plus the amount absorbed and removed equals zero. "Carbon Neutral vs. Net Zero: Understanding the Difference," National Grid, June 6, 2022, https://www.nationalgrid.com/stories/energy-explained/carbon-neutral-vs-net-zero-understanding-difference.

18. AI could play an important role in improving energy efficiency in the economy. Amy Myers Jaffe, "AI Is Going to Consume a Lot of Energy. It Can Also Help Us Consume Less," *Wall Street Journal*, September 22, 2025.
19. Charles Schmidt, "Environment: California Out Front," *Environmental Health Perspective* 115, no. 3 (2007): A144–A147.
20. "The One Big Beautiful Bill Act: Key Provisions," Reuters, August 2025, https://www.reuters.com/practical-law-the-journal/transactional/one-big-beautiful-bill-act-key-provisions-2025-08-01/.
21. Susannah Shoemaker, "NREL Researchers Reveal How Buildings Across the United States Do—and Could—Use Energy," National Laboratory of the Rockies, September 14, 2023, https://www.nlr.gov/news/detail/features/2023/nrel-researchers-reveal-how-buildings-across-the-united-states-do-and-could-use-energy.
22. "North Carolina State Energy Conservation Code Amendments," NC Department of Insurance, January 1, 2019, https://www.ncdoi.gov; Cassie Gavin, "North Carolina's Safety and Energy Savings on the Chopping Block," NC Sustainable Energy Association, June 12, 2024, https://www.energync.org/blog/sb166-puts-north-carolinians-safety-and-energy-savings-on-the-chopping-block/.
23. Energy-efficient homes can be 5 percent to 10 percent more costly than homes without the energy-efficient features. "Elemental Green," Zero Energy Project, 2024, https://elemental.green.
24. While there are various definitions of the state's Downeast region, a common definition includes Bladen, Columbus, Duplin, Greene, Jones, Lenoir, Robeson, Sampson, and Wayne Counties. Michael Walden, "The Human, Environmental, and Economic Impacts of Safely Removing Hog Waste: An Application to Eastern North Carolina," report prepared for Montauk Ag Renewables, LLC, July 2023, https://www.montaukrenewables.com.
25. "Tailpipe Greenhouse Emissions for a Typical Vehicle," US Environmental Protection Agency, May 30, 2023; "Livestock and Poultry," Environmental Learning Community, March 5, 2019.
26. "Livestock and Poultry."
27. Josh Torres and Andrew Howell, "With Early Progress in Reducing Livestock Methane, It's Time for Finance to Lean In," Environmental Defense Fund, September 16, 2024, https://business.edf.org/insights/with-early-progress-in-reducing-livestock-methane-its-time-for-finance-to-lean-in/.
28. "Residential Wood Burning," American Lung Association, November 2, 2023, https://www.lung.org/clean-air/indoor-air/indoor-air-pollutants/residential-wood-burning.
29. Ryan December, "Firm Looks to Power AI with Wood," *Wall Street Journal*, December 19, 2024.
30. Laura Oleniacz, "Textile Filter Testing Shows Promise of Carbon Capture," *NC State News*, June 2, 2022, https://news.ncsu.edu/2022/06/textile-filter-testing-shows-promise-for-carbon-capture/.
31. Cameron Oglesby, "What's the Deal with Carbon Capture and Storage?, *Yale Climate Connections*, October 20, 2023, https://yaleclimateconnections.org/2023/10/whats-the-deal-with-carbon-capture-and-storage/.
32. Victoria Masterson, "9 Ways AI Is Helping Tackle Climate Change," World

Economic Forum, February 12, 2024, https://www.weforum.org/stories/2024/02/ai-combat-climate-change/.

33. "End-Use Energy Consumption in North Carolina," Energy Information Agency, US Department of Energy, 2022, https://www.eia.gov/state/seds/seds-data-complete.php?sid=NC.
34. Sam Wigness, "What Is the Carbon Footprint of Solar Panels?," Solar.com, August 32, 2023, https://www.solar.com/learn/what-is-the-carbon-footprint-of-solar-panels/.
35. "North Carolina Clean Energy Plan," NC Department of Environmental Quality, 2019; "2022 Duke Energy Climate Report," Duke Energy, 2022, https://investors.duke-energy.com/esg/governance-documents/default.aspx.
36. "North Carolina Energy Profile," Energy Information Agency, US Department of Energy, 2022, https://www.eia.gov.
37. Gareth McGarth, "High Costs Prompt Duke to Move Away from North Carolina Offshore Wind Projects, Including Brunswick," *Star News Online*, August 13, 2025, https://www.starnewsonline.com/story/news/local/2025/08/13/duke-energy-scraps-wind-projects-off-nc-coast-including-brunswick/85631545007/.
38. José Reyes, "The Hydrogen Rush: Ushering in a New Era of Energy with Small Nuclear Reactors," NuScale Power, September 10, 2024, https://www.nuscalepower.com/smr-insights-blog/the-hydrogen-rush-ushering-in-a-new-era-of-energy-with-small-modular-reactors.
39. Logan Stewart, "US Department of Energy Awards Duke Energy $57 Million in Cost-Share Funding to Enhance North Carolina's Energy Grid," Duke Energy, August 6, 2024, https://investors.duke-energy.com/news/news-details/2024/U.S.-Department-of-Energy-awards-Duke-Energy-project-57-million-in-cost-share-funding-to-enhance-North-Carolinas-energy-grid/default.aspx; Treavor Lewis, Isaac Orr, and Mitch Rolling, "Lighting the Path: Meeting North Carolina's Energy Needs," John Locke Foundation, October 2024, https://www.johnlocke.org/wp-content/uploads/2024/10/Lighting-the-Path-Web.pdf.
40. "North Carolina Energy Profile."
41. Ralph Mureti, "The Rise of Electric Vehicles in North Carolina," Diminished Value Carolina, September 17, 2024, https://diminishedvaluecarolina.com/rise-of-nc-nc.
42. "Lithium Mining for EVs: How Sustainable Is It?," APM Research Lab, February 22, 2024, https://www.apmresearchlab.org/10x/lithium-mining-for-evs-sustainability.
43. "Mining Permit Granted for Controversial Carolina Lithium Project," *WTTV News*, May 7, 2024.
44. "Batteries for Electric Vehicles," Alternative Fuels Center, US Department of Energy, 2024, https://afdc.energy.gov; Andrew Moseman, "Are Electric Vehicles Definitely Better for the Climate than Gas Powered Vehicles," *MIT Climate Portal*, October 13, 2022, https://climate.mit.edu/ask-mit/are-electric-vehicles-definitely-better-climate-gas-powered-cars.
45. Kanishk Shah and Fiyanshu Kaka, "Reduction of Carbon Footprint of Electric Batteries Using Battery Alternatives and Integrated Photovoltaics," *Materials Today—Proceedings* 57, no. 1 (2022): 106–11; Niki Jennings, "North Carolina State University Joins National Energy Innovation Hub, Boosting Battery

Research," Department of Materials Science and Engineering, NC State University, September 12, 2024, https://mse.ncsu.edu/2024/09/north-carolina-state-university-joins-national-energy-innovation-hub-boosting-battery-research/.

46. Matt Brannon and Evelyn Pimplaskar, "Nearly 50% of EV Buyers Say the Tax Credit Was a Deciding Factor—How Will Ending It Affect Sales?," Insurify, May 22, 2025, https://insurify.com/car-insurance/insights/ev-tax-credit-survey/.
47. "Electric Vehicle Ownership Costs," *Consumer Reports*, October 2020.
48. Thea Riofrancos, Alissa Kendall, Kristi Dayemo, Matthew Haugen, Kira McDonald, Batul Hassan, Magaret Slattery, and Xan Lillehei, "Achieving Zero Emissions with More Mobility and Less Mining," Climate and Community Institute, January 2023, https://climateandcommunity.org/research/more-mobility-less-mining/.
49. "Pro-Environment, Pro-Climate," Housing Development Consortium, November 19, 2020, https://www.housingconsortium.org.
50. Stefan Redding Lallinger, "Fair Housing Reform in a Southern City: The Case of Charlotte," Century Foundation, December 21, 2023, https://tcf.org/content/report/fair-housing-reform-in-a-southern-city-the-case-of-charlotte/; "Zoning Reform Is Creating Opportunities for More Housing," City of Raleigh, October 17, 2023, https://www.raleighnc.gov.
51. "New Development Could Create Game-Changing Residential Growth in RTP," *WRAL Techwire*, January 10, 2024.
52. "Housing America's Older Adults, 2023," Joint Center for Housing Studies, Harvard University, 2023, https://www.jchs.harvard.edu/housing-americas-older-adults-2023.
53. "2024 Home Buyers and Sellers Generational Trends Report," National Association of Realtors, 2024, https://www.nar.realtor/sites/default/files/documents/2024-home-buyers-and-sellers-generational-trends-04-03-2024.pdf.
54. Yanqui Tao, Yang Longqi, Sonia Jaffe, and Fengqi You, "Climate Mitigation Potentials of Teleworking Are Sensitive to Changes in Lifestyle and Workplace Rather Than ICU Usage," *Proceedings of the National Academy of Sciences of the United States of America*, September 18, 2023, https://www.pnas.org/doi/10.1073/pnas.2304099120.
55. "Overview of Greenhouse Gases," US Environmental Protection Agency, April 11, 2024.
56. "Economic Impact of the Pork Industry in the US," US Department of Agriculture, August 7, 2024; "Agricultural Statistics: 2024," NC Department of Agriculture and Consumer Services.
57. "Road Quality 2025," *US News*, February 21, 2025.
58. "What Is the State of America's Highway Bridges?," USAFacts, January 1, 2024, https://usafacts.org/articles/what-is-the-state-of-americas-highway-bridges/.
59. "Newly Released Scorecard Ranks States for Efficiency and Sustainability Values," Alliance for Water Efficiency, January 18, 2023, https://allianceforwaterefficiency.org/newly-released-scorecard-ranks-states-water-efficiency-and-sustainability-policies/.
60. Michael Chiulli, *The New Panama Canal and North Carolina: Potential Economic Impacts and Opportunities* (Sanford School of Public Policy, Duke University, 2014).
61. "NC Ports Moves Up Three Spots to #1 for Container Terminal Efficiency," North Carolina Ports, May 22, 2023, https://ncports.com/about-the-ports/news

/north-carolina-ports-moves-up-three-spots-to-1-in-north-america-for-container-terminal-efficiency/; "NC Ports Breaks Intermodal Volume Record, Sees Solid Results in FY14," North Carolina Ports, July 25, 2024, https://ncports.com/about-the-ports/news/nc-ports-breaks-intermodal-volume-record-sees-solid-results-in-fy24/.
62. Christopher Otts and Mike Collins, "Battery Belt Counts on EV Success," *Wall Street Journal*, January 8, 2025; Eric Niler, "As Nuclear Gains, Its Waste Piles Up," *Wall Street Journal*, March 6, 2025.
63. Elizabeth Ouzts, "Former Critics Set to Coalesce Around Duke Energy's Plans for More Gas, Solar in North Carolina," *Energy News Network*, August 26, 2024.
64. Marco Visscher, *The Power of Nuclear* (Bloomsbury Sigma, 2024).
65. Mark Holt and Lance Larson, "Considerations for Reprocessing Spent Nuclear Fuel," Congressional Research Service, January 23, 2025, https://www.congress.gov/crs_external_products/R/PDF/R48364/R48364.2.pdf.
66. Michelle Kurilla, "What Is the CHIPS Act?," Council on Foreign Relations, April 29, 2024, https://www.cfr.org/articles/what-chips-act.
67. Dan Way, "Moore County's Residents Worry About Solar's Long-Term Environmental Impacts," *Carolina Journal*, May 25, 2017.
68. Sharon Terlep, "Ford Plans Low-Cost EV Models as It Eyes China Rivals," *Wall Street Journal*, August 12, 2025.
69. Lee Jinjoo, "Solar and Wind Power Can Thrive Without Subsidies," *Wall Street Journal*, August 23, 2025.

Chapter 9: North Carolina's Position in the Nation and World

1. Population of the States, 2024, US Census Bureau.
2. Population of the States, 1970 and 1990, US Census Bureau.
3. Regional Data, US Bureau of Economic Analysis.
4. Regional Data, US Bureau of Economic Analysis.
5. Weldon Cooper Center for Public Service, University of Virginia, July 1, 2024, https://www.publicservice.virginia.edu.
6. Weldon Cooper Center for Public Service, July 1, 2024.
7. Gavin Wright, *Old South, New South* (Basic Books, 1986).
8. Evan Moore, "People Are Moving to North Carolina from These 10 States the Most, New Census Data Show," *Charlotte Observer*, October 24, 2024.
9. Regional Data, US Bureau of Economic Analysis.
10. US Bureau of Labor Statistics, State and Area Employment, Hours, and Earnings, https://www.bls.gov/help/one_screen/sa.htm.
11. Regional Data, US Bureau of Economic Analysis.
12. "Natural and Scenic Attractions in North Carolina," North Carolina Travel and Tourism Board, November 21, 2024, https://www.visitnc.com; Randi Moultrie, "North and South Carolina Voted Among States That Have the Best Weather Year Round," Beasley Media Group, February 7, 2023, http://www.bbgi.com.
13. Phillip Joonbae Gong, "Raleigh, Charlotte Make Top 10 List for Fastest-Growing Large Metros in the US," *Carolina Demography*, February 2, 2023, https://carolinademography.cpc.unc.edu/author/phillip-joonbae-gong/; "Comparing the Carolinas' Top Real Estate Markets," Henderson Properties, November 1, 2024, https://www.hendersonproperties.com.
14. Tom George and Maggie Green, "'Heat Keeps Getting Worse': Climate Data

Predicting Dangerous Summers by 2050," *WTVD*, August 17, 2023, https://abc11.com/post/weathering-tomorrow-climate-change-heat-new-data/13653271/.

15. Russ Schumacher and Kathie Dello, "Why Are So Many Historically Rare Storms Hitting the Carolinas? Climate Puts These States at Risk, and the Climate Is Changing," *The Conversation*, October 10, 2024, https://theconversation.com/why-are-so-many-historically-rare-storms-hitting-the-carolinas-geography-puts-these-states-at-risk-and-climate-change-is-loading-the-dice-240178.
16. Laura Brumment, "Foreign Investment, Jobs, on the Rise in North Carolina," *Triangle Business Journal*, March 27, 2023; "Key Industries in North Carolina," NC Department of Commerce, November 2024, https://www.commerce.nc.gov.
17. "See Why Charlotte Region Is One of the Most Connected Locations on the East Coast," Charlotte Regional Business Alliance, November 11, 2024, https://charlotteregion.com/do-business-here/regional-connectivity/; "RDU History," Raleigh-Durham International Airport, November 24, 2024, https://www.rdu.com/airport-authority/history/.
18. "List of US Representatives from North Carolina," Ballotpedia, accessed November 25, 2024, https://ballotpedia.org/List_of_United_States_Representatives_from_North_Carolina.
19. "Almost All (94 Percent) of the 2024 Presidential Campaign Was Concentrated in Seven States," National Popular Vote, November 22, 2024, https://www.nationalpopularvote.com/almost-all-94-2024-presidential-campaign-was-concentrated-7-states.
20. Linus Blomquist, "Rising Agricultural Yields Spares Land," Breakthrough Institute, March 13, 2024, https://breakthroughinsitute.org.
21. Rose Hoban, "Planting the Seeds for a Farm to Help People with Mental Health Needs," *NC Health News*, May 8, 2024, https://www.northcarolinahealthnews.org/2024/05/08/planting-seeds-care-farm-help-people-mental-health-needs/.
22. "State Price Deflators," US Bureau of Economic Analysis, bea.gov; "Commuting to Work, 2010, 2022," US Census Bureau; "More Working from Home, but Longer Commutes for Those Who Don't: An Update to Cross-County Commuting Patterns," NC Department of Commerce; National Agricultural Statistics Service, US Department of Agriculture, 2014 and 2024.
23. Reeve Bull and Bryan Horn, "Virginia Is a Model for Lowering Housing Costs," *City Journal*, January 31, 2025, https://www.city-journal.org/article/home-prices-housing-market-virginia; Samantha Fu and Nyla Holland, "Can Factory-Built Housing Contribute to Greater Affordability and Climate Resiliency?," Urban Institute, December 2024, https://www.urban.org/sites/default/files/2024-12/Can_Factory_Built_Housing_Contribute_to_Greater_Affordability_and_Climate_Resiliency.pdf.

Chapter 10: North Carolina in 2050

1. "North Carolina's Innovation Performance Continues to Improve," NC Department of Commerce, July 29, 2024, https://www.commerce.nc.gov/news/press-releases/2024/07/29/north-carolinas-innovation-performance-continues-improve.
2. "Gross Domestic Happiness," Wellness Research Centre, University of Oxford,

2023, https://www.worldhappiness.report/; "Better Life Index: France," Organisation for Economic Co-operation and Development (OECD), 2023, https://www.oecd.org/en/data/tools/well-being-data-monitor/better-life-index.html.

3. Javier Andres and Hernando Ignacio, "Does Inflation Harm Economic Growth?," Working Paper No. 6062, National Bureau of Economic Research, December 1, 1997, https://www.nber.org.; Diane Coyle, *The Measure of Progress: Counting What Really Matters* (Princeton University Press, 2025). The lower estimate of GDP in graph 10.1 is based on Andres and Ignacio's finding that the economic growth rate slows by half the increase in the inflation rate. Graph 10.1 assumes the faster rise in prices in North Carolina after 2023 reduces the state's cost advantage by 1 percent every decade, the same as occurred during the 2012–22 decade.
4. High-earning occupations include those in management, finance, utilities, information, and professional services. Middle-earning occupations are defined as those in wholesale trade, mining, manufacturing, real estate, health care, public administration, transportation/warehousing, and education. Administrative support, agriculture, personal services, arts/entertainment, retail trade, and accommodations/food service comprise the low-earning occupations. There are natural break points in average weekly earnings for the three categories. Michael L. Walden, "Economic Growth and Income Distribution in North Carolina and Introduction of the NC-Growth and NC-Share Indices, Update to 2022," Working Paper, Department of Agricultural and Resource Economics, North Carolina State University, January 2023.
5. David Autor, "Applying AI to Rebuild Middle Class Jobs," Working Paper No. 32140, National Bureau of Economic Research, November 4, 2023, https://www.nber.org/papers/w32140. See also Anton Korinek and Joseph E. Stiglitz, "Artificial Intelligence and Its Implications for Income Distribution and Unemployment," Working Paper No. 24174, National Bureau of Economic Research, December 2017, https://www.nber.org/papers/w24174.
6. A. Georgieff, "Artificial Intelligence and Wage Inequality," OECD Artificial Intelligence Papers, April 10 2024, https://www.oecd.org/en/publications/artificial-intelligence-and-wage-inequality_bf98a45c-en.html.
7. Sam Manning, "AI's Impact on Income Inequality in the US," Brookings, July 3, 2024, https://www.brookings.edu/articles/ais-impact-on-income-inequality-in-the-us/.
8. Nathan Wilmers, "Generative AI and the Future of Inequality," *An MIT Exploration of Generative AI*, March 27, 2024, https://doi.org/10.21428/e4baedd9.777b7123.
9. "Housing Needs Assessment, North Carolina," NC Realtors, 2024, https://www.ncrealtors.org.
10. Michael L. Walden, "Economic Impact of Closing the Housing Gap in North Carolina," January 2025, North Carolina Chamber of Commerce, https://ncchamber.com/wp-content/uploads/Report-on-the-Economic-Impact-of-Closing-the-Housing-Gap-in-NC.pdf.
11. Gleb Tsipurty, "The AI Revolution Transforming Hybrid and Remote Work and the Return to the Office," *Forbes*, May 9, 2023; Penny Redlin, "AI and the Future of Remote Work," *Edvisors*, September 10, 2024, https://www.edvisors.com/blog/ai-and-remote-work/.

12. "The Impact of Large Corporations on the Housing Market," Housing and Education Alliance, April 2024, https://www/heausa/org.
13. Joshua Coren, "The Impact of Institutional Investors on Homeownership and Neighborhood Access," Stern School of Business, New York University, August 8, 2023, https://www.chen.institute/workingpapers.
14. US Bureau of Labor Statistics, "Consumer Price Index for All Urban Consumers," https://www.bls.gov/help/one_screen/sa.htm.
15. "How AI Can Impact Agriculture," National FFA Organization, August 18, 2023, https://www.ffa.org/technology/how-ai-can-impact-agriculture/.
16. Martin Gaynor, Farzad Mostashari, and Paul Ginsburg, "Making Health Care Markets Work: Competition Policy for Health Care," Brookings, April 13, 2017, https://www.brookings.edu/articles/making-health-care-markets-work-competition-policy-for-health-care/.
17. Zarek Brot-Goldberg, Zack Cooper, Stuart Craig, Lev Klarnet, Ithai Lurie, and Corbin Miller, "Who Pays for Rising Health Care Costs? Evidence from Hospital Mergers," Working Paper No. 32613, National Bureau of Economic Research, December 2024, https://www.nber.org/papers/w32613.
18. Bruce Allain, "North Carolina Supreme Court Address Certificate of Need Challenge," *Source Blog*, November 11, 2024, https://sourceonhealthcare.org/north-carolina-supreme-court-addresses-certificate-of-need-challenge/.
19. Electricity prices by state are available at RateWatt, https://ratewatt.com/; US Energy Information Administration, "Analysis and Projections," https://www.eia.gov/analysis/.

INDEX

NOTE: Pages in *italic* type refer to illustrative matter.

absenteeism, 56
Abundant University, The (Smith), 71
age of population, statistics, 5–7. *See also* aging population; population statistics
aging population, xiv, 2, xviii, 5. *See also* age of population, statistics; population statistics
agricultural industry, 44, 77–78, 82–83, 111, 117, 120, *129*, 133, 146, 164n10
AI (artificial intelligence), xvi–xvii, 43–53, 134; climate change and, 111–12; education and, 60–65; effects on labor force, 79–80, 145; energy use and data centers for, 109, 170n18; labor-saving changes from, 33, 138–39; remote work and, 16, 38, 139–40. *See also* technological innovations; workforce
airports, 127
AI tutors, 68–69, 76, 145
Albemarle lithium mine, 88
Amazon (company), 36, 59, 97, 156n42
American Indians, 7
Anxious Age, concept overview, xvii–xx, 145–46
Apple (company), 82, 88
Asheville, NC, 4, 124
Asian population, 8, *9*. *See also* population statistics
automobile industry, xvii, 24, 36, 97, 120. *See also* EV (electric vehicle) manufacturing
Autor, David, 138

banking industry, 44–45, 79, 84
Barclays, 63
basketball, 127
battery manufacturing, xvii, 36, 85, 88, 98, 101, 104, 115, 119–20. *See also* EV (electric vehicle) manufacturing
Bhutan, 134
Big Five economy, xviii, 78–82, 100–101. *See also names of specific industries*
Big Three economy, xiii, 78, 79, 80–85, 90, 100, 101. *See also names of specific industries*
birth rate, 1–2, *xxii*, 10, 26, 150n3, 151n19. *See also* population statistics
Black population, 7, *8*, 150n3, 159n5
BMW, 97
Boeing, 97
Boom Supersonic aircraft production, 101
broadband internet, 18
Burlington, NC, 124

California, 4, 121, 122
capital investments, 87–88. *See also* economic geography
carbon footprint, 117–18
Carolina Hornets (basketball team), 127
Carolina Hurricanes (hockey team), 127
Carolina Panthers (football team), 127
Cary, NC, 14
cattle, 117
censuses, 5, 19, 24, 148n1. *See also* population statistics
Chapel Hill, NC, xiv, 153n36. *See also* Triangle (Raleigh–Durham–Chapel Hill)
Charlotte, NC, xv, 19, 45, 124, 153n36; industry changes in, xiv, xv, xvi
climate change, xiv, xvii, xix, 104, 106, 111–12, 115–19, 126. *See also* energy usage
"closed shop" regulations, 35
CO_2 emissions, 107, 109–17, 119, 146, 169n9

coal, 112, 113
commuting, xv, 14, 16, 21–22, 24, 39, 99, 116–17, 128–29, *129*. *See also* remote work
Congressional Budget Office (CBO), 10
Connected Age, xiii–xiv
construction industry, 25, 32, 70
corridor development, 77, 98–100, 104–5
cost of living, 122–24, 126, *129*, 135, 139–41. *See also* income (in)equality
Council on Foreign Relations, 4
COVID pandemic, xv–xviii; effects on education by, 55–56; workforce changes, 25–27, 45–47
cyberbuying, 16–17
cybersecurity, 50

data centers, 109
death rate, 1, 2, 9, 10, 11, 150n4, 151n19
Democratic Party, 36
demographic trends, xviii–xiv, *xxii*, 1–12. *See also* population statistics
Denmark, 38–39
disaster recovery, 18
diversity of population, 7–9. *See also* population statistics
driverless vehicles, 24
drone delivery, 17
Duke Energy, 112, 113, 114, 119
Durham, NC, xiv, 153n36. *See also* Triangle (Raleigh–Durham–Chapel Hill)
Durham County, xiv

East Carolina University, 5, 57
economic geography, 13–24, 87–95, 101–2, 121. *See also names of specific industries and locations*
economic growth of North Carolina, 121–31, 146. *See also* prosperity
education: AI and, 60–65; attainment statistics in, xiii, 45, 149n2; challenges and changes to, 32, 67, 75–76; higher education, 56–60, 69–74; K-12 schools, 55–56, 67–69, 75–76, 145, 159n5. *See also* job training
elderly population. *See* aging population
electricity, 112, 167n54
energy efficiency, 110–12, 170n18
energy industry, xiv–xv, xvii, 102–5, 109–20
energy sources, 112–15, 145
energy usage, 105–9. *See also* climate change
EPA (Environmental Protection Agency), 87
EV (electric vehicle) manufacturing, xvii, 85, 88, 115, 118. *See also* automobile industry; battery manufacturing

farming, 77–78, 82–83, 86, 111, 120, *129*, 133, 146, 164n10. *See also* livestock industry
Federal Reserve Bank, 35, 84
Felten, Edward, 60
Fletcher, Angus, 52
Florida, 4, 121
football, 127
Ford (company), 120
foreign immigration, 2–3, *3*, 5, 10–11, 19, 26–27
forestry, 78, 85
Fort Bragg, 80, 86
France, 134
freelance work, xviii, 37–38. *See also* workforce
Fujifilm Biotech, 90
furniture industry, 85
future predictions, 133–44

GDH (gross domestic happiness), 134
GDP (gross domestic product), 134
Generation Z, 14
geographic shifts, 12–24, 87–95, 101–2. *See also names of specific locations*
Georgia, 1, 117, 121
gig work, xviii, 37–38. *See also* workforce
gold, 78
Goldman Sachs, 50
Goldsboro, NC, 123
Google, 97
Grant, Ulysses, 38

GREAT (Growing Rural Economies with Access to Technology), 18
Great Depression, 34
Great Recession, 37
Great Resignation, 29
Greensboro, NC, xiv, 19, 124. *See also* Triad (Greensboro–Winston Salem–High Point)
Greenville, NC, 123, 124
guaranteed-income programs, 53, 75, 164n25. *See also* workforce

healthcare industry, 32, 146, 152n13
higher education, 56–60, 69–74, 145. *See also* education
High Point, NC, xiv, 153n36. *See also* Triad (Greensboro–Winston Salem–High Point)
high-speed internet, 17–18
Hispanic population, *8*, 9, 159n5. *See also* population statistics
hockey, 127
hog production, 111, 117
home delivery, 16–17
home prices, *129*
household movements, 19–24. *See also* migration
housing construction, 146
housing density, 116
Hurricane Helene (2024), 18, 104, 126
hydrogen power, 113, 114, 119, 143, 145

IBM, 63
Illinois, 121
immigration. *See* migration
income (in)equality, 63–64, 65, 134, 136–39, 143. *See also* cost of living; wages
Industrial Revolution, 103, 149n9
industry changes, xiii–xvii, 60–63. *See also* Big Five economy; Big Three economy; labor market; *and names of specific industries*
inequality. *See* income (in)equality
information industry, 32
in-migration population statistics, 1, 2, 4, 19–20, *20*, 122. *See also* population statistics
internet access, 17–18
"iron law," 15

Job Openings and Labor Turnover Survey (JOLTS), 27, *28*
job openings rate, 27, *28*
job shortage, 74–75
job training, 141–42, 145. *See also* education; workforce

K–12 schools, 55–56, 67–69, 75–76, 145, 159n5. *See also* education
Keynes, John Maynard, 74, 75
Khan, Salman, 68
Khan Academy, 68

labor force participation rate (LFPR), 27–28
labor market, xv, xvi, xviii, 25–41, 141–42. *See also* industry changes; workforce
labor unions, xviii, 26, 33–36, 154n9, 156n42. *See also* workforce
land-based economy, 77–78
leisure/hospitality industry, 25, 32
lifelong education, 73
lithium, 85, 88, 101, 105
livestock industry, 111, 117. *See also* agricultural industry
Lombard, Hamilton, 19
lumber industry, 78, 85

manufacturing industry, *94*, 95
Marshall, Alfred, 15
McDonald's, 33
McKinsey Global, 50
meat industry, 117
Mecklenburg County, xviii–xiv
megasites, 98
mental health, 146
methane emissions, 117
migration: changes in North Carolina, xvii; foreign immigration, 2–3, *3*, 5, 10–11, 19, 26–27; of households, 19–24; in-migrant population statistics, 1, 2, 4, 19, *20*, 122. *See also* population statistics

military complex, 80–81
mining industry, 86, 101. *See also* lithium

National Assessment of Educational Progress (NAEP), 55, 56
National Bureau of Economic Research, 4
National Institutes of Health, 87
Natron Energy, 88
natural gas, 112–13
New Bern, NC, 4, 124
New York, 4, 121
North American Free Trade Agreement (NAFTA), 34, 78
North Carolina Beyond the Connected Age (Walden), xiv
North Carolina Chamber of Commerce, 139
North Carolina in the Connected Age (Walden), xviii
North Carolina State University, 57, 111
Norway, 38–39
Novo Nordisk, 90
nuclear power, 112, 113, 145, 169n9

Ohio, 121
oil and gas industry, 112
online shopping and home delivery, 16–17
open spaces, 130, 146
Organisation for Economic Co-operation and Development, 63, 138

pandemic. *See* COVID pandemic
parks, 75, 130
Pennsylvania, 121
pharmaceutical industry, 79, 90, *90–92*
phosphate, 101, 105
politics, 128
population statistics, xiii–xiv, xxii, 1–12. *See also* censuses; demographic trends
prosperity, 134–35. *See also* economic growth of North Carolina
pure silicon, 101, 105

quarrying industry, 101
quit rates, 27–29

Raj, Manav, 60
Raleigh, NC, 19, 124; industry changes in, xiv, xv, xvi; WFH rates in, 14. *See also* Triangle (Raleigh–Durham–Chapel Hill)
real estate industry, *129*, 146, 152n13
remote work, xv, 14–16, 22, 77, 116, 139–40, 145, 152n13
renewable energy manufacturing corridor, 104–5. *See also* energy industry
Republican Party, 36
Research Triangle Park (RTP), 82, 98, 116
right-to-work laws, 35, 36, 156n44. *See also* unions; workforce
Rocky Mount, NC, 123, 124
rural/urban divide. *See* urban/rural divide

Sanders, Bernie, 38
Seamans, Robert, 60
semiconductor manufacturing, 88
silicon, 101, 105
Smith, Michael D., 71
SNAP (Supplemental Nutrition Assistance Program), 29
solar energy, 113, 120
South Carolina, 4, 36, 44–45, 117
sports, 127
Starlink, 18
state economic growth, 121–31
State of North Carolina, 112–13

Tar Heel: as term, 78
taxation, 97, 145, 146, 166n48
technological innovations, xiv, 44–45, 48–49, 79, 133, 149n9. *See also* AI (artificial intelligence)
technology investments, 88
Tennessee, 36, 117, 126
Texas, 4, 14, 121
textile industry, 35, 80, 84–85
timber industry, 78, 85
tobacco, xiii, 44, 77, 78, 80, 84, 89, 101
tourism industry, 86, 101
Toyota, xvii, 88, 97, 98
transportation industry, 79. *See also* battery manufacturing; EV (electric vehicle) manufacturing

Triad (Greensboro–Winston Salem–High Point), xiv, 4, 88, 153n36
Triangle (Raleigh–Durham–Chapel Hill), xiv, xv, 4, 88, 153n36. *See also* Raleigh, NC
Trump administration, 87

unions, xviii, 26, 33–36, 154n9, 156n42. *See also* right-to-work laws; workforce
University of North Carolina, 5, 89
urban/rural divide, xiii–xiv, xv, 13–16, 22–24, 63, 154n40
US Bureau of Labor Statistics, 27, 96
US Department of Transportation, 117
US Supreme Court, 87

VinFast (company), xvii, 36, 88, 98, 101
Virginia, 117
visitor statistics, xv–xvi
Volvo, 97

wages, 30–33, 124–26, 131, 167n61. *See also* income (in)equality
Wake County: population statistics, xviii
warehousing industry, *93*
white population, 7, 159n5
Wilmington, NC, 4
wind energy, 113
Winston Salem, NC, xiv, 153n36. *See also* Triad (Greensboro–Winston Salem–High Point)
Wolfspeed (company), xvii, 88
workforce: AI and, 46–53; changes to, overview, xv, xvi, xviii, 40–41; COVID and, 25–27, 45–47; education and skills of, xviii, xix, 141–42, 145; gig work, xviii, 37–38; guaranteed-income programs for, 53, 75, 164n25; labor unions, xviii, 26, 33–36, 33–36, 154n9, 156n42; remote working, xv, 14–16, 22, 77, 116, 139–40, 145, 152n13; by sectors, *46*, *62*; shortages of, 27–30; wages, 30–33, 124–26, 167n61; work-week changes, 38–40, 41. *See also* AI (artificial intelligence); industry changes
work-from-home (WFH). *See* remote work
workweek changes, 38–40, 41
World Trade Organization (WTO), 34

www.ingramcontent.com/pod-product-compliance
Lightning Source LLC
LaVergne TN
LVHW051156241026
850939LV00025B/279
* 9 7 8 1 4 6 9 6 9 7 9 2 5 *